Visions of
Addiction

Visions of Addiction

Major Contemporary Perspectives on Addiction and Alcoholism

Edited by

Stanton Peele

Lexington Books

D.C. Heath and Company/Lexington, Massachusetts/Toronto

Library of Congress Cataloging-in-Publication Data

Visions of addiction.

Includes bibliographies and index.
1. Substance abuse. 2. Alcoholism. 3. Compulsive
behavior. I. Peele, Stanton. [DNLM: 1. Alcoholism.
2. Personality. 3. Substance Dependence. WM 270 V831]
RC564.V57   1988   616.86   86–45054
ISBN 0–669–13092–3 (alk. paper)

Published simultaneously in Canada
Printed in the United States of America
International Standard Book Number: 0–669–13092–3
Library of Congress Catalog Card Number: 86–45054

The paper used in this publication meets the minimum requirements of
American National Standard for Information Sciences—Permanence of
Paper for Printed Library Materials, ANSI Z39.48 – 84.

88 89 90 8 7 6 5 4 3 2 1

For Mary Arnold,
without whom this would not be possible;
Don't Forget to Dance

Contents

Preface

The field of addiction has grown dramatically in the last decade. Professionals from a host of disciplines and backgrounds, interested in a variety of drugs and other behavioral problems and compulsions, have all joined ranks in the study of addiction. The question is: Have we progressed as a result of all this work? *Visions of Addiction* answers this question by showing how far we have come, how much of a shared vision of addiction has been created, and how much disagreement remains.

Important researchers, clinicians, and theorists from the major disciplines concerned with addiction research were asked to contribute chapters summarizing their areas of expertise. All were asked to describe how *they* see addiction. Addiction was not limited to alcohol or specific drugs; rather, all of addiction was to be included in the authors' answers. Authors were further instructed to explain why they think of addiction in this way. What is their evidence, their personal experience, their indications that their view will be helpful? In addition to presenting research and clinical data, the authors describe what their approaches offer in the way of solutions for addiction, both for individual addicts and for our society as a whole.

I can only offer thanks to my distinguished colleagues, first for joining me in this venture, and second for the excellent way in which they did their jobs. The contributors present the range of approaches to addictive problems: social learning, Freudian, genetic, neurobiological, sociological, medical, existential, moral, adaptive, and conditioning. All of these professionals and teams, moreover, have concrete recommendations that reflect their experience and research. The result is a volume that covers every aspect of addiction. Sometimes the similarities in the perspectives are striking—as in the large role all the contributors see social forces playing in addiction. In other areas, such as in views of the validity of a disease approach to addiction, the disagreement is just as striking.

The final product thus does justice to the range of knowledge and visions in this field, to the commonality in these visions, and to their differences. No reader, however, can fail to learn from any contributing author or group. To explore the variety of these contributions is to gain an essential understanding of the addiction field today that could not have been provided by any individual author. I am indebted to all the contributors for this final product. In addition, I thank Richard Rachin for giving me the support and original mandate to create this volume as a special double issue of the *Journal of Drug Issues*. Finally, I thank my wife, Mary Arnold, for creating an environment in which I could do this work, and my friend and colleague Archie Brodsky for helping me to give this volume its final form.

Introduction:
The Nature of the Beast

Stanton Peele

Joseph Frawley in this volume is not the first person to liken those searching for the shape of addiction to the blind men who, each feeling a disparate section of the elephant, develop wholly different visions of the nature of the beast. In the opening chapter, Alan Marlatt and Kim Fromme liken different views of addiction to metaphors. For these authors, metaphor describes the nature of the divergent views different specialists and practitioners take of addictive phenomena, while it also presents an important tool for addicts to use in eliminating their addictions. As a tool, it helps the addict to discover new ways of conceiving of the problem and the self that can aid the therapeutic process.

Marlatt and Fromme are at particular pains to point up the drawbacks of the medical or disease model of addiction. This model conceives of addicts as being incapable of self-control while at the same time it holds them morally responsible should they give into the temptation of a slip (e.g., having a drink). The disease model deprives addicts of the sense of self-efficacy necessary both to plan their lives in the face of their addictions and to overcome individual lapses in their overall journey to freedom from the enslavement of an addiction. Marlatt and Fromme instead describe addiction as a learning process and develop with addicts a set of personalized coping techniques for avoiding relapse and progressing further and further from addictiveness.

Frawley elucidates what he calls a neurobehavioral model, although the model is essentially the medical model of alcoholism (and addiction) as a primary disease that requires abstinence (supported by spiritual redemption) for recovery. I must at this point apologize because we were unable to publish the some 400 references covering over 30 pages that Dr. Frawley appended to his chapter. The book simply could not support this lengthy reference section (not to mention the listing of references in the text that sometimes included 25 citations in an individual set of parentheses). We also were able to include only 8 of the 26 figures (along with one table) he attached to his chapter, and those interested in his fascinating and inclusive set of citations along with his complete list of figures are asked to write directly to Dr. Frawley to obtain copies.

However, I don't think the strength of Frawley's argument was affected by these deletions. I say this because the article originally arrived without any references and did not rely in any place on a specific citation or research finding. Indeed, the absence of specific references emphasizes the schematic nature of Frawley's presentation, which finds its strength in the translation of medical and Alcoholics Anonymous precepts into neurological and behavioral terms. The figures included here indicate that this schema can be applied not only to biological feedback loops but also to learning about drug effects and even to family functioning. For example, the same model shows (in figures 2–7 and 2–8) how people respond both to experiential and metabolic stimuli.

Indeed, as a clinician, Frawley relies on exactly this schematic clarity to teach alcoholics how to cope with their feelings and situational stresses. It is this heuristic value that may recommend the model more than any detailed research findings that tend to prove or disprove its assumptions. These assumptions, however, are quite opposite from Marlatt and Fromme's. What, then, are we to make of results indicating that the Schick Shadel aversion model Frawley expounds and Marlatt's relapse prevention model have both demonstrated unusually good success in treating alcoholism (cf. Chaney et al., 1978; Wiens and Menustik, 1983)? The tempting conclusion is that more important for outcomes than the type of therapy or treatment philosophy are therapists' commitment to the philosophy and their skill in applying it, along with clients' acceptance of the model.

Bruce Alexander, in the third chapter in this volume, leaps into the debate over the disease model by comparing this framework with what Alexander terms the adaptive model. Alexander's concerns are broader than the individual clinical outcomes on which Frawley and Marlatt and Fromme base their arguments. In Alexander's view, the disease framework disregards the methods people have developed to deal with a lack of personal integration. To disavow the personal meaning of an addiction in this way leads to coercive forms of treatment, a militaristic social order, and a denial of a humane and communal basis for approaching individual and social problems. For Alexander, those who fail to achieve mature integration because of personal or environmental deficiencies seek a range of addictive adaptations, including drugs, alcohol, and other addictions (including addictive love relationships) in order to forestall further disintegration.

Each contributor to this volume presents an implicit or explicit model of the nature and sources of addiction, of which Alexander's adaptive model is one. Marlatt and Fromme see alcoholism as a socially learned, pharmacological means for addicts to transform themselves magically into more acceptable people, both in their own eyes and in the eyes of others. This view combines the adaptive notion with a view of addiction as self-destructive fantasy. Frawley's model (in line with Alexander's characterization of disease views) sees alcoholism and drug addiction as biological mechanisms that have replaced personal methods for coping. Unlike the adaptive view, the disease view finds that these pharmacological mechanisms are imprinted due to inherited susceptibility to drug effects and a continued exposure to drugs that interferes with and replaces the individual's natural coping mechanisms.

As a part of his argument against the hegemony of disease views of addiction, Alexander takes on the seminal genetic research of Goodwin. He finds this work is less than it claims to be and, even put in the most favorable light, is far from the deterministic model of alcoholism often presented by popularizers such as Franks (1985). Ralph Tarter and Kathleen Edwards in this volume also recognize the difficulty in identifying a genetic source for alcoholism. These authors, however, express a faith that the topology of alcoholism must include a sizable genetic component. They trace alcoholism back to several potential inherited factors, among which their favored candidate is an inherited temperament marked by volatility and impulsiveness. Nonetheless, they believe the path to expression of this temperament in the form of alcoholism is a complex one. Environmental factors may play the largest role, including social stressors (as in the case of American Indians) and availability of a given drug.

Creating a deterministic model may be fundamentally limited by the possibility that the same temperament can lead to a wide variety of compulsive or antisocial behaviors. Tarter and Edwards believe that such diagnostic categories as the manias (among which could be included *dipsomania,* the term by which alcoholism was once designated as a psychiatric category) may all be different outcroppings of a similar dispositional disorder. Overall, these authors believe, the underlying disorder must be addressed directly to prevent addiction. Although availability of a substance will affect any individual addictive manifestation, to eliminate one addictive manifestation is mainly to enhance the possibility that addiction will surface in some other behavioral area. Although Tarter and Edwards, along with Alexander, express this viewpoint most directly, all the models presented up to this point view different addictions as alternate attempts at coping with environmental and internal pressures.

Shepard Siegel, Marvin Krank, and Riley Hinson present the most formal model of addiction effects in this collection in outlining the role of classical conditioning in tolerance and withdrawal. That is, the defining traits of addiction comprise learned, anticipatory reactions by the organism to drugs or to their withdrawal. To separate addictive phenomena in this way from actual administration of a substance suggests similar learned processes that operate in immunology, exercise, and stress reactions to augment, imitate, or counteract basic physiological processes. This entire fascinating area of experimental investigation opens up the concept of addiction to proprioceptive or endogenous contributions by the organism beyond any (or in the complete absence of) contributions from drugs themselves.

If tolerance and withdrawal occur without current or recent administration of a substance, then these are not necessarily pharmacological phenomena and may result from other interactions between organism and environment. Siegel and his colleagues indicate these responses occur where physiological changes are produced by such nonpharmacological means as exercise, illness, or stress. However, it would seem physiological changes occur as a result of all major interactions with the environment, such as sex, eating, and emotional reactions of all kinds (Leventhal, 1982). Furthermore, we may wonder about the role of cognitions and values in these responses. In what sense, for example, is the pitter-patter of the heart when a lover comes into view conditioned by fantasy, ideals about love, and simple sound judgments about the type of person it is good to form a love relationship with (Peele, in press)? The conditioning analysis presented here opens up whole new dimensions for conceiving addictive phenomena.

Ovide and Cynthia Pomerleau synthesize such psychological and physiological elements into a biobehavioral model of addiction. That is, models of addiction regularly posit separate psychological and physical dependence components (Peele, 1985). Pomerleau and Pomerleau recognize such distinctions may be meaningless and may even create incorrect assumptions about addictive behavior. Their resolution is to define addiction to allow a place for changes in the "internal milieu" (changes in consciousness and feeling) as long as these are indicated by "neurochemical or neuronal activity." Is the person then addicted who compulsively pursues a harmful involvement where no neuronal activity has been measured? If neuronal activity measures do not jibe with such behavior, is the person then not addicted? Pomerleau and Pomerleau report that the urge to take drugs (which in itself is related in unknown ways to neuronal activity) is very inexactly linked to actual drug use (cf. Tiffany and Baker, 1986).

For their paradigmatic addiction, the Pomerleaus refer to cigarette smoking. They caution that smoking produces genuine physical dependence, although they claim not on the order of other, unspecified drugs. Yet general epidemiological data and phenomenological observation qualify smoking as addictive without reservation, which the Pomerleaus indicate cannot be accounted for strictly in terms of pharmacological dependence. Other factors they find relevant to addictive behavior include subjective states (like anxiety) and familiar settings and activities, which they analyze in a learning framework. They explore the neurochemical effects of nicotine in relation to smoking sensations and, further, construct a model involving individual susceptibility, setting, behavior, and consequences, all of which include genetic, developmental (such as idiosyncratic social-learning), and sociocultural components.

Pomerleau and Pomerleau, as do all authors in this collection, deduce therapeutic and preventive techniques from their model. For example, in common with Siegel et al., they discuss modification of environmental stimuli in eliminating addiction. In common with Marlatt and Fromme, they deal with the creation of alternate coping abilities in the addict. And, along with Frawley, they discuss finding pharmacological or neuroactivating substitutes for drug use. The Pomerleaus do not discuss sociocultural modifications or developments that could remove or prevent addictions, of the kind outlined by Alexander, even though they find influences at the cultural level (as do Tarter and Edwards) to be crucial for the expression of an addiction. Oetting and Beauvais, reviewing the range of models of substance abuse, find the social level to be the most important in determining drug use.

Oetting and Beauvais focus on the immediate peer group because of the strong consistencies in drug use within the peer group (compared with the minimal role played by the *type* of substance or by individual personality traits). Their own data examine gradations of involvements with drugs and alcohol among thousands of adolescents from a variety of social backgrounds. Along with their own data, Oetting and Beauvais refer to other important data bases and to clinical observations of the development of substance abuse that support their views. Individual exceptions to the peer-group model are almost nonexistent; at the same time (as these authors indicate) they "have only moved the problem one step back." That is, how do some children become so heavily involved in unhealthy peer groups? For answers to this question they look to the family and to socioeconomic factors (particularly disadvantaged and minority status).

Social-level factors like these are normally given short shrift not only in disease, neurobehavioral, and genetic models, but in learning—even social learning—approaches. The specific recommendations Oetting and Beauvais make for combatting drug and alcohol abuse are to attack the predisposing social forces that lead the person toward addiction. Simply addressing drug use in therapy, or even removing a child to a non–drug-using therapeutic community, offer little chance for a permanent reorientation for the young person. This social analysis raises questions about whether we can combat addiction in the absence of attacking underlying social-environmental problems in our society. Again and again the importance of overriding social forces has been adumbrated by the authors in this collection, even those dealing with genetic and neurobehavioral explanations.

Craig MacAndrew analyzes our society's addiction-proneness at an entirely different level. MacAndrew, one of the few addictionologists to have done significant work both at a sociocultural (MacAndrew and Edgerton, 1969) and an individual-clinical (MacAndrew, 1981) level, here delves into our modern cultural ethos, finding it to be in some essential way addictive. Addiction, he argues, is not limited to simple objects such as alcohol or narcotics. Rather, it pervades every aspect of our object and personal relationships. Drawing on philosophy, psychoanalysis, abnormal psychology, Christianity, Eastern religion, and the writings of AA, MacAndrew understands addiction as a byproduct of America's—and modern humans'—pre-occupation with self. Oddly, in this madcap pursuit of self-gain, we have lost both the worldly benefits we seek and spiritual wholeness, while endangering our civilization.

MacAndrew avers both that our civilization inflicts undue guilt and that society members should be guilty because they are so extremely self-centered. John McFadden addresses the role of guilt in modern society, particularly its role in alcoholism, from the perspective of neo-Freudian ego analysis. For McFadden, guilt is at the root of nearly all emotional disturbance, and alcoholism represents a search for relief from guilt. Even social learning theorists recognize the intense aversiveness of self-contempt; it makes sense to McFadden that the individual seeks alcoholic unconsciousness rather than to confront guilt-inspiring thoughts and feelings. The primary step to curing addiction then becomes to alleviate clients' guilt, which McFadden accomplishes through empathy and acceptance.

McFadden does not find the disease approach helpful, despite its claims that it eliminates guilt and self-recrimination for the alcoholic. He notes that the disease model encourages guilt by accusing of denial those who are not comfortable at Alcoholics Anonymous meetings, who don't believe they are alcoholic, or who don't wish to abstain or follow other disease precepts—the large majority of those with alcohol problems. Peele objects to the disease model for reasons exactly the opposite of McFadden's. For Peele, the disease theory and other approaches to addiction claiming the mantle of scientific discovery actually represent the imposition of an ideology, one that replaces individual and social responsibility with mythical disease, biochemical, and clinical accounts of behavior.

Yet, Peele notes, individuals and groups that insist on personal accountability and do not accept intoxication as an excuse for misbehavior have the lowest rates of addiction and substance-related misconduct. Peele is not optimistic about the impact of modern approaches to addiction on society. He finds they justify and reinforce trends that attack the core of our social fiber and individual self-conceptions with results that will be quite the opposite of those the modern addiction movement claims it will achieve. The world as seen by the addiction specialist and increasingly conveyed to young people is not, in Peele's view, a world worth living in. In place of this world view, Peele recommends a value-oriented approach that emphasizes what is positive in the world and in the individual, whether addicted or a substance abuser or not.

I used the third person in summarizing my chapter because my job as an editor is to present in as evenhanded a way as I can the opposing points of view represented in this collection. In writing my chapter I had an entirely different goal—to present as persuasively as possible a point of view I feel needs urgently to be put forward. Each reader of this volume needs to consider seriously all the points of view that appear, while at the same time developing a definite, workable model of addiction for himself or herself. Most people come to this task with strong prejudices in favor of one model—or type of model—or another. Nonetheless, I ask them to identify while reading each article with the perspective of its author(s). Why does the model each author (or set of authors) presents make sense to the authors in terms of their data, goals, and backgrounds?

In terms of evaluating all points of view from a larger framework (as Alexander attempts in his chapter), I respectfully suggest the following test questions: What function does the view expressed serve for the author(s); what does it do for addicted individuals; what impact does the view have on our society as a whole; how well does it make sense out of the research data; how well does it conform to the reader's personal observations and experiences; and, lastly, if everybody in the world held this view, what would our world be like? At the present time, as MacAndrew suggests, views of addiction in our advanced, medicotechnological society reduce addiction to an impersonal force viciously assailing us and the world we know. But the animal all of us are trying to get our hands around may be something far vaster and yet nonetheless incorporeal. It may be so hard to grasp because it is both a part of us and yet as large as our world.

References

Chaney, E.F., M.R. O'Leary, and G.A. Marlatt. 1978. Skill Training and Alcoholics. *Journal of Consulting and Clinical Psychology* 46:1092–1104.

Franks, L. 1985. A New Attack on Alcoholism. *New York Times Magazine,* October 20:47–50, 61–69.

Leventhal, H. 1982. The Integration of Emotion and Cognition. In M.S. Clark and S.T. Fiske, eds., *Affect and Cognition: The 17th Annual Symposium on Cognition.* Hillsdale, NJ: Erlbaum.

MacAndrew, C. 1981. What the MAC Scale Tells Us about Men Alcoholics: An Interpretive Review. *Journal of Studies on Alcohol* 42:604–625.

MacAndrew, C., and R. Edgerton. 1969. *Drunken Comportment: A Social Explanation.* Chicago: Aldine.

Peele, S. 1985. *The Meaning of Addiction.* Lexington, MA: Lexington Books.

———. In press. Fools for Love: The Romantic Ideal, Psychological Theory, and Addictive Love. In R.J. Sternberg and M. Barnes, eds., *Anatomy of Love.* New Haven: Yale University Press.

Tiffany, S.T., and T.B. Baker. 1986. Tolerance to Alcohol: Psychological Models and Their Application to Alcoholism. *Annals of Behavioral Medicine* 8:7–12.

Wiens, A.N., and C.E. Menustik. 1983. Treatment Outcome and Patient Characteristics in an Aversion Therapy Program for Alcoholism. *American Psychologist* 38:1089–1096.

1
Metaphors for Addiction

G. Alan Marlatt
Kim Fromme

Introduction

Having been a poor young man, Midas, when he became king, desired great riches and power. To this end, he gathered enormous amounts of gold but was not satisfied.

One day Midas offered comfort to his venerable teacher, Bacchus, god of wine. For this kindness, Bacchus offered to grant one wish to Midas. Midas wished to have the magical power to turn everything he touched into gold. Bacchus, although warning Midas against this foolhardiness, cast a spell over Midas, granting his wish.

At first Midas was overjoyed with his magical power and ordered his servants to prepare a grand feast for him to celebrate his great happiness at being granted his desire: to be the richest king in all the world. Alas, as each piece of food and each glass of wine he touched turned to gold, his happiness soured. "How will I ever eat or drink again?" Midas wondered.

Deep in thought, he stepped wearily into his magnificent garden where his little daughter saw him. Upon seeing her running joyfully to kiss and hug him, Midas forgot his woe and eagerly outstretched his arms for her. At the moment he touched her, she instantly turned to gold. "How foolish am I!" Midas exclaimed. "How foolish to have desired so much power and to have wished for a golden touch!"

In great despair for his daughter's sake, Midas prayed to the god of wine to restore his child to him. "Please, Bacchus," he prayed, "bring back my child—and take this cursed magical power away from me!"

Bacchus, on hearing Midas's prayer, pitied him and instructed Midas to bathe in a special pool of water, whereupon his power to turn everything into gold would vanish. And if Midas brought some of this water back with him and poured it over the golden statue of his darling child, she would once again laugh and sing, Bacchus said.

Most happily, Midas did as he was told: He brought his daughter back to life and no longer had—or desired—the power to create gold with his very touch. Never again did Midas think of power and gold as more valuable than all else or anyone.

Although usually interpreted as a story about greed, avarice, and the quest for gold, the Midas metaphor can also be applied to the basic attachment or "greed for pleasure" that characterizes the addictive experience. The attachment to gold in the Midas story is reminiscent of descriptions of alchemists who searched for the magic elixir that would transform lead into gold. Some drugs, particularly alcohol, have been similarly described as magic elixirs, capable of transforming the lead of negative emotions into a golden glow of intoxication (Marlatt, in press). Feeling himself deficient in several areas of life, Midas turned to Bacchus, god of wine, for power and wealth. This parallels research that has identified desires for enhanced personal power and feelings of self-worth as motivations for drinking alcohol (McClelland et al., 1972). Initial positive effects of Midas's gold-making ability are similar to the positive experiences reported from the initial effects of drinking (Conners and Maisto, 1979; Conners and Sobell, 1986). However, like Midas—who began to discover significant problems related to his new powers—the magical qualities associated with moderate drinking or drug use can ultimately become problematic with increased use over time. A behavior over which Midas had once exercised control began to control him, as so often happens in the addictive cycle. Alienation of loved ones, illustrated by Midas's loss of his daughter, leads some drug users to give up their "magical behaviors," cleansing themselves in the waters of abstinence.

The theme of drugs and the transformation of emotional states is exemplified *par excellence* in the mythical stories of the Greek god, Dionysus (also known as Bacchus), the god of wine. Dionysus was a god with a dual nature, one who could both be kind and beneficent, on the one hand, or cruel and frightful on the other. Often he drove people mad (the Maenads, or Bacchantes, were women frenzied with wine). These opposing personality characteristics (the best modern example of which is exhibited by Robert Louis Stevenson's characters, Dr. Jekyll and Mr. Hyde) metaphorically represent the dual qualities of wine, with its capacity to evoke both pleasure and pain. The positive qualities of Dionysus border on the ecstatic and divine. In a commentary on Dionysus, Edith Hamilton (1942:60) notes that

> Under his influence courage was quickened and fear banished, at any rate for the moment. He uplifted his worshipers; he made them feel that they could do what they had thought they could not. All this happy freedom and confidence passed away, of course, as they either grew sober or got drunk, but while it lasted it was like being possessed by a power greater than themselves. So people felt about Dionysus as about no other god. He was not only outside of them, he was within them, too. They could be transformed by him into being like him. The momentary sense of exultant power wine-drinking can give was only a sign to show men that they had within them more than they knew; "then could themselves become divine."

Dionysus's negative side was just the opposite, a heartless god, savage, brutal, as he "hunts his prey/Snares and drags him to his death/With his Bacchanals" (Hamilton, 1942:59).

The myth of Dionysus exemplifies what we could call today the biphasic effect of alcohol and other psychoactive drugs (Marlatt, in press)—the immediate gratification associated with the initial effects, followed by the delayed "opponent-process" of negative aftereffects, particularly in the addicted individual (Solomon, 1980). Recent research on expectancies about the effects of alcohol shows that problem drinkers often harbor unrealistically positive beliefs about alcohol's global transformation effect; namely, that drinking will make one feel good no matter how one feels before imbibing (Goldman et al., 1987). Stories about Dionysus and his various adventures help exemplify the role that these positive outcome expectancies play in the development of addiction. Such expectancies can be considered to be at the very root of *psychological dependency,* the belief that alcohol/Bacchus can transform negative feelings into the "exultant power" of Dionysian intoxication.

What Are Metaphors?

Literary scholars and rhetoricians have been defining, redefining, and confining the definition and use of metaphor for centuries. There is basic agreement that metaphor is a figure of speech that makes a comparison between two otherwise unlike entities. However, the importance of distinguishing metaphor from other similar prose, such as allegory, proverb, and simile, has been debated. Based on Aristotle's definition of metaphor, Turbayne (1970) suggests that one consider parable, fable, allegory, and myth as subclasses of metaphor. Technical distinctions among these subclasses are beyond the scope of the present chapter. We will consider metaphor to be "a way of speaking in which one thing is expressed in terms of another, whereby this bringing together throws new light on the character of what is being described" (Kopp, 1971:17).

Applications of Metaphor

Various forms of metaphor have been used throughout history to transmit important cultural, sociological, and moral information. Stories can be used to give instructions or suggestions for action, present different opinions or ways of viewing a situation, or offer possible solutions to problems. The Bible is particularly noteworthy for the wealth of metaphor contained within its pages. Behavioral instructions and consequences for one's actions are clearly evidenced in Jesus' parables. Likewise, Greek mythology communicates many behavioral principles and related sociological implications. As an example, the myth of Daedalus and Icarus is cited by Barker (1985) with reference to addiction. As will be recalled, in order to escape their prison island (Crete), Daedalus and his son, Icarus, constructed four wings from seagull feathers and melted wax, which they affixed to pairs of wooden frames. After days of practice, father and son embarked on their escape flight to Athens. Daedalus warned his son not to fly too high or the sun would melt the wax and send him to the ocean far below. At first Icarus followed closely behind his father, but as he grew more confident he went higher and higher. No man had ever been so high before. As Icarus got closer to the sun, the hot rays melted the wax holding the feathers to his wings, and he plunged to his death. The implications of the dangers of getting "too high" from drugs are clearly spelled out in this myth.

Another Greek myth referred to by Barker (1985) is the story of Pandora's box, an allegory of giving into temptation. Once Pandora gave in and lifted the lid of the box, contrary to the commands of Zeus, all hell broke loose in the form of the troubles that now plague humankind—pain, decay, craving, hunger, envy, revenge, and hatred, along with all the diseases that cause sickness and death (including addiction, we presume). As Barker (1985:180) notes

> This tale is rich in symbolism. Pandora, artificially created by Zeus as a punishment for mankind, seems to me a rather nice metaphor for euphoriant drugs—beautiful, much to be desired, but in the end cruel and destructive and bringing unhappiness. The box, too, could represent drugs of addiction. Once you start them, it is hard to go back, just as Pandora couldn't quickly close the box again; the damage had been done.

Fairy tales and children's stories are other classic examples of the use of metaphor to communicate cultural and moral information to children (Bettelheim, 1975). A child need not live in the countryside to learn the dangers of "crying wolf," or work in a puppet store to understand the consequences of lying. Walt Disney's character, Dumbo the elephant, could metaphorically represent an addicted individual. Dumbo was convinced that he was able to fly only because he held a "magic feather" in his trunk. When Dumbo dropped the feather, he fell to the ground, forgetting that he was able to fly by flapping his giant ears. In the current context, we can conjure up the picture of Dumbo the Dope Fiend, who relies on his magic feather/drug to fly high.

In addition to general teaching purposes, metaphor has been used extensively in some forms of psychotherapy (Kopp 1976). Less threatening and confronting than direct communications, metaphor can be helpful in establishing rapport and in defining or explaining the nature of the client's problems. Fears over entering therapy, for example, might be desensitized through a story about learning to ride a bicycle; the need for training wheels at first, but the ability to later ride on one's own.

By paralleling the client's particular situation and problem, metaphor can also be used to reframe and redefine presenting complaints (Brandler and Grinder, 1982). For the client who exacerbates his or her situation by moral brow-beating, a disease metaphor might assist in positive reframing of the problem. Furthermore, the positive aspect of alleviating moral responsibility for the problem may motivate the individual to seek treatment. If the therapist has reason to expect the client to be unwilling to accept the therapist's formulation, metaphor might also be used to summarize conceptualizations of the problem. Any time direct expression of ideas might be upsetting to the client, indirect, embedded messages can be presented via metaphorical expression.

For the pessimistic client, metaphor can be used to increase self-efficacy and motivation through stories about other people overcoming similar problems (Rosen, 1982). Available resources can be reviewed, and the client may be helped to see his or her potential for change. In addition, metaphor might be a way to assist the client in setting believable goals for therapy. Both proximal and distal goals (Bandura, 1986) might be presented metaphorically. For example, a distal goal of life-long abstinence could be represented as a long journey. The proximal goals could be likened to reviewing the map and preparing the route prior to leaving on the journey.

Milton Erickson was a master of metaphor in the therapeutic relationship (Lankton and Lankton, 1983; Rosen, 1982). Erickson saw metaphor as a means of circumventing the biases, limiting beliefs, and rigid perceptual patterns of the conscious mind (Lankton and Lankton, 1983). Through metaphor, unique ideas can be presented, and the clients' awareness and understanding of their problems expanded. In combination with hypnosis, Ericksonian therapy views metaphor as a powerful mechanism for therapeutic change.

Disease Metaphors for Addiction

Disease metaphors for addiction have profound implications for the ways one conceptualizes both the etiology and treatment of addiction. Biomedical approaches to addiction continue their search for the key to the disease process, presumably to be found in some deranged physiological process or genetic aberration. Once the key etiological mechanism is uncovered, it is assumed that a medicinal "magic bullet" will follow as a cure for the disease—much as occurred in the case of tuberculosis once the etiological role of the tubercle bacillus was established. The search for biological markers to detect the young who are prone to addiction is illustrated by the recent establishment of the National Foundation for Prevention of Chemical Dependency Disease by a group in Omaha, Nebraska. The Mission Statement for this foundation is as follows: "To sponsor scientific research and development of a simple biochemical test that can be administered to our young children to determine any predisposition for chemical dependency disease; to promote greater awareness, understanding and acceptance of the disease by the general public so prevention or treatment can be commenced at the age youngsters are most vulnerable, thus giving all persons born with predispositions to the disease a maximum opportunity to lead normal, healthy lives" (Isaacson, 1984).

To date, however, the underlying biomedical mechanism of addiction has yet to be found, despite decades of diligent searching (Peele, 1985). New hope that the discovery is near is garnered by the use of sophisticated high-tech instrumentation and advanced technology. The recent use of "imaging techniques" to visually trace specific drug actions (e.g., alcohol) on brain functioning has inspired new optimism that the key will soon be discovered (Chao, 1986). But are we looking in the right place for the key? One is reminded of the old joke about the drunk who lost his car keys late one night. When asked where he lost them, he replied, "Down the street, near my car." When asked why he was restricting his search to the area under a bright street-light, he replied, "Why, the light's better here, of course!" Modern technology may permit us to shine a brighter light into the body's physiological processes, but there is no guarantee that this will illuminate a biological key to addiction.

The quest for the endogenous physical etiology is predicated on the notion that addiction is primarily a biomedical disease, such that the overt *behavior* of addiction is driven by genetic/physiologic processes that act beyond the individual's volitional sphere of control. It follows that alcoholism is defined as a disease characterized primarily by parameters such as tolerance, physical dependency, withdrawal, and associated "loss of control" symptomatology. But, as Szasz (1974) and other critics have noted, the fact that behavioral disorders such as alcoholism appear to be *similar* to other medical disorders such as diabetes does not necessarily imply that these conditions actually *are* disease entities. Although metaphors can be useful verbal representations of events, they are *not* the events themselves. Indeed, in developing metaphors, it is crucial to heed the cautious statement of Korzybski (1933:58): "A map *is not* the territory it represents, but, if correct, it has a similar *structure* to the territory, which accounts for its usefulness." As Szasz (1974:5) points out, addiction-as-disease concepts have

progressively metamorphized disagreeable conduct and forbidden desire as disease—thus creating more and more mental diseases; second, they literalized this *medical metaphor,* insisting that disapproved behavior was not merely *like* a disease, but that it *was* a disease—thus confusing others, and perhaps themselves as well, regarding the differences between bodily and behavioral "abnormalities."

The disease metaphor for addiction has important implications for the alcoholic or other addict. The alcoholic is told that there is no known "cure" for the disease, that alcoholism is progressive, extending inexorably downwards to the depths of degradation, despair, and eventually death unless the condition is "arrested" by continuous abstinence. The metaphorical message is that the alcoholic is a helpless pawn of a powerful disease entity that grips the victim in a downward slide until he or she "hits bottom." Because there is no known magic bullet to pharmacologically stave off the disease process or instill abstinence, the alcoholic is told to turn elsewhere for help. Membership in self-help groups such as Alcoholics Anonymous (AA) or Narcotics Anonymous is typically recommended by advocates of the disease model.

Strange bedfellows: a physical disease is alleviated by a quasi-religious, self-help fellowship that encourages reliance on a higher power to facilitate behavioral change. It is as though a higher power is needed to offset the ravages of a lower power manifested in the form of a physical disease process. That a physical disease such as alcoholism can be arrested through involvement in a spiritual discipline such as AA illustrates the following critical point regarding the determination of change: the parameters of determinants of behavior change (e.g., abstinence from drugs) may be independent or causally unrelated to the factors that led to the development of the problem in the first place. As Brickman and his colleagues (1981) have pointed out in a brilliant attributional analysis of various models of helping and coping, determinants of etiology may be independent of determinants of change.

Brickman et al. (1982) outlined a fourfold analysis of models of etiology and change that has significant implications for the addictions field. Two questions are asked from an attributional perspective: (1) Is the individual (addict) considered to be personally responsible for the *development* (etiology) of the addiction problem (yes/no), and (2) is the addict considered the responsible agent for *changing* the problem (yes/no)? The four models that emerge from this 2 × 2 contingency table are as follows: (1) the medical/disease model, which assumes that the addict is considered free from personal responsibility for the development of the addiction, but that change is impossible unless one submits to some kind of medical treatment program (presumably geared toward the alleviation of the underlying disease); (2) the moral model, which holds that the addict is to blame for becoming addicted (e.g., due to lack of willpower or moral fiber) and that he or she is also to be held responsible for changing or failing to change the addictive behavior; (3) the so-called enlightenment model, which holds that the addict is to some extent personally responsible for the emergence of the addiction but must give up the notion of personal control in order to change (as in AA, where the alcoholic becomes enlightened to the notion that change is possible only by relinquishing personal control to a "higher power"); and (4) the compensatory model, which holds that the individual learns to "compensate" for a problem by assuming active responsibility and self-mastery in the change process but that the individual is not held personally responsible for the problem (e.g., addiction develops as a function of multiple biopsychosocial determinants, and not as a failure in personal will).

Each of Brickman's four models can be considered a different metaphor for addiction (see also Shaffer, 1985). Each model provides a framework for understanding the problem and for formulating an approach to change. Behavior change, such as abstinence, can either be self-initiated, by the exercise of willpower (moral model) and/or by acquiring compensatory coping skills (compensatory model), or be the product of external professional treatment (disease model) or reliance on a self-help group or "higher power" (enlightenment model). Along similar lines, relapse (itself a medical model term) can be "reframed" by each model as a return of disease symptomatology (medical model), a sinful act (moral model), a consequence of getting out of touch with one's higher power (enlightenment model), or a mistake or error in compensatory coping (compensatory model). Each of these metaphoric alternatives has a differential impact on the addict's understanding of the problem, motivation to change, seeking treatment or initiating self-change, or response to lapses and setbacks in the process of recovery. It is for this reason that theorists and clinicians should understand the implications of the metaphorical model they adopt and inculcate with the addicted person. Metaphors are more than just stylistic figures of speech; they provide both an overarching model of causation and a blueprint for change.

Metaphors Based on the Compensatory Model of Addiction

Our own approach to the prevention and treatment of addiction favors the compensatory model. Although we do not assume that the addict is considered personally responsible for the development of the addiction (defined as an acquired habit or dependency locked in by the combined influence of powerful reinforcement contingencies, classical-conditioning effects, and higher-order cognitive factors), the individual is held responsible for assuming an active role in the change process. Cognitive-behavioral approaches to relapse prevention emphasize the learning of new coping responses (alternatives to addictive behavior), modifying maladaptive beliefs and expectancies concerning drug use, and changing one's personal lifestyle. Our work on relapse prevention (Marlatt and Gordon, 1985) includes the use of metaphors as a critical adjunct to the therapeutic change process. In the material to follow, we review some of these previously described metaphors and introduce others that may be effective in facilitating both the understanding of addiction and the process of recovery.

Metaphors and the Stages of
Addictive Behavior Change

Recent conceptual accounts of behavior change with addiction problems have emphasized a *stage model* of change (Brownell et al., 1986; Prochaska and DiClemente, 1984; Marlatt and Gordon, 1985). Most such models posit at least three stages: motivation and contemplation of change (prechange), commitment and action (initiation of self-change or commitment to treatment), and maintenance/relapse (postchange). The primary advantage to a stage model approach is that it describes change as an ongoing *process,* a series of stages over time, rather than a sole emphasis on quitting or abstinence as the primary factor of significance. Different assessment and treatment procedures (or self-change processes) appear to be associated with specific stages, thereby permitting a process-oriented sequencing of interventions. Many people who are engaged in an attempt to change an addictive habit fail to recognize the different stages involved and often overemphasize the outcome of the middle stage (initiation of change) as the critical one. Yet the problems they experience may be related to factors in other stages, such as inadequate motivation, inattention to developing adequate coping skills during the maintenance stage, etc.

In order to reframe the experience of habit change to conform with a stage or process model, we recommend the use of a *journey metaphor* (Marlatt and Gordon, 1985). Clients are told that there are three important stages to any journey: preparation, departure, and the trip itself. Preparation involves activities such as picking a destination or goal (motivation regarding desired objective of abstinence or moderation), finding a suitable vehicle for the trip (the methods of change, whether self-initiated or choice of type of treatment), locating maps, training in survival skills, and so forth. In the addiction field, most potential travelers are in a state of conflict about the impending trip. Part of them wants to stay addicted and part of them wants to leave the addiction behind—many continue to postpone their intended departure indefinitely (I'll quit tomorrow, and tomorrow . . .). These conflicts need to be recognized and dealt with during the preparation stage. Premature departure (i.e., a sudden decision to quit) often leads to lapses and setbacks in the early part of the trip.

A detailed description of a metaphorical journey for smoking cessation is provided in our account of a trip from "Tobacco Road" to "Freedom Mountain" (Marlatt and Gordon, 1985:ch. 4). This story illustrates that the initial act of quitting smoking is similar to one's *first steps* when embarking on the road to Freedom Mountain. Many people see the act of quitting as the final stage—as if quitting per se was the equivalent to having arrived at one's ultimate goal. In order to emphasize the importance of the maintenance stage, we tell our clients that it may take some time before they successfully attain their ultimate goal—escape from Tobacco Road, once and for all. For most clients, the third stage of the trip is the longest: relapse rates are particularly high during the first three months after quitting; many people take much longer, sometimes several years, before they finally attain the peak of Freedom Mountain (Brownell et al., 1986; Schachter, 1982). Although some may reach their goal on the first ascent, most take several tries before they succeed; some are never successful. For example, in a recent two-year follow-up study of smokers who quit on their own without treatment, only about one out of five people reached their goal without a single lapse; the majority moved back and forth, in and out of abstinence, as they slowly proceeded on their zig-zag journey of change (Marlatt et al., 1986). For most people, the journey is not smooth sailing—like Odysseus, we must attempt to cope with the Sirens of temptation as we sail toward our goal.

What if all fails, and a lapse occurs? In order to prevent the initial lapse from escalating into a full blown relapse, reframing the experience metaphorically may be of benefit. The target of this reframing is the abstinence violation effect (AVE), the tendency for people to blame themselves and give up trying in the face of a setback (Marlatt and Gordon, 1985:ch. 3). Attributions of the cause of an initial lapse to personal weakness (e.g., due to lack of willpower) or to disease factors that are beyond one's personal control may set the individual up for a total relapse (Curry et al., in press). From the compensatory model perspective, a lapse is redefined as an error, a mistake that can be benefited from. Errors and mistakes are to be expected when one attempts to master any new habit or skill, such as learning to ride a bicycle, play a musical instrument, or acquire a foreign language. The point is to extract whatever useful information can be derived from the mistake (e.g., the skater who is learning to maintain balance during a turn on the ice) and to try again. In some cases one learns so much from a single lapse that it may turn out to be the last such experience—every successful period of recovery begins with the end of the last relapse. When this happens, we refer to the episode as a "prolapse" in which the "fall" is "forward" as opposed to the back-sliding of relapse (Marlatt and Gordon, 1985:ch. 1).

A story to illustrate the shortcomings of "willpower" as a means of resisting temptation and avoiding relapse has been described in Marlatt and Gordon (1985:ch. 4). The story concerns a man in India who was attempting to control a poisonous snake. To keep himself safe from the snake (symbolizing temptation and danger, a role the snake has played since its first appearance in the Garden of Eden), the man strapped it securely in a wicker basket, tying down the lid with strong cords and ropes. The story illustrates the use of strong willpower as a means of "keeping the lid on" temptation. Once the snake was securely fastened in the box, the man's curiosity began to grow about the snake. Was the snake alive or dead in the box? Like Pandora's, his curiosity grew to the point where he could no longer stand the suspense, and he began to untie the cords and sashes from the lid to peek inside and ascertain the snake's state of being. Just as he finally pried open the lid enough to take a quick look inside, the snake sprang out and delivered a fatal bite. The moral of the story concerns the best way to "control" the snake of temptation. By suppressing temptation by the sheer force of willpower, the strength and danger of the tempting forces increase correspondingly. An alternative method of "control" would be much more effective. Rather than keeping the snake locked in the box where it cannot be observed, the snake might be let out so that its natural behavior could be observed and studied. Only by fully understanding the behavior of the snake (i.e., how the snake reacts to enclosed spaces, how it feeds itself, how it reacts to human beings, etc.) can we fully protect ourselves from its dangers. Similarly, the person who is attempting to overcome an addictive habit will benefit from a full understanding of how temptation works—the cues that trigger craving, the expected time-course of urges, etc.—so that an adequate and effective means of coping with temptation can be developed. Willpower alone will not do the job; it takes both awareness and active coping to keep the snake at bay. Willpower can be reframed as the *motivation* to change, but it is not the *means* of change. As the saying goes, where there's a will, there's a way.

Even if a lapse has been successfully dealt with, the reactions to the setback can continue to be a problem for both the individual with the addiction problem and his or her friends and family. Sometimes the sense of failure triggered by the lapse continues to exert a negative influence long after the actual event has passed and may increase the likelihood of further backsliding. To counter this sense of continued failure, the following story may be told. This story is about two Buddhist monks who were walking through the forests of Southeast Asia on their way to a ceremonial gathering. Buddhist monks adopt a number of religious precepts when they are ordained. One precept prohibits the monk from any contact with persons of the opposite sex. Monks are not allowed to touch, or even to look at, women. As the story goes, our two monks were walking along the forest path when they suddenly came around a bend to find a beautiful woman standing in front of a rushing muddy stream that was blocking the path. Dressed in a spotless white gown, she stood there helplessly, trying to figure out how to cross the stream, surging with water from the recent monsoon. Without speaking a word, one of the monks came up behind the woman, picked her up in his arms, and silently carried her across the stream, placing her down on the opposite side before continuing along the path. His companion monk could not believe what he had just witnessed. His fellow monk had broken the Buddhist's precept! Not only had he looked at a woman, he actually touched one and held her in his arms! Nothing could be as bad as this lapse in the monk's behavior, thought his companion, as the two monks trod on in Noble Silence. Finally, as the hours wore by, he could stand it no longer, and he impulsively blurted out his misgivings to his companion. "You touched a woman!" he gasped at long last. His friend looked at him and replied, "I put her down hours ago; it's clear that you are still carrying her."

Relapse is often part of the journey, often marked by warning signals, detours, crossroads, and slippery curves. Clients can learn from other people's mistakes on the road to recovery. We have made use of one individual's misfortune, a compulsive gambler from Seattle who experienced a significant relapse in Reno, Nevada. This story, based on an actual case study outlined in Marlatt and Gordon (1985:ch. 1), serves as a metaphor for the relapse process and points out the role of "set-ups," apparently irrelevant decisions (rationalization and denial components), high-risk junctions, and warning signs in the relapse process. The "moral" of the story is to show how relapse can be anticipated and possibly prevented if one accepts responsibility for change and acquires the awareness and skills of productive self-management. In the Reno story, the gambler drove from Seattle to Reno, a distance of approximately 1,000 miles. When we present the story to clinical audiences, we illustrate it with photo-slides depicting highways on the way to Reno (including the "Highway Paved with Good Intentions"), junctions (decision points that lead toward or away from Reno), highway roadsigns (e.g., "warning signs" announcing the Nevada state border), and ending with dramatic shots of slot machines and gambling casinos in downtown Reno, where the actual relapse occurred. The story line can be stopped at various points, allowing clients to discuss their personal reactions, outline alternative means of coping, etc. Because the story involves a gambler, it can be told to other addiction clients (such as alcoholics, smokers, or cocaine addicts) without raising their resistance or provoking denial.

Driving provides a useful analogy for the process of habit change (Stephens and Marlatt, in press). There are a number of parallels between driving and drug-taking. Both behaviors are learned and both can be extremely dangerous, if not fatal. Both behaviors can become largely automatic and habitual, once the individual has mastered the essentials. There are many dangers on the road and one must become a *skilled* driver to survive; the person at the wheel is in charge and responsible for keeping the vehicle from going into skids, or slipping off the shoulder or other potential mishaps. A skilled driver learns to anticipate problems, plan ahead (by consulting the roadmap, etc.), take detours when necessary, fix flat tires, and add fluids to the engine to prevent breakdowns. In a similar fashion, individuals who are attempting to free themselves from the grip of an addiction must "drive defensively," learn new ways of coping with problems, know how to cope with slips should they occur, and so on. In short, a good driver learns to be his or her own "maintenance man" (Marlatt and Gordon, 1980).

Coping with urges and craving along the road to Freedom Mountain represents a serious problem for any traveler, from Odysseus' time to the present day. Although most people may not follow Odysseus' lead in chaining themselves to the mast to resist the Sirens of craving (thereby avoiding a wreck on the rocks of temptation), they do need to learn alternative ways of dealing with urges and craving. Here again, the use of metaphor may be helpful. Many addicts experience drug cravings as coming from endogenous ("inside the body") sources. Disease theories of addiction frequently posit craving as a symptom of some underlying physiological imbalance or addictive need that gets stronger over time as the disease moves through its progressive intensification (Marlatt, 1987). To view craving in these terms is to see it as a force beyond one's personal volition, an intense physical desire that precipitates binging and other forms of loss of control. An alternative approach is to define craving as a conditioned response to some exogenous cue or stimulus, particularly those associated with prior drug use (Marlatt, 1978; Marlatt, 1987). Viewed from this perspective, an urge or craving becomes more intense over time only if reinforced by subsequent drug use. If the conditioned craving response is not reinforced, on the other hand, the urge should gradually extinguish and become *less* intense over time (Cooney et al., 1983; Hodgson and Rankin, 1982). Clients may perceive themselves as having more control over urges if they believe those urges first will rise in intensity and then reach a plateau of strength before eventually subsiding. A metaphor we often use with clients to drive home this point is to describe the urge or craving as an ocean wave—a wave that arises, crests, and subsides as it washes up on shore. We then encourage the client to think of him- or herself as a "surfer"—someone who has acquired the skills of balance and can ride the wave gracefully without being "wiped out" in the process. The "surfer" analogy, along with other metaphorical means of coping with craving (e.g., the Samurai warrior, who is constantly on guard against threats to his life) is described in greater detail by Marlatt and Gordon (1985:ch. 4).

Why Use Metaphors?

The advantage of choosing metaphorical prose, as opposed to straight exposition, for relating information may lie in its relative palatability. Direct teaching of moral or behavioral principles often meets with resistance because the message is too aversive, too difficult to understand, or arouses reactance (Brehm and Brehm, 1981). As an indirect form of communication, metaphor can be a more gentle way of transmitting difficult or unwanted lessons. In addition, metaphors are usually more interesting than straight expositions and hold the potential for capturing the recipient's attention and imagination. Novel ways of viewing a situation or problem might therefore be more likely.

Why Metaphors Are Effective

Several theories have been offered for the apparent effectiveness of metaphor to facilitate increased understanding and to promote change. Neurological arguments (e.g., Watzlawick, 1978) suggest that metaphor is the language of the right cerebral hemisphere. According to Watzlawick (1978:1415), there are two languages involved:

> The one . . . is objective, definitional, cerebral, logical, analytic; it is the language of reason, of science, explanation and interpretation, and therefore the language of most psychotherapy. The other . . . is much more difficult to define. . . . We might call it the language of imagery, of metaphor, of *pars pro toto,* perhaps of symbols, but certainly of synthesis and totality, and not of analytical dissection.

Cited by Barker (1985), Lamb's 1980 review of the relationship between hemispheric laterality and storytelling provides some support for such a contention. She concluded that the left hemisphere processes data in a sequential fashion, and as such, is best suited to logical, temporal, verbal, and analytic concerns. The right hemisphere, on the other hand, is assumed to process information in a simultaneous, holistic manner (Ornstein, 1977). Spatial, structural, kinesthetic, gestalt, and metaphoric considerations are more in the right hemisphere's domain. It has been suggested that conscious awareness, in effect, is the left hemisphere's attempt to "understand" and verbalize the activities and memories of the right hemisphere (Mahoney, 1980). Through its combination of linguistics and abstract imagery, metaphor may assist in such a process.

Neurolinguistic programming (NLP) emphasizes the use of metaphor in facilitating human change (Gordon, 1978; Bandler and Grinder, 1982). NLP, based on analysis of Cricksen's communication, considers metaphors useful for describing patterns of how people communicate their experience of the world. As such, metaphors might be considered verbal representations of what Watzlawick (1978) calls the individual's "world image," or holistic style of ordering experience. Although such ordering systems help organize experience, they also limit one's perceptions. Analogous to the Necker cube, it is impossible for an individual to hold two opposing perceptions or world images simultaneously. It would seem likely that metaphor might be used to communicate with, and possibly change, an individual's world image. Central to psychological change is the ability to alter one's representation of significant choice-limiting experiences. As a predominantly right-brain phenomenon, metaphor could be a means for accessing these holistic ordering processes. Metaphor might serve to help the individual see the "big picture," or as Gordon (1978) explains, to "provide an opportunity to step out of the trees and look at the forest."

According to Gordon (1978), an effective metaphor should include characters and events that are "isomorphic" (i.e., equivalent) with those individuals and events that characterize the client's situation and problem. All parameters of the situation and the processes involved should be represented, but the actual content and setting of the metaphor are unimportant. Metaphors can therefore be vehicles for indirectly suggesting and/or implementing changes in the client's world image.

An overall heightened awareness through metaphor has also been offered as an explanation for how metaphors work. Because of their unique and somewhat ambiguous content, metaphors are thought to stimulate an unconscious search for meaning, and to

> enhance normal comprehension mechanisms of the mind more effectively than logical speech. While conducting a massive mental search for related associations, the mind brings together the common symbols and elements of a new perceptual framework by entertaining the metaphoric theme. (Lankton and Lankton, 1983:80)

The mental search for associations to the metaphorical content is subsequently thought to make possible the blending of ideas and the creation of new ways of looking at the situation or problem.

As is alluded to in earlier comments about Ericksonian therapy, metaphor is also thought to work by circumventing conscious resistance. According to Hayek (1978), a metaphor may be a direct route to the "super-conscious," which he describes as consisting of abstract rules for being, and which appear to "govern the conscious processes without appearing in them." Our models of reality and our personal meaning systems are thought to be based on such abstract principles (Mahoney, 1982). Metaphorical content is consequently filtered through an individual's personal meaning systems, and results in idiosyncratic interpretations. This process of personal interpretation allows somewhat "generic" metaphors to have personal meaning for and consequently powerful effects on a variety of individuals.

The association between metaphor and emotion is related to the idea of tapping into the unconscious. Some theorists suggest that the power of metaphor lies in its ability to touch an affective component of the individual's experience (Barker, 1985). Emotions are presumed to make up "feeling memories," which then furnish individuals with a more or less automatic unconscious reaction repertoire to affectively meaningful stimuli (Guidano and Liotte, 1983). By providing affectively meaningful stimuli that are incongruous with the individual's current ways of seeing him- or herself or situation, metaphor may necessitate structural changes in the person's reality system. This is what Watzlawick refers to as "second-order change." Whenever a system cannot accommodate new information, structural changes are necessary to allow assimilation to occur (Guidano and Liotte, 1983).

As a consequence, the individual's thoughts, behavior, or emotions may be altered.

Conclusions

Throughout this article we have attempted to illustrate how metaphor is related to understanding, research, and treatment of addictive behaviors. Greek myths, traditional stories, and clinical anecdotes were used to illustrate metaphors of addiction. In conclusion, we would like to offer our own metaphorical dramatization of the addictive process.

Such a metaphor should include several components, common to all addiction. First, there is a need to represent the individual's life experiences leading up to the point of addiction. For example, what are the life circumstances and personal attributes that might influence development of the addiction? A second consideration involves depicting the positive aspects of the addictive substance or activity. Why is the potentially hazardous drug or action appealing? What are the actual, or expected benefits of consuming the substance or engaging in the behavior? Social influences at both the cultural and peer levels also need to be included in any addictive behavior metaphor. How do peer pressure and modeling effects influence acquisition of the addiction? Later stages of addiction may be represented by negative consequences of the process and by related denial of the problem. Recognition of the problem, motivation to change, and possible means to achieve change are important parts of the metaphor's resolution. Goal setting, lapses, and the role of personal responsibility for change are additional important considerations. The following story is our attempt to represent metaphorically commonalities among addictions.

Freddy the Flying Fish

Off the coast of southern California, not too far from Santa Catalina Island, a group of flying fish found their home. Among them lived Freddy, a teenage flying fish, who loved to shoot upwards through the water as fast as he could, breaking through the surface, gliding above the wavetops sparkling with sunbeams, and finally diving deeply back into the ocean. Unlike many of his fellow flying fish who resorted to flying only as a means of escaping such predators as the deadly shark (too heavy to fly in pursuit of his prey), Freddy and a few of his friends liked to fly for the sheer pleasure of the experience. A few flying fish had even gone on to set speed and distance records at the Ocean Olympics at Atlantis, but Freddy did not aspire to this kind of competitive flying. He simply loved the exhiliration of breaking through the resistance of the waterworld into the light airiness above the surface. Unlike most fish who had no knowledge or experience of the airworld above their heads, Freddy had direct experience with a higher level of awareness, one that existed just above the surface level. This special experience was something he had difficulty explaining to his friends who could not fly, such as Clara the Codfish and Tony the Tuna.

Freddy had two close friends. Frank was a level-headed, serious flying fish who harbored ambitions to set up an accredited flying-fish school. Another flying-fish friend was Flipper, a school-of-fish dropout, who spent most of his time looking for new ways of getting high (mostly through sex, drugs, and rock and roll).

Freddy met his girlfriend Francine while they both were flying. One golden sunset evening, Freddy soared above the waves in one of his longest flights ever. He glanced to his left just in time to see a beautiful young flying fish gliding gracefully by in the opposite direction. Their eyes met briefly as they flashed by, and Freddy felt warm sensations of romantic excitement as he dove back into the depths to seek her out. Freddy and Francine soon became boyfriend and girlfriend and spent more and more of their time together, frequently flying in tandem like two stones skipping over the surface of the sea from one wavecrest to another. It was clear to both Frank and Flipper that Freddy and Francine were in love.

One day, after a particularly long and exciting flight with Francine, Freddy was approached by Flipper. Flipper was acting strangely—he was hyperexcited and actually appeared to glow in luminescent colors as he spoke to Freddy. Frank and Francine swam by to join in the conversation. As it turned out, Flipper was high from eating a neonfish, a little known fish that he discovered one day off the south coast of Santa Catalina Island. "These neonfish are great!" Flipper raved. "They make you feel even better than when you're flying—better because you don't have to do any work, just swallow one neonfish and you'll feel high for hours! Come on, Freddy! I know where we can find some if we leave right away—the neonfish are just getting out of school about now. Let's split!" Francine, although saying nothing, looked upset because it was obvious that Freddy was tempted.

Suddenly, Frank spoke up, his voice grave and concerned. "According to the teachings of Moby Dick, some neonfish have hooks in them—but there's no way of telling just by looking at them which ones have hooks and which ones do not. But if you bite one with a hook—ZAP! You're a goner! Many fish have disappeared from the face of the ocean after biting into a hook, and no one saw them again!" There followed a long discussion concerning the risk of getting hooked. Flipper insisted that only about 1 out of every 1,000 neonfish actually contained a hook. Frank countered that the risk was much higher, that as many as 1 out of every 10 neonfish had a hook in it. Francine said that it didn't seem worth the risk. "I only have one life," she exclaimed. "Why should I take a chance even if the odds were only 1 in a million? If I get the one with the hook, I'm dead!" But it was no use. Freddy swam off with Flipper. Frank and Francine stayed behind. They both looked worried.

Freddy's first neonfish made him feel higher than he had ever felt before. Moments after swallowing his first bite, he felt a warm glow pulse throughout his body. Flipper laughed uproariously, and he saw Freddy turn a series of phosphorescent colors, first a deep ruby red and electric blue, followed by a lingering golden glow. Not only is there no hook in this neonfish, Freddy exulted, but this feels *fantastic!* He felt powerful and masculine, even more so than when things were going great with Francine. Most important to Freddy was the realization that the feelings he got from the neonfish were more exciting than those he experienced while flying. "I feel on top of the ocean!" he yelled to Flipper as they swam up behind a pair of unsuspecting neonfish. "And yet, here we are, many fathoms below the surface! It's wild!"

As the days passed into weeks and months, Freddy spent more and more of his time with Flipper. Together they sought out neonfish wherever they could find them. They both became increasingly preoccupied with neonfish, following them home each day after school, concerned that their supply might run out. Freddy spent less time with either Francine or Frank. Having gained weight from eating so many neonfish, both Flipper and Freddy became sluggish and slow in their swimming. Neither had flown above the surface in many weeks. Francine finally decided to confront Freddy with her concerns. She told him that she thought he was addicted to the neonfish and that, if he didn't do something soon, he was likely to hit bottom. Freddy shuddered for a moment as he thought of the dangers of the murky ocean-bottom—the sharks, octopus, and the deadly manta ray, the devilfish himself. "Don't worry, Francine—there's no way I'm going to hit bottom. I'm still myself— I'm alive, right? I've eaten hundreds of neonfish and not a single one had a hook inside! So how can I be hooked?" He grinned, trying to minimize the growing sense of guilt he felt whenever Francine or Frank tried to talk to him about his behavior. Francine swam away sadly.

A week later, something terrible happened to Flipper while he and Freddy were pursuing some neonfish to deeper and deeper levels. Just as Flipper was about to lunge at a particularly attractive purple and gold neonfish, a hammerhead shark appeared ominously nearby. The shark took after Flipper. "Watch out! SHARK!" Freddy screamed, but it was too late. Overweight and out of shape, Flipper could not build up enough speed to escape the shark. Just before hitting the surface of the ocean and flying off to freedom, Flipper was grabbed by the tail by the hammerhead and snatched under. Although he struggled desperately, it was over in an instant.

Flipper's death shocked Freddy into action. After Flipper's funeral, Freddy vowed to give up neonfish forever. He decided to seek help from others, turning to Frank and Francine for suggestions. Frank recommended that he spend three weeks in treatment in the Electric Eel clinic, where they offered an aversion therapy program for neonaholism. Francine, on the other hand, suggested he attend a self-help school of fish called NA (Neonaholics Anonymous), made up of fish who were all recovering from the same addiction. After several months of participation in both programs, Freddy committed himself to a lifelong period of total abstinence from all neonfish. He was told that because of his disease, he must avoid neonfish forever, that even so much as a tiny nibble of neonfish flesh would reactivate the disease. He was told that neonaholism was an inherited progressive disease and that there was no cure. All he could do was to arrest the disease by staying away from neonfish for the rest of his life. After several weeks of abstinence, Freddy started to feel his old self. He lost some weight and soon was able to fly again, just as in the old days. Francine and Freddy began dating again. They both spent a lot of time with Frank.

Three months later, Freddy had a slip. After a painful fight with Francine one night, Freddy was swimming home alone when he suddenly saw a lone neonfish, brilliantly glowing green and orange a fathom below. At first he tried to ignore the temptation, but he found himself thinking the following thoughts: "I'm feeling angry and pissed off with Francine. I know I would feel instantly better if I had a hit of neonfish. Surely just one can't hurt—after all, I never was *really* hooked before. I ate hundreds of neonfish and not a single one ever had a hook in it. Since no one is around, why not? Who would know? I think I'll swim a little deeper, drop down a level, just to get a better look at those flashing colors.

Freddy gobbled down the neonfish. He felt a mix of reactions—the spreading fire of the neonglow inside his belly (it felt particularly intense since he was no longer as tolerant to the effects), but coupled with a sense of guilt and failure. It's no use, Freddy thought—this just proves I have no willpower. Why should I try? I can't fight the disease. The more miserable he became, the greater became the lure of the neonfish as an instant relief. Soon he was back into his old addictive pattern, feeling both helpless and victimized. The neonfish became both the problem and the cure: the worse he felt, the more he was tempted to eat another neonfish to escape his bad feelings. The neonglow always felt good for a little while, but the long-range effects grew much more painful. His friends started to see less of him. Francine was particularly upset, but she did not know where to turn for help.

Finally Freddy could stand it no longer. There's no use, he thought. I can't seem to live without neonfish; yet, I can't live with them either—look at what happened to Flipper. These things will kill me in the end. But what can I do? Tired and at his wit's end, he finally decided to turn to Moby Dick for help. Although never a religious fish, Freddy opened his heart and asked for help from the Great White Whale. "I can't do it on my own," he cried. "Please help me."

That night, Freddy had a vision. He was visited by a beautiful white sailfish who said she had swum all the way from Hawaii especially to see him. The sailfish seemed so real that Freddy was not sure if he were dreaming or awake. "My name is Sarah, Freddy. Come with me," she said warmly, taking Freddy by the fin. "We're going to fly higher than you have ever been before." Freddy was amazed at how easy and effortless it was to swim alongside Sarah, who seemed to glow brighter the faster she swam. Their speed increased to an incredible velocity as they neared the surface of the water. When they at last broke through, the surface exploded as a mirror shattering into thousands of brilliant shards. Bursting through the crest of a huge wave, a Tsunami wave triggered by an undersea earthquake somewhere near the Hawaiian Islands, Freddy soared effortlessly through the midnight air. As the light of the huge golden moon glittered on the waves below, Freddy felt as though he was sailing between stars on the water and stars in the sky above. The Pacific waves surged below as Freddy and Sarah flew together in graceful silence, buoyed up by the currents of the warm summer wind. They skipped off the wavetops as they sailed along, Sarah with her long white sailfins stretched out like the wings of an albatross. After what seemed like an eternity, they dove back down into the warm ocean currents. Freddy felt totally exhilarated. His body was filled with a golden glow, warmer and more joyful than any he had experienced before, even after eating the finest neonfish. The glow of the neonfish seemed dull and lusterless compared with the brilliance of the glow he now experienced. Sarah smiled. "Now you know how high you can go. And even though I was with you, you were flying on your own, and you now know you can do it anytime you wish. It's so much higher than you can ever get with the neonfish. But, you know, the poor neonfish doesn't know how to fly above the water. That's why Moby Dick gave them the luminescent glow so that they could experience the fire within, even though they never reach the surface. But you, Freddy, you can fly on your own, higher and better than any neonfish can take you. Rely on yourself, you don't need a crutch. Just keep your heart open to your own higher power within, and you'll find that there is no limit as to how high and far you can fly." With those words, Sarah swam slowly off into the dark night waters, her body glowing as if from some inner light.

Freddy never saw Sarah again, but he never forgot that night of flying above and below the stars. He began to work on his own flying skills more and more, finding that he could improve on his performance each time he practiced. Within a year, he entered some flying competitions and soon developed a reputation as a champion flier. A year and a half after his experience with Sarah, Freddy won a gold medal at the Atlantis Ocean Olympic games for the longest, highest flight ever recorded for a California flying fish. Freddy and Francine were friends and lovers once more. Frank opened his own professional flying school, with Freddy as his co-partner. One day, while Freddy and Frank were swimming home after a day of teaching new fish how to fly, they both spotted a very attractive neonfish, glowing in bright rainbow colors, next to some seaweed. "Look at that neonfish!" Frank exclaimed. "Do you think that one has a hook in it, Freddy?" Freddy smiled slowly and looked at his friend. "Yes," Freddy said with quiet but firm conviction. "They all have hooks in them."

References

Bandler, R., and J. Grinder. 1982. *Reframing: Neuro-Linguistic Programming and the Transformation of Meaning.* Moab, Utah: Real People Press.

Bandura, A. 1986. *Social Foundations of Thought and Action.* Englewood Cliffs, NJ: Prentice Hall.

Barker, P. 1985. *Using Metaphors in Psychotherapy.* New York: Brunner/Mazel.

Bettelheim, B. 1975. *The Uses of Enchantment.* New York: Alfred Knopf.

Brehm, S.S., and J.W. Brehm. 1981. *Psychological Reactance: A Theory of Freedom and Control.* New York: Academic Press.

Brickman, P., V.C. Rabinowitz, J. Karuza, Jr., D. Coates, E. Cohen, and L. Kidder. 1982. Models of Helping and Coping. *American Psychologist* 37:368–384.

Brown, S.A., M.S. Goldman, A. Inn, and L.R. Anderson. 1980. Expectations of Reinforcement from Alcohol: Their Domain and Relation to Drinking Patterns. *Journal of Consulting and Clinical Psychology* 48:419–426.

Brownell, K.D., G.R. Marlatt, E. Lichtenstein, and G.T. Wilson. 1986. Understanding and Preventing Relapse. *American Psychologist* 41:765–782.

Chao, H.M., ed. 1986. Symposium on Imaging Research in Alcoholism. *Alcoholism: Clinical and Experimental Research* 10:223–259.

Conners, G.J., and J.R. Maisto. 1979. Effects of Alcohol, Instructions, and Consumption Rate on Affect and Physiological Sensations. *Psychopharmacology* 62:261–266.

Conners, G.J., and M.B. Sobell. 1986. Alcohol and Drinking Environment: Effects on Affect and Sensations, Personal Perception and Perceived Intoxication. *Cognitive Therapy and Research* 10:389–402.

Cooney, N.L., L. Baker, and O.F. Pomerleau. 1983. Cue Exposure for Relapse Prevention in Alcohol Treatment. In R.J. McMahon and K.D. Craig, eds., *Advances in Clinical Behavior Therapy.* New York: Brunner/Mazel.

Curry, S., J.R. Gordon, and G.A. Marlatt. In press. Abstinence Violation Effect: Validation of an Attributional Construct with Smoking Cessation. *Journal of Consulting and Clinical Psychology.*

Goldman, M.S., S. Brown, and B. Christiansen. 1987. Expectancy Theory: Thinking about Drinking. In H.T. Blaine and H.E. Leonard, *Psychological Theories of Drinking and Alcoholism.* New York: Guilford Press.

Gordon, D. 1978. *Therapeutic Metaphors.* Cupertino, CA: Meta Publications.

Guidano, V.F., and G. Liotte. 1983. *Cognitive Processes and Emotional Disorders.* New York: Guilford Press.

Hamilton, E. 1942. *Mythology: Timeless Tales of Gods and Heros.* New York: Mentor Books.

Hayek, F.A. 1978. *New Studies in Philosophy, Politics, Economics, and the History of Ideas*. Chicago: University of Chicago Press.

Hodgson, R.J., and H. Rankin. 1982. Cue Exposure and Relapse Prevention. In W.M. Hay and P.E. Nathan, eds., *Clinical Case Studies in the Behavioral Treatment of Alcoholism*. New York: Plenum.

Isaacson, F.R. 1984. *Memorandum on Research Grants for Potential Biochemical Markers for Early Detection of Alcohol and Drug Addiction*. March. Omaha, Nebraska: National Foundation for Prevention of Chemical Dependency Disease.

Kopp, S. 1971. *Guru: Metaphors from a Psychotherapist*. Palo Alto: Science and Behavior Books.

Korzybski, A. 1933. *Science and Sanity*. Clinton, MA: Colonial Press.

Lankton, S.R., and C.H. Lankton. 1983. *The Answer Within: A Clinical Framework of Ericksonian Hypnotherapy*. New York: Brunner/Mazel.

Mahoney, M.J. 1980. Psychotherapy and the Structure of Personal Revolutions. In M.J. Mahoney, ed., *Psychotherapy Process: Current Issues and Future Directions*. New York: Plenum Press.

———. 1982. Psychotherapy and Human Change Processes. In J.H. Harvey and M.M. Parks, eds., *The Master Lecture Series: Vol. 1. Psychotherapy Research and Behavior Change*. Washington, DC: American Psychological Association.

Marlatt, G.A. 1978. Craving for Alcohol, Loss of Control, and Relapse: A Cognitive-Behavioral Analysis. In P.E. Nathan, G.A. Marlatt and T. Loberg, eds., *Alcoholism: New Directions in Behavior Research and Treatment*. New York: Plenum.

———. 1987. Craving Notes. *British Journal of Addiction* 82:42–44.

———. In press. Alcohol, the Magic Elixir: Stress, Expectancy, and the Transformation of Emotional States. In E. Gottheil, ed., *Stress: Alcohol and Drug Interactions*. New York: Brunner/Mazel.

Marlatt, G.A., and J.R. Gordon. 1980. Determinants of Relapse: Implications for the Maintenance of Behavior Change. In P.O. Davidson and S.M. Davidson, eds., *Behavioral Medicine: Changing Health Lifestyles*. New York: Brunner/Mazel.

Marlatt, G.A., and J.R. Gordon, eds. 1985. *Relapse Prevention: Maintenance Strategies in the Treatment of Addictive Behaviors*. New York: Guilford Press.

Marlatt, G.A., J.R. Gordon, and S. Curry. 1986. *Smoking Cessation: A Prospective Analysis of Unaided Quitters*. Unpublished Manuscript, University of Washington.

McClelland, D.C., L.N. Davis, R. Kalin, and E. Wanner. 1972. *The Drinking Man*. New York: Free Press.

Ornstein, R.E. 1977. *The Psychology of Consciousness*. 2nd ed. New York: Harcourt, Brace, Jovanovich.

Peele, S. 1985. *The Meaning of Addiction: Compulsive Experience and Its Interpretation*. Lexington, MA: Lexington Books.

Prochaska, J.O., and C.C. DiClemente. 1984. *The Transtheoretical Approach: Crossing Traditional Boundaries of Therapy*. Homewood, IL: Dow Jones/Irwin.

Rosen, S. ed. 1982. *My Voice Will Go with You*. New York: W.W. Norton.

Schachter, S. 1982. Recidivism and Self-Cure of Smoking and Obesity. *American Psychologist* 37:436–444.

Shaffer, H.J. 1985. The Disease Controversy: Of Metaphors, Maps and Menus. *Journal of Psychoactive Drugs* 17:65–76.

Solomon, R.L. 1980. The Opponent-Process Theory of Acquired Motivation: The Costs of Pleasure and the Benefits of Pain. *American Psychologist* 35:691–712.

Stephens, R.S., and G.A. Marlatt. In press. Creatures of Habit: Loss of Control over Addictive and Nonaddictive Behaviors. *Drugs and Society.*

Szasz, T. 1974. *Ceremonial Chemistry: The Ritual Persecution of Drugs, Addicts, and Pushers.* New York: Anchor.

Turbayne, C. 1970. *The Myth of Metaphor.* Columbia, SC: University of South Carolina Press.

Watzlawick, P. 1978. *The Language of Change.* New York: Basic Books.

2
Neurobehavioral Model of Addiction: Addiction as a Primary Disease

P. Joseph Frawley

Introduction

To many observers, the addiction field must seem like the ten blind men and the elephant—each faction grasping a part but not having a unified concept of the whole. Thus, the need for a model to aid us in coordinating our efforts and advancing research is paramount. With an adequate model we can test our beliefs regarding this illness. It will help us track individuals through their illnesses and into their recoveries, and it will add structure to our therapeutic efforts.

The model must be useful to physicians, psychologists, biochemists, researchers, therapists, patients, nurses, allied health professionals, self-help groups, and families. The model that I have used in treating patients over the past five to six years is the subject of this chapter. The model is based on our current knowledge regarding the normal human survival system and encompasses various aspects of addiction. There is a place in it for genetics as well as behavior, biochemistry, and learning. I have been able to use it with patients to discuss the disease progression, the process of treatment, and recovery.

The underlying philosophy behind this model is that the addict is trying to live, not die; that the survival system is "lied" to in a peculiar way by addictive drugs, and that recovery involves reversing that lie.

The Model—The Human Survival System

What we know about the human survival system is that there are apparently built in drives and needs, some of which need to be responded to in a matter of minutes, others in terms of days, and others in terms of biorhythms. Certain parts of the brain apparently are designed to monitor whether or not those needs are being met, and if so, a chemical message is sent to a reward center after which we experience a feeling of well-being or satisfaction.

Our habits are controlled by reward that maintains behavior and distress that
motivates change of behavior.

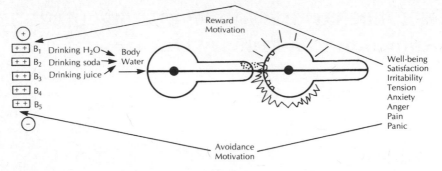

Figure 2–1. Human Survival System

In a simplified model of the human survival system, one cell monitors
needs and is able to release chemical messengers to a second cell, which we
would call a reward center (see figure 2–1). As long as behavior results in
meeting needs, that message is picked up by the monitoring cell and results in
stimulation of the reward center.

The key element in this model is the relationship between (1) behavior
that meets needs and the monitoring system and (2) the transmission of information to the reward center. When a need is not being met (for example, the
need for water), the monitoring cell stops sending out its chemical reward
message. The reward center responds to this lack of input by activating a
biochemical/emotional alarm system. We have this alarm system from the
time we are born to the time we die. There is a hierarchy to this alarm system
so that attached to thirst is an intensity measure beginning with irritability,
then tension, then anxiety, then anger, then pain, and finally panic. The
greater the deficit of the need, the higher the alarm signal. This alarm system
is nondirective in that it does not point the way to proper behavior but is
primarily something that makes us uncomfortable enough to motivate us to
change what we are doing. It brings discomfort to our awareness. Anyone
who has taken care of a six-week-old baby recognizes the distinction between
this alarm that the baby sends out and the parent's process of going through a
laundry list of needs, trying to find out why the baby is crying.

Drinking water results in satisfying thirst and, when recorded by the
monitoring cell, results in the release of a chemical messenger stimulating the
reward center. With this we experience a feeling of well-being or satisfaction.
The important thing here, however, is that the positive feeling is stored. We
have within us "reward circuits" that cause that positive feeling to feed back
and result in strengthening of the behavior that led to meeting this need. This

procedural memory is experience-based. What has become apparent is that the brain is both like and unlike a computer. It is like a computer in that we can talk about the hardware of the nerves and the software of the information coming in. However, it is unlike a computer in that it appears that the information itself alters the structure of the hardware and the type of connections that the hardware will make. Hence, when we ask if training is physical or mental, we find ourselves caught in the middle of the mind/body dispute.

However, we do not need to be there as long as we understand that the brain stores information and that information results in a physical alteration of the brain. Certain pathways are strengthened; others are weakened by our experience.

The Role of Memory

It has become evident through a variety of routes of research that there are several types of memory. We are familiar with the process of what is called declarative memory—that is, the memory that may be called up consciously and voluntarily that has certain factual information. There is also a procedural memory that appears to be based on conditioning and experiential learning that has been measured to be active in persons who are amnestic from the standpoint of declarative memory but can still demonstrate that they have learned procedures. There apparently is a third type of memory that has been called *imprinting* and is related to certain important biologic drives and critical learning periods that direct those drives. Examples have been found in geese and a variety of other birds with regard to identifying the parent to be followed and in salmon with regard to identifying the spawning grounds by the chemical composition of the water they grew up in.

With regard to the declarative and the procedural memory, the strength of the learning appears to be influenced by the state of arousal and the level of need satisfaction in the organism.

Procedural memory, however, is particularly dependent on appropriate timing, association, and repetition. Volumes have been written about the importance of conditioning from either the Pavlovian or Skinnerian models and its influence on procedural memory.

I have used the term *subconscious memory* with patients in discussing procedural memory and have likened it to a tape recorder that simply records and plays back previous experience. Declarative memory is more like a calculator that may call up a variety of specific facts stored in memory and may be used to calculate or plan future actions. This model emphasizes the power of the procedural memory when it becomes involved in training the survival system. A good example of this is learning to drive in the United States. Initially, an individual may have to carefully think about each one of the steps in driving, but over a period of time the procedural memory becomes programmed so that driving becomes automatic. This works well until the individual moves to England. The reasoning or declarative memory can read the new laws, which indicate that driving must be done on the left-hand side of the street; however, the procedural memory that has been responsible for the individual's survival on the road is still programmed to seek safety on the right-hand side of the road. This has resulted in the British government placing signs at tourist locations that read, "Americans look to the right before crossing the street."

The importance of procedural memory or subconscious memory is that it, rather than declarative memory, governs nearly all survival learning. Procedural memory provides programs for rapid mobilization for survival. It is the power of addictive drugs to train this memory that makes it difficult for the addict to get the monkey off his or her back.

The Drug

Over the past fifteen years, understanding of the nature of addictive drugs has blossomed. Experiments showing that narcotics were able to fit into receptors for endorphins, that GABA was enhanced by benzodiazepines, that cocaine enhanced dopamine/norepinephrine, and that barbiturates enhanced GABA as well, have caused us to focus on the fact that addictive drugs in general appear to mimic various neurotransmitters. We have long known that nicotine was able to stimulate and then suppress receptors for acetylcholine. In fact, a category of acetylcholine receptors was named *nicotinic receptors*. The role of alcohol is apparently more complex and may involve THIQs or THPs or membrane alterations that result in receptor or neurotransmitter shifts or some other as yet unknown mechanism. What comes out as important is that these drugs apparently are able to artificially stimulate or enhance the stimulation of receptors for neurotransmitters (see table 2–1).

These drugs are able to artificially stimulate the reward center and produce a feeling of well-being (see figure 2–2). It may be that there are a variety of reward centers with different drugs interacting with different centers and different drives. Nevertheless, the positive feeling of well-being produced automatically activates the built-in reward circuits and reinforces the drug behavior. This is a chemical short circuit of the survival system because, in fact, no needs were actually met. But because of the ability of the drug to lie to the brain, the drug behavior is registered as reality. The drug-induced pleasure is able to produce more rapid, predictable and powerful pleasure than can be obtained regularly and reliably through the normal reward system. Hence, the drug impact can be very powerful. It is the memory of this effect that drives the addictive behavior.

Table 2–1
Addictive Drugs Mimic Normal Chemistry Action, Act to Suppress Normal Chemistry Production

Drug	Immediate Action	Normal Brain Chemical	Delayed Effect
Nicotine	Looks and acts like	Acetylcholine	Depletion/suppression
Narcotic	Looks and acts like	Endorphin/Enkefalin	Depletion/suppression
Valium	Increases action of	G.A.B.A.	Depletion/suppression
Barbiturates	Increases action of	G.A.B.A.	Depletion/suppression
Amphetamines	Increases action of	Noradrenaline Dopamine	Depletion/suppression
Cocaine	Increases action of	Noradrenaline Dopamine	Depletion/suppression
Alcohol	Increases action of	G.A.B.A. Endorphin Dopamine Other?	Depletion/suppression

Genetics no doubt play a major role in determining how pleasurable the drug impact is, the rate of tolerance that may or may not develop, and the type of effect (euphoria, dysphoria, sedation, exhilaration) produced. The amount of pleasure produced by a drug appears to be partially related to the rate of change of its concentration in the blood and, hence, the acceleration of its effect on the brain. The drug effect appears to be greater on the rising side of the blood drug curve than on the falling side of the blood drug curve. The more pleasure a rising drug concentration can produce, the more dysphoria a falling concentration may produce.

Repetition of the use of the drug results in a new procedural memory or subconscious memory that, in many cases, appears to have the characteristics of a new drive. Receiving the drug and procuring the drug appear to become new goals. Thus the new drug drive or appetite begins to compete with other habit patterns for time and resources. Drug-seeking behavior is somewhat reminiscent of the persistent behavior elicited by malimprinted geese or salmon on their way to spawning. The behavior is goal directed and stereotyped and has conditioned stimuli that elicit both the behavior and a state of readiness to receive the drug.

Something appears to occur in the addiction, however, that goes beyond the pleasure produced by the drug. This is the adaptation of the system not only to become tolerant to the drug's effect but also to shut down or suppress the function of the normal reward system (see figure 2–2). Manifestations of this are what we call *physical dependence*. It would appear that the drug is not only able to "lie" to the reward center that receives the drug stimulation but also to the parts of the brain that produce normal chemicals that stim-

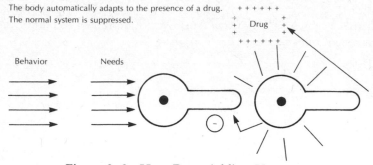

The body automatically adapts to the presence of a drug.
The normal system is suppressed.

Behavior   Needs

Figure 2–2. How Drug Addicts Users

ulate the reward center. Work with narcotic addiction has demonstrated that the pain-relieving effects of narcotics can be separated from the withdrawal-inducing effects. In other studies tolerance has been separated from withdrawal.

A common example of withdrawal occurs in nasal spray addiction, in which case an individual adapts to using a nasal spray to produce vasoconstriction. When the effect of the spray wears off there is a rebound vasodilitation because of a suppression in function of the normal sympathomimetic nerves. This rebound response is called *withdrawal*. Similar rebound appears to occur in the central nervous system to all types of addictive drugs, including cocaine, amphetamines, barbiturates, benzodiazepines, opiates, nicotine, and alcohol.

When the drug is removed or the effects have worn off and the normal system has been suppressed, withdrawal is the result. The addict experiences a reemergence of the biologic alarm systems beginning with irritability, then tension, anxiety, anger, pain, and finally panic. The level appears to be related to the amount of use of the drug and, hence, the amount of suppression. Genetics probably play a role in not only the amount of tolerance that an individual will experience with a drug but also probably the amount of suppression and adaptation that they will undergo in response to a drug.

It is equally important to note that during the period of withdrawal, the normal response to these alarm signals (to take an action to meet a need) is ineffective due to the biochemical suppression of the normal system. The normal response may also be ineffective due to the tolerance developed and to an expectation of immediate superreinforcement that has been "trained in" by the drug. The addict once again takes the drug and experiences a relief of discomfort and a return to a feeling of well-being or satisfaction. The basic brainwashing that all addicts go through as a result of memory programming and chemical adaptation and that seems to characterize their beliefs about themselves and the drug can be stated as, "the drug works and I don't work."

Repetition of the drug reward/withdrawal cycle is a physical conditioning process that reinforces the drug taking and at the same time reinforces that the individual does not have what it takes to feel good. This will particularly worsen any low self-esteem or self-doubt that may be there to begin with, but as has been shown repeatedly, loss of self-esteem is most likely the result of addiction rather than its cause.

When the addict begins to get to this level of addiction we begin to hear him or her make statements like "I needed that." This is a relatively late stage in addiction in that the individual, on a conscious level, begins to become aware of the adaptation that has been progressively occurring over a period of time.

Loss of Control

Fundamental to the disease concept of addiction is that the addict is not able to return to controlled use of the chemical. Loss of control then is manifested by loss of control over one or all of the following:

1. Amount of use
2. Effects of use
3. Urge or craving to use

Operationally, this loss of control occurs in essentially one of two situations. The individual understands that if they drink or use, they will lose control. Regardless of that, the individual cannot resist the urge or craving to use the drug. The individual believes that they should be able to control the drug, but once the drug enters into their system they find that they cannot control the amount they use and/or its effect on them.

Within the disease model, then, the disease is manifested by the involuntary biochemical adaptation (tolerance, physical dependence, and perhaps other unknown changes) *and* a patterning of the nervous system in terms of the procedural memory and perhaps also a kind of imprinting to seek the drug for its effect.

There are undoubtedly genetic predispositions and addictive reactions to these chemicals, and there also may be certain biochemical/behavioral states where imprinting of the chemical may be quite powerful.

Training to Use a Drug

Consequences influence behavior. During the addict's progression on his or her disease, the alcohol or drug habit "trains" multiple habits that feed into it. People, places, activities, friends, weekends, emotional reactions, thinking patterns, vacations become "trained" to meet the alcohol or drug need. This is a gradual process of training and of increasing the behavior that facilitates drug or alcohol use and eliminating behavior that interferes with or does not lead to drug or alcohol use. This leads to a kind of "tunnel vision" on the part of the addict and may be imperceptible to those watching on a day-to-day basis but is obvious to those who have not seen the individual for a while. Some of these patterns are relatively obvious and involve new friends, new haunts, loss of interest in certain activities, and money increasingly going toward alcohol and drug use and away from other sources of reward and responsibilities.

More subtle is the role in which the drug rewards patterns of allowing tensions, frustrations, anger to build up, in expectation of the drug to be there to take care of those feelings rather than finding behavioral ways to meet the needs and reduce the state of alarm.

Fundamental to the thinking patterns that are reinforced by the drug is the basic belief that the drug works and the addict does not. This is fundamental to the individual's denial and, hence, their difficulty in seeing the drug as the problem and a tendency to blame self and others as problems occur. In this way the addiction reinforces patterns of anger toward self or others and ultimately sets the stage for the next drink or dose or drug. There is also a growing disappointment with self and others because the drug seems to be able to provide rewards so much more powerfully and faster than the other normal behavioral resources.

Consequences

Although the consequences of alcoholism in general are not necessarily dependent on the model, there are certain internal consequences and effects on relationships that seem to make sense to be included here. The first and foremost of these is the impact on self-esteem.

Self-esteem, self-image, or how one perceives oneself appears to have five fundamental components:

1. Successes (confidence)
2. Feedback from others
3. Physical health
4. A sense of being in control of oneself
5. A feeling of going toward the things one values

In the beginning there may be an artificial feeling of enhanced self-esteem due to the feeling of being able to control the drug and its effect, but this changes with progression of the disease.

Addiction appears to affect and damage all parts of self-esteem. The intoxicated state interferes with the ability to have successful behavior; the resulting failures lead to negative feedback both from self and others. Physical health is damaged in general, and in particular the drug's disorganization of the neurochemistry leads to feelings of agitation and alarm. As "the monkey on the individual's back" increases and more and more control is wrested from the individual's grasp and placed in the hands of the addiction, procedural memory, or subconscious, the individual no longer trusts themselves with money in their pocket or to honestly be able to say they will be somewhere or not be there or to predict future behavior. Finally, as more and more behavior becomes drug or alcohol-oriented and less and less oriented toward normal values, individuals experience guilt and an awareness that they are not going toward the things they value. Time, money, resources, and relationships are being diverted from the individual's values, commitments, and responsibilities.

It appears that *timing* is important in preventing the subconscious or procedural memory from registering a revulsion to alcohol or other drugs following problems related to their use. Although the human reasoning or declarative memory can understand that drinking has led to problems, the procedural memory that is able to learn only through association in very short time periods registers only that the drug works and later after some time delay that negative consequences may occur. When they do occur, the association is with self as the cause of failure, the timing necessary to make a connection has been missed. This contributes to the drug-induced denial and prevents the anger that the individual experiences from being focused on the drug. Hence, anger is turned in on self or others. The hangover the following morning, in fact, may be relieved by another dose of the drug.

Where individuals may have had other damage to their self-esteem, the addiction appears to deepen the scars, and there tends to be an intensive focus on past negatives, which is rewarded by the next dose of the drug. Focusing on the past that leads to drinking reinforces the focusing on the past.

Figure 2–3 demonstrates, in a graphic manner, the effect of the addiction on self-esteem.

The individual who is immobilized by addiction and is in a state of pain because of guilt, needs not being met, or conflicts, experiences an intensive feeling of depression, frustration, anxiety, and a desire to run away. Suicide may look like an appropriate option to the individual. They may be overcome with self-pity and unable to see the drug as the problem.

As the individual becomes more and more immobilized, anger, guilt, and negative emotions tend to become pushed onto others in order to motivate the others to take care of the individual's needs that are not being met and as another focus for that anger besides self. Hence, resentment seems to develop as a byproduct of the continued need to use the drug and the immobilization caused by the drug. Because of denial addicts very often are in the position

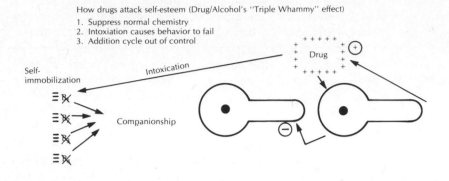

Figure 2–3. Habits Rewarded by Drug

of defending who they were while they were drinking or using, in order to protect the drug. Those around them—family, employers, friends—react to this by "throwing the baby out with the bath water." Unable to separate the addict from the drug and feeling a lot of pain, the tendency is to try to push the individual away.

Another important effect on relationships, of course, is the effect on communication. We need to remember that addictive drugs are "lies" to the brain and as such, distort reality and prevent accurate perceptions of what another individual may be communicating. When there is a conflict and both parties are upset, the addict's use of the drug to allay angry feelings prevents the couple from finding a way to behaviorally allay feelings through interaction with the other individual. In the same way, the drug becomes the confidant of the addict and is perceived as more responsive and understanding than the actual partner.

Development

It is a truism that one's needs as a child are different from those as an adolescent, which are, in turn, different from those as a young adult, which are, in turn, different from those as an older adult. Appropriate behavior for one set of needs may not be appropriate and, in fact, may be counterproductive for another set of needs. Anyone who has observed the transition from childhood to adulthood (which we call adolescence) will be aware of the emotional upheaval as the individual goes through the process of changing behavior to meet adult needs and eliminating behavior that primarily met childhood needs. Drugs, by "lying" to the brain, interfere with this learning process and delay or distort development. Drug values and drug skills may be well learned but of no value to the user to get rewards out of life. In addition, the necessary feedback from life has been distorted through the addiction process.

Family Adaptation

The modern viewpoint of addiction is that it is not only a disease of the individual but, in fact, a family disease. This view transcends the traditional mechanical body definitions of disease and incorporates the concept of a dysfunctional system and the need to treat the individuals involved in that system as a unit. The desperation and feelings of futility experienced by the family members who are living with an addict can be aided by understanding this disease model of addiction. Initial attempts at control of the addiction usually lead to bitterness and resentment, and in order to stay in the situation the family adapts its behavior to the addict. From the family's perspective, the persistence of the addict in seeking the drug is reminiscent of the salmon seeking to go up river and spawn despite the presence of multiple dams and turbines that have been placed in their way. They do not seek other rivers to go up but continue relentlessly trying to get back to the waters in which they were initially spawned.

Within the family the initial attempts to adapt to the addiction are described in figure 2–4. This same diagram, however, might be just as true for any other type of chronic illness that causes one member of a family unit to be immobilized. Other family members take over to maintain a sense of homeostasis. The normal boundaries between people and patterns of demonstration of respect are crossed leading to defensiveness and a trust in the addict to be sick. With addiction, as more and more painful events occur, family or work or other units may push the individual away because they are unable to separate the addict from his or her drug.

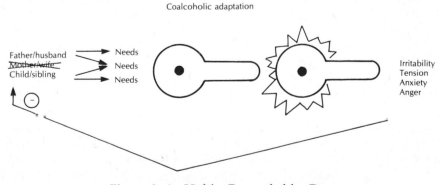

Figure 2–4. Habits Rewarded by Drug

Recovery

For a model to be effective it must not only describe the disease process but facilitate the understanding of treaters and patients of the role of treatment and the process of recovery. The decision to stop drug or alcohol use usually comes gradually over a period of time and is accentuated by some acute crisis. The development of the intervention process has demonstrated that a crisis can be induced in a therapeutic manner. At other times mini "hitting bottoms" occur that provide motivation for the addict to seek treatment. The addict's understanding of the problem, however, may not be synonymous with their desire to seek help. Pain/crisis is a tremendous motivator to change; however, it is not necessarily directive as to what the most productive way of dealing with the pain is.

Step I—Stopping the Drug

A certain percentage of addicts are unable to stop their use of a drug due to the discomfort of withdrawal. Other addicts are able to stop it for a period of time, but attempts are temporary and ultimately result back to drinking. In either case, an initial step in the recovery is to stop the drug in a safe manner and allow the natural chemistry to return. There is a time course for that return both of an acute nature and a subacute nature, and much has been written regarding the management of both acute withdrawal and the nature of the postacute withdrawal syndromes. Our assessment of this recovery is mostly clinical using signs (such as pulse, tremor, sweating, or agitation) or symptoms (such as insomnia, depression, anxiety, lowered sex drive). Recovery from the chemical toxicity of alcohol is different from the biochemical recovery from its addictive effects. Hence, liver, pancreas, peripheral nerves, memory (brain), or testicle all go through a healing process as well.

With modern techniques of brain-imaging, perhaps we will be able to better understand the recovery from the addictive process and discover improved methods to facilitate it.

Step II—Education

Addicts need to understand that they have the type of nervous system that adapts to alcohol in a way that prevents them from being satisfied with a particular dose of drug and leads to an involuntary demand for additional drug. This demonstrates the progressive nature of addiction and the fact that there is some type of physical memory that will cause the individual to readapt back to the same level of use that they were in before they stopped. The addict also needs to receive specific education regarding addictive drugs in general and the process of recovery that will be described further on.

Counterconditioning to alcohol/drug gives a new negative
association immediately with drug. This blocks the
conditioned-reflex craving to drink alcohol/use drug.

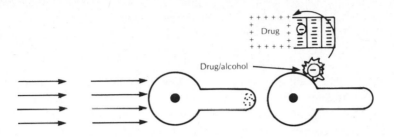

Figure 2–5. Schick Program of Recovery

Step III—Counterconditioning

Reprogramming procedural memory is most effectively done through the use
of specific experiential retraining, associating a particular behavior or action
with a negative, immediate consequence. Timing, repetition, and association
are essential for the appropriate retraining to take place. The conditioning is
enhanced in a state of arousal, and the treatment program should provide for
periodic reinforcements of that new learning at periodic intervals. This is
somewhat similar to the need to provide boosters to the immune system
regarding the polio virus.

Counterconditioning also, with regard to alcohol, needs to encompass a
variety of alcoholic beverages so that beer is dealt with separately from wine,
which, in turn, is dealt with separately from scotch, etc. However, ultimately
there is a generalization to alcohol as a chemical. During the counterconditioning, there is also the opportunity for individuals undergoing treatment to
allow their anger to become focused on the drug and the drug behavior rather
than on self or others. Figure 2–5 graphically demonstrates the role of counterconditioning in treatment to specifically block and countertrain the drug
reward learning and disrupt the drug reinforcement cycle.

Counterconditioning is extremely effective at breaking down denial. It
opens the way for individuals to see they have been lied to by the drug and to
seek other rewards. The conditioning is a retraining process only carried out
in the presence of the drug and stopped in the absence of the drug.

Step IV—Habit Change

The aversion therapy is able to block the drive to seek the drug and craving.
The process of recovery is to eliminate those patterns that primarily fit into

the alcohol/drug use and to facilitate the growth and development and nurturing of those patterns that provide reward through life.

To start, the individual, as already mentioned, needs to change the people, places, and activities that primarily led into drinking and develop activities with individuals who do not have alcohol or drugs as a primary reward system. The process of treatment and recovery involves reevaluation of attitudes that tended to feed into the alcohol or drug use and point out that their primary reward is the next dose of the drug.

This is a process of, in particular, challenging denial and resentment that has developed over the course of the addiction. Confrontation as well as acceptance, caring, honesty, and a variety of other tools play a role in bringing this to surface and in facilitating the patient's looking at it in a different manner. Counterconditioning, again, aids this process by breaking down denial and allowing the individual to look at their addiction from a different perspective.

The use of sodium pentothal interviews has also facilitated monitoring the level of aversion that an individual may be developing in treatment as well as assessing denial, resentment, and particular problems that the addict sees that may prevent recovery.

Self-esteem. Hugs are a significant therapeutic modality in reestablishing self-esteem. One of the main barriers to this recovery of self-esteem is misinformation from the past. Much of this misinformation is stored in procedural memory as self-put downs, guilt, etc.

This program emphasizes the need to devalue the past and the importance of both professionals and support groups in enlarging the awareness of options and providing training and support to meeting today's needs. Companionship is one example of a need among many that could be used.

Thus, placing the past in the past and taking the recovery process one day at a time is essential and is reinforced by "hugs" in a professional environment and a support group that is not carrying excess "baggage" from the past with regard to the individual. The professional environment and support group then are able to provide honest feedback and acceptance of the individual, and through the education and treatment process individuals are able to focus their anger on the chemical rather than themselves.

Over a period of time as successes begin to develop utilizing the normal reward system, self-esteem will develop as the individual experiences a renewed feeling of self-control. As he or she moves once again toward the things that he or she values, self-esteem will increase. Forgiveness also plays a role in self-esteem, and this is aided through the understanding of the disease process, support, and time (see figure 2–6).

Self-esteem takes time to be rebuilt and needs to be specifically addressed during the treatment process. Family work is often essential in altering the type of feedback the individual is receiving which again will assist self-esteem.

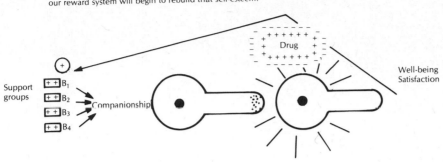

Figure 2–6. Schick Program of Recovery

Getting Rewards Out of Life. Part of the treatment process is to train in new patterns that will get rewards for the individual through life rather than a chemical. Some of this will take place acutely in the treatment setting and may involve such things as assertion training, relaxation training, self-acceptance training, communication skills training, and training to use a support group and life-acceptance training. However, a significant part of this recovery process usually takes place outside of the treatment setting in the individual's natural environment and involves such things as return to work, family recovery, health recovery, development of new recreational activities and hobbies that do not involve alcohol or other drugs and a continuing growth of the individual's skills and attitudes. There may also be time for the development of new goals that the individual now perceives as important for their own needs being met and awareness of a new meaning to life, free of chemicals.

The above is a time-dependent process requiring continued nurturing, understanding, training, education, and limits. These can be provided both through support groups and self-help groups as well as professionals.

Response to Stress. Figure 2–7 demonstrates that the addict begins to learn that alarm feelings are not the problem; they are just signals to the individual that a need is not being met. The acronym HALT stands for, don't get too Hungry, Angry, Lonely, [or] Tired. This primarily means to monitor feelings at a low level and take action to meet the needs. The addict also then begins to redirect those feelings away from self and others and toward the problem that is bothering him or her. The addict gets out of the past and away from procedural memory, blaming and self-put downs, and uses the ongoing support of others to help with recovery. The feeling of a need to blame becomes lessened and there is more of a response to do what can be done and to let

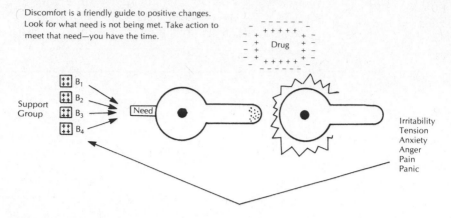

Figure 2–7. Schick Program of Recovery

go of the rest. This takes practice and can be reinforced through a support group, continued training, therapy and/or family recovery.

Support. Support is essentially feedback and information presented in a caring, accepting, open, honest, and hopeful manner with empathy but not sympathy. It can come from a variety of sources; Alcoholics Anonymous is the most widespread and well-known support program with a specific outline of a spiritual recovery program. This is reinforced by its members, who provide a fellowship made up of other individuals who are recovering. Sponsors may be provided to give more directive and individual support. Alanon is a support group for spouses.

Most treatment programs provide ongoing support groups for both patients and family. These may be run by professionals or peers (most often who are recovered) and serve to provide a structured support program with a common fellowship made up of those who are treated at that program. Spouses are very often encouraged to attend.

An individual's church may also be a powerful source of support and emphasizes that a part of support is the fact that both the patient and the group share a common belief system that is revalidated each time the support group meets. For the addict, the number one priority needs to be sobriety. Those who are successful in recovery emphasize that as problems mount or tension occurs, returning to the priority of sobriety has aided them. In particular, they are aware of the need to not allow a drug to "lie" to their brain at those times and the need to let other things go if this affects sobriety. A support group reinforces this.

Spirituality. Spirituality in recovery is the addict's acceptance of his or her ability to deal with life within his or her limits. Underlying this is maintaining the priority of sobriety and the acceptance of his or her inability to be responsible for things beyond his or her control. The support group reinforces this as well. This is summarized in the often quoted *Serenity Prayer.*

Family/Relationship Recovery. In many cases there is a time lag in family recovery. Addict recovery is first, with family recovery lagging behind. A period of time is necessary for new behaviors to be consistent and expected before trust is reestablished. During that time, however, the family can provide ongoing support and can receive support for themselves. As much as possible, the family needs to be assisted to stay out of the past and take one day at a time. The ultimate goal for family recovery is that each individual is once again taking over his or her responsibility to meet the family's needs. The goal of treatment should be to enable the patient and family to be an effective support group for each other. Treatment needs to aid families in getting out of the past, keeping anger focused on the drug, facilitating honesty and forgiveness, and renewing a commitment to health.

Para-illnesses. A word should be said regarding illnesses associated with chemical dependency. The most prominent of these are affective disorders, chronic pain, disability, hyperactivity, post-traumatic stress disorder, eating disorders, and panic attacks/agoraphobia.

The above disorders emphasize the need for professional evaluation in chemical dependency. Awareness of these and possibly other disorders will facilitate the individual's recovery; lack of understanding may prevent such a recovery. Treatment of the primary addiction must be undertaken first before these other disorders can be dealt with effectively.

With what we understand regarding affective disorders and their biochemical components, some individuals may be unable to utilize their normal reward system because the neurotransmitters are not being properly released (see figure 2–8). Antidepressant medication apparently allows that neurotransmitter system to function more appropriately, and, thus, when an individual engages in rewarding activity, the reward center is able to experience the positive result. This is quite different from tranquilizers, which provide reward artificially. Most antidepressants take two to three weeks to take effect, and one will still be depressed if, in fact, positive things are not happening. Tranquilizers, on the other hand, tend to work quite rapidly and can effectively "lie" to the individual regarding whether or not their needs are being met. Hence, antidepressants apparently allow for appropriate feedback, while tranquilizers provide false feedback. It takes skilled clinicians to be able to determine what is, in fact, normal "depression" related to addiction versus the disorder of depression. At times it is appropriate to wait to see whether or not the imbalances created by the addiction will right themselves and when it is appropriate to medicate the individual.

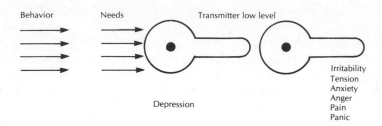

Identify biochemical imbalances that create mood dysfunction.

Behavior   Needs   Transmitter low level

Depression

Irritability
Tension
Anxiety
Anger
Pain
Panic

Figure 2–8. Schick Program of Recovery

Chronic pain is another disorder that is highly interactive with chemical dependency. Specific therapy may need to be addressed to the pain behavior and the source of pain.

Disability is another disorder or condition that interferes with the normal reward system functioning and facilitates the use of chemicals. Specific evaluations and assessments need to be carried out to assess an individual's extent of disability and provide a program for their meeting their optimal potential and regaining self-esteem.

Hyperactivity is a diagnosable condition in children, and children often are medicated to manage it. These medications are in the category of addictive drugs, and clinicians need to be aware of these disorders and the possibility of an adult residual type of hyperactivity and appropriate methods for managing this disorder and allowing the patient to function.

Eating disorders are commonly associated with chemical dependency. Most experts emphasize that the chemical dependency needs to be dealt with first before the eating disorder. However, the eating disorder should not be ignored, and appropriate referral and management should be undertaken.

Panic attacks and agoraphobia are disorders that apparently have biochemical bases and, at times, are responsive to antidepressant medication and, at other times, are manageable through behavioral techniques. Ignoring these disorders is likely to lead to resurgence of chemical dependency.

Posttraumatic stress disorder is a disorder commonly associated with chemical dependency. Clinicians need to be aware of it and evaluate the need for specific treatment.

Anxiety in addicts needs to be managed without chemicals. The use of chemicals to deal with this symptom nearly invariably leads to loss of control and continued problems. Whether or not there is a true biochemical disorder of anxiety has yet to be determined, but at the present time anti-anxiety drugs are contraindicated in the alcoholic.

Summary

The above model has been useful in planning treatment and explaining the disease of addiction to patients. It provides an interactive system with which to test hypotheses and to measure parts of recovery.

The model is based on a biological/behavioral foundation and sees addictive drugs as creating a primary illness, for which there is a progression to a diagnosable state and from which there is a systematic process of recovery.

3

The Disease and Adaptive Models Of Addiction: A Framework Evaluation

Bruce K. Alexander

The value of a disease model of addiction[1] has been at issue among scholars since the nineteenth century. In the interest of resolving this issue, this chapter formalizes an adaptive model[2] as the alternative to the disease model. It also discusses how conflicting models can be evaluated, in light of recent advances in the history and philosophy of science. I hope to show, through a framework evaluation, that the adaptive model is superior to the disease model and to combinations of the two models. This chapter also discusses two final steps that seem necessary to bring closure to the issue.

Two Models of Addiction

The disease and adaptive models both provide comprehensive, logically coherent analyses of the development of addiction. However, they are seldom examined formally. To permit a critical comparison, therefore, detailed representations of both models are sketched in figure 3–1.

These diagrams are distillations of innumerable versions of each model that I have encountered in the past fifteen years. I believe that they capture the essence of both models as typically applied to addiction (rather than to drug use that does not cause serious problems). The diagrams could be drawn somewhat differently by different theorists, and there are many ways of combining elements from both models. However, considering the models in this essential, distinct form enables critical comparison.

There are technical vocabularies from psychoanalysis, psychiatry, cognitive and behavioral psychology, physiology, sociology, and existential philosophy that have been used to express the two models, but they are stated here in plain language. They are familiar ideas open to public scrutiny, not technical theories accessible only to experts.

Figure 3–1a. Disease Model

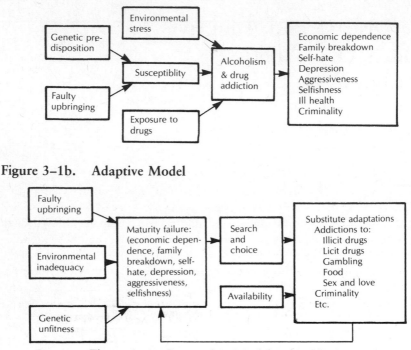

Figure 3–1b. Adaptive Model

Figure 3–1. Competing Models of Addiction

The Disease Model

The disease model is depicted in figure 3–1a as a set of causal relationships, each represented by an arrow. The casual links are arranged in a process whereby people first become "susceptible" to addiction, then addicted, and finally self-destructive. The susceptibility could be caused by any disease process, but in contemporary forms of the disease model it is attributed either to a genetic predisposition or to psychological damage that occurred during childhood, or both. Susceptible people are seen as vulnerable to drugs much as people with other genetic defects might be vulnerable to diabetes or people with other kinds of childhood trauma might be vulnerable to psychosis.

When a susceptible person is exposed to drugs (including alcohol) and/or to environmental stress, drug addiction or alcoholism is likely to result, which typically leads to a familiar set of problems: economic dependence, family breakdown, self-hate, depression, and a host of other problems that are sampled in figure 3–1a.

In different variations of the disease model, different contributing factors are emphasized. For example, "genetic predisposition" could be drawn larger and "faulty upbringing" smaller, indicating that genetic factors are given paramount importance in developing susceptibility (Goodwin, 1985). In another current version, the "exposure to drugs" component could be drawn very large and the others correspondingly small, indicating prepotency of the addictive properties of drugs over all other factors (e.g., Gold and Rea, 1983; Goldstein, 1979). This special case of the disease model has been previously termed the "exposure orientation" (Alexander and Hadaway, 1982).

The Adaptive Model

The adaptive model is also depicted as an organized set of causal relationships (figure 3–1b). The process starts with some combination of faulty upbringing, inadequate environmental support (e.g., ghetto conditions, societal breakdown), and genetic unfitness (i.e., inborn physical or psychological disability). These problems, and the way that the person understands them, result in failure to achieve the levels of self-reliance, competence, social acceptance, self-confidence, and so on that are the basic expectations of society. In short, some people fail to "grow up" or to maintain adult integration.

Failure to reach or maintain adult integration is a grave problem. It invites social ostracism, despair, mental disintegration, and ultimately suicide. Therefore, it creates an urgent need to search out and choose substitute ways to provide meaning, organization, and social support. Various "substitute adaptations" may be, consciously or unconsciously, adopted for this purpose. Substitute adaptations do *not* provide the abiding satisfactions of adult integration but at least provide a basis for survival and allow hope for the future. Therefore they are seized and held desperately when their availability is threatened.

From an adaptive viewpoint, drug addiction or any other "substitute adaptations" are *adaptive* because the alternatives are worse. The substitute adaptations may be visibly harmful, but they provide something essential. For example, the despised identity of an addict is more bearable than the hellish void of none at all, and deep immersion in drug culture at least guarantees distraction from self-hate. In desperate situations, it is adaptive to choose the lesser evil.[3]

It might seem outrageous to assert that harmful addictions are adaptive. I believe this is because, in the present atmosphere of a war on drugs, it is hard to see drug use in the same way as other actions. In a parallel case, regular use of crutches can produce painful blisters or bruises, but it is clearly adaptive for injured people. The alternatives to using crutches are worse—aggravating the injury or remaining bedridden. According to the adaptive view, drug addiction, like crutch use, is adaptive in spite of its drawbacks.

Differences between the Models

Although the adaptive model includes most of the same component terms as the disease model, the two differ in at least four major ways. Most important, the disease model assumes that addicted people are sick. The adaptive model posits no disease, pathology, or disorder and assumes that addicted people are responding adaptively within the limitations of their own abilities, perceptions, and environments. Second, a critical cause-and-effect relationship is reversed in the two models. Drug addiction and alcoholism are seen as causing a host of problems in the disease model, but in the adaptive model they are seen primarily as a *result* of the same problems (although the addiction may well exacerbate their problems). Third, similar components in the two models are construed differently. For example, *environmental stress* in the disease model is termed *environmental inadequacy* in the adaptive model, reflecting a more critical view of the social environment. Likewise, as the next section will show, *genetic predisposition* means something quite different from *genetic unfitness*.

Finally, there are two central terms that do not translate from one model to the other because they have no counterparts—these are *susceptibility* in the disease model and *search and choice* in the adaptive model. *Susceptibility* has probabilistic, actuarial connotations that do not fit the adaptive model in which actions are seen as purposive, as the term *search and choice* indicates. Thus, the two models fall on opposite sides of the cleavage between mechanical and purposive interpretations of human behavior that have long riven psychology.

Empirical Research

Observations from clinical practice, scientific research, and historical studies can be found to provide some empirical support for each causal hypothesis (i.e., each arrow) in both models. However, the support is not *strong* for any of the hypotheses, and it cannot confirm either model as a whole. The entire body of empirical data cannot be reviewed here, but one causal hypothesis will be evaluated as an example before proceeding to the framework analysis of the two models.

The "Genes → Susceptibility" Hypothesis

The inconclusiveness of the empirical research will be illustrated with data concerning the link between genetic predisposition and susceptibility in the disease model. (This will be referred to as the genes → susceptibility hypothesis). There is only weak support for this hypothesis and no real foundation for the extravagant claims being trumpeted in the popular press (cf. Franks, 1985).

By most accounts, the strongest support for the hypothesis comes from two teams of investigators headed by Vaillant and Goodwin, respectively. Both sets of research will be considered briefly.

Although Vaillant is frequently cited in support of the genes → susceptibility hypothesis, he himself acknowledges that his data provide only weak and indirect support for it (Vaillant, 1983:67–70). Some of his strongest data involve comparing the prevalence of alcoholism among men with no alcoholic relatives to that of men with several alcoholic relatives. In two large, carefully studied samples, 10 and 14 percent of the men with no alcoholic relatives became "alcohol dependent" at some time in their adult lives, but 29 and 34 percent of men with several alcoholic relatives did so.

However, Vaillant (1983) judiciously points out that these data are not as powerful as they seem at first glance, and certainly not as powerful as some popularizers have taken them to be. The men with several alcoholic relatives very likely grew up in homes where alcoholism and its related stresses were much more prominent, so genetic determinants are completely confounded with environmental factors.

There is no way Vaillant's (1983) naturalistic research can control the effect of the family environment. Vaillant, however, identified an environmental factor that could be statistically controlled. In one of his samples, where ethnic backgrounds were diverse, ethnicity was highly correlated with frequency of alcoholism. For example, Irish-American men were much more likely to become alcoholic than Italian-Americans or Jews. Vaillant (1983) attributed this ethnic effect to subcultural differences in attitudes toward drinking and drunkenness. Obviously, in a mixed ethnic sample, this could have accounted for part of the correlation between alcoholism prevalence and number of alcoholic ancestors.

When ethnicity was controlled by looking separately at each ethnic group for the relationship between alcoholism and the number of alcoholic relatives, the correlation was greatly reduced. In fact, the correlation disappeared in some (not all) of the ethnic groups.

Such evidence provides only a weak support for the genes → susceptibility hypothesis. Vaillant (1983) acknowledges this but maintains that stronger support for the hypothesis can be found in Goodwin's adoption studies, which provide a more substantial opportunity to control environmental factors. However, when Goodwin's research is examined closely, it provides no stronger support for the hypothesis than Vaillant's.

Goodwin clearly endorses the genes → susceptibility hypothesis (Goodwin, 1979, 1985), but there are many problems with the data he provides as evidence. In general, the research is not of the same high quality as Vaillant's. For example, the classification of people as alcoholic was based on interviews conducted in Danish in Copenhagen, transcribed into English, and then diagnosed by an American psychiatrist in St. Louis. The frequency of alcoholism determined in this way was, in some of the studies, then compared to the Danish estimates of alcoholism in the general population that were obviously determined in a different way, although the Danish method is not explained in the reports (cf. Goodwin et al., 1974). There are too many differences in the two methods of determining the prevalance of alcoholism for comparisons of data obtained in this way to be regarded as strong evidence.

Another serious problem is that differences that could be attributed to heredity were found only in males. In fact, the results for females ran contrary to the prediction of the genes → susceptibility hypothesis, although the contrary data did not reach statistical significance (Goodwin et al., 1977). This fact is overlooked in most generalizations that are drawn from the data, including Goodwin's own statement of conclusions (Goodwin, 1979), which fails to mention finding only contrary evidence for the genes → susceptibility hypothesis in females.

Still another problem is that even in the best-controlled experiments, when the methodology is given the full benefit of the doubt, the influence of a genetic predisposition was small. The strongest finding is that 15 percent of male offspring of alcoholics that had been adopted by nonalcoholic parents were diagnosed as currently alcoholic, whereas only 4 percent of adopted males whose biological parents were not alcoholic were so diagnosed. In one sense this seems like a large effect—the likelihood of alcoholism is almost four times greater for men with the genetic predisposition. In another sense, however, this means that 85 percent of men with alcoholic parents do not become alcoholic. Studies of male identical twins show that about 25 percent of those with an alcoholic twin (with whom they share identical genotypes as well as very similar upbringing) themselves became alcoholic—and 75 percent do not (Murray et al., 1983). This is not evidence for a strong genetic effect.

The final weakness in the data is that the genetic effect does not appear to be specific for alcoholism. Goodwin himself argues strongly that his data support a specific effect, but his logic is tortuous (cf. Goodwin et al., 1973). As well, two facts from the more recent literature (Tarter et al., 1985) indicate major flaws in the specificity argument. Alcoholics have special temperamental traits that are measurable before they begin to drink as well as after. These include hyperactivity, reduced attention span, increased sociability and social aggressiveness, and heightened emotionality. Therefore, if alcoholism is to be considered a partially inherited trait, it is hardly a specific inclination to drink that is inherited but a much broader constellation of traits that can lead to alcoholism or a variety of other problems.

The second fact is that, whereas the male relatives of alcoholics have a somewhat elevated likelihood of alcoholism, the same can be said of relatives of people afflicted with hysteria, borderline personality, bulimia, anorexia nervosa, antisocial personality, and schizophrenia—their relatives are more likely to be alcoholic as well (Tarter et al., 1985). Again, these data do not support a specific predisposition to alcoholism.

The existing data can validly be taken as weak support for the genes→susceptibility hypothesis. However, when viewed differently, these data offer at least as much support for the genetic unfitness→maturity failure hypothesis from the adaptive model. This hypothesis predicts the kind of weak, nonspecific inheritance that has been found. Genetic unfitness of many sorts would hinder a person's efforts to reach or maintain adult integration. Such unfitness would manifest itself in signs of distress throughout life, difficulty in achieving adult integration, and, possibly, in alcoholism or some other substitute adaptation.

It is not possible here to evaluate the genetic evidence further. A more extensive critique of the research on genetic predispositions to alcoholism is available in two excellent review articles (Murray et al., 1983; Peele, 1986). Finally, it should be noted that the research connecting genes to alcoholism provides the *best* support for the genes→susceptibility hypothesis; research on no other drug has provided even this degree of support for a genetic predisposition towards drug addiction.[4]

In this article, the review of empirical evidence is limited to a single component hypothesis of the disease model, chosen because it is widely, but wrongly, believed to have conclusive empirical support. Critical examinations of other component hypotheses of the disease model, particularly the exposure→drug addiction hypothesis, are available elsewhere (Alexander and Hadaway, 1982; Alexander, 1984; Falk, 1973; Fingarette, 1979; Peele, 1985). Excellent reviews of the (also inconclusive) empirical support for the adaptive model can be found in Chein et al., (1964), Kaplan and Wieder (1974), Peele (1985), and Shiffman and Wills (1985).

Suitability of the Empirical Method
for Evaluating Models

Beyond the historical fact that empirical methodology has not resolved the conflict between the two models after a century of application, there are other indications that this method may not be adequate.

Falsifiability. Both models appear to be *unfalsifiable*. That is, it is hard to conjure up even a hypothetical fact that could disprove either one, when they are taken in their general forms. For example, if it could be proven that neither genes nor upbringing had any influence on the suceptibility to addiction, addiction could still result from some *other* kind of disease. It could result from cancer in areas of the brain that produce endorphins, resulting in a chronic insufficiency, or from an auto-immune response to dietary factors that make drugs unnecessary, etc. There is always a new disease-type explanation because there are undoubtedly still undiscovered disease processes.

Likewise, it is impossible to rule out the possibility that an addiction is serving some kind of adaptive function. Powerful needs are often idiosyncratic and may be unconscious. How then could it be proven that any person, even an outwardly successful one, had *not* failed to "achieve or maintain adult integration" with respect to their own needs? How could it be proven that any addictive behavior was not providing some kind of substitute satisfaction?

If a model can absorb any conceivable evidence it cannot be disproven. But if it cannot be disproven, how can it ever be considered proven? An unfalsifiable model cannot be validated by exclusively empirical methodology.

Unfalsifiability is not unique to models of addiction. Every field of science is based on frameworks that can neither be empirically proven nor falsified.[5] This once controversial idea is now widely accepted by the leading philosophers of science. For example, Lakatos (1978:19) describes frameworks as: "not only equally unprovable, and equally improbable, but . . . also equally undisprovable." This conclusion is supported by working empirical scientists as well as philosophers of science. For example, W.R. Uttal (1978:80), in his book on psychobiology writes: "The naive model of a totally objective science collapses in almost every instance that one penetrates its fragile surface. What is always found inside is something like a working 'paradigm' . . . that substitutes for a totally objective analysis."

Detachment.   There is a second indication that empirical methodology is not sufficient to choose between the two models. Empirical hypothesis testing is a detached, objective business—people can agree because they accept the hegemony of data. However, the theoretical literature on addiction has little feel of detachment or objectivity. Rather, addiction research is conducted in insular groupings of scholars who ignore or distort conflicting data, instead of using it to check their own conclusions. Where discordant views are discussed, remarkably undetached hostility sometimes erupts (cf. Bean-Bayog, 1986a). This seems the antithesis of detached empirical investigation and more like evidence of the "incommensurability" that exists between frameworks or "paradigms" (Kuhn, 1970).

Combining Models

Many scholars have attempted to combine elements of the disease and adaptive models. Others have argued for such amalgamations on principle (Reich and Filstead, 1986), but there are historical and logical reasons to resist combination.

Historically, scientific advance has often required that competing models be completely rejected in favor of a single conception that captures the imagination of society and the scientific community (Kuhn, 1970). For example, biological theory prior to the nineteenth century was dominated by the concept of a perfect and continuous ordering of species that served as the necessary basis of classification and pre-established goal of any progressive change in species (Foucault, 1970:ch. 5). Darwin's achievement was not to compromise with this universally held conception but to abandon it completely in favor of an undirected evolutionary process.

In his turn, however, Darwin tried to reconcile a proto-Mendelian and a Lamarckian view of inheritance in his development of evolutionary theory (Mayr, 1982). Those who brought evolutionary theory into the twentieth century preserved Darwin's essentially Mendelian ideas but completely rejected Lamarckian inheritance. The result of this series of theoretical rejections is the modern synthetic theory of evolution, which owes much of its elegant unity and productive simplicity to jettisoning surplus baggage. Tortuous compromise is appropriate in many situations but often out of place in the development of scientific theory.

There are logical as well as historical objections to combining the adaptive and disease models. Consider, for example, the view that adaptive factors explain the initial attraction of people to drugs but that continuing use and addiction are maintained by some disease process. The problem is that the adaptive model is *not* a model of drug experimentation but a model of the addictive process itself (Peele, 1985). Therefore, this putative sequential combination of the models is actually just an acceptance of the disease model of addiction, augmented by the trivial assertion that people are drawn by their needs to try drugs in the first place. Therefore it is no better supported than the disease model alone.

Combining parts of each model into a single whole leads to problems of coherence. A person who is behaving adaptively is not a patient who requires treatment, adaptation cannot be maladaptive, an addict's environment cannot be both benign and inadequate to support normal development, and behavior cannot be both mechanically determined and purposive. Each model comprises a logically coherent whole. When parts from each model are combined, the coherence dissolves.

Framework Evaluation

It is not possible to choose between the two models on the basis of logical coherence (both are amply coherent) or on the basis of empirical support (neither has very much). Moreover, the choice cannot be evaded by combining them, for the reasons just given. Therefore, scholars should choose between them on the basis of analysis, argument and values more than on the basis of empirical research. I will call this process *framework evaluation*.

This call for framework evaluation is neither unscientific, pessimistic, nor irrational, although it may appear so when examined superficially. Most modern philosophers of science (although they agree on little else) concur that accepted frameworks are not empirically proven. To a large degree, they are instead established, sustained, and eventually replaced by changing scientific conventions, social movements, and personal motives (Carnap, 1952; Feyerabend, 1978; Foucault, 1970; Hacking, 1983; Kuhn, 1970; Lakatos, 1978; James, 1910/1963).

Once a framework has been accepted, a different phase of science ensues in which researchers employ empirical methodology rigorously to test specific hypotheses, quantify functional relationships, and extend theory. These two aspects of science are completely dependent on each other. Frameworks are vacant constructions until filled in by rigorous empirical research. However, empirical research is not productive until a framework has been adopted because the framework gives terms distinct meanings, tells which predictions are important to test, and provides working assumptions that make hypothesis testing possible.

Philosophers of science differ sharply on how much social factors should influence the choice of scientific frameworks. I hold with those who believe that social influence on the acceptance of frameworks is both inevitable and desirable. *Inevitable* because scientists are inevitably human beings, enmeshed in their society. That one's own views on addiction, one of the deeply emotional issues of our times, could be coldly objective and detached would seem to express unsupportable vanity and inexplicable disregard for findings of contemporary psychology, psychiatry, and history of science.

It is also *desirable* that social factors influence frameworks. If they did not, the frameworks that guide science would be cut free of human concern, and the immensely powerful force of empirical science could become an unleashed menace—a Frankenstein monster—rather than a benefactor. Moreover, social influence on frameworks takes nothing from the rigor of the more rule-governed empirical research that ensues when frameworks are accepted (Kuhn, 1970).

Effective scientists should be able to participate openly in empirical research *and* framework evaluation and to recognize when each is appropriate. In the case of addiction, framework evaluation is needed now because the unresolved framework issue has prevented clear understanding of addiction for many years and because the confusion cannot be resolved by empirical research or by combining the two models. Scientific scholars are uniquely suited to the task of framework evaluation because they are well informed on the issue. By contrast, dogged loyalty to a pure empiricism that cannot resolve the framework issue leaves the field of addiction perpetually embattled, chaotic, and impotent.

The remainder of this chapter is a framework evaluation of the two models, from several perspectives.

History

The disease model is sometimes seen as a humane conception that supplanted an earlier view of addicts as criminal or evil. It is sometimes seen as a scientific achievement, the discovery of a medical entity called *addiction*. Historically, neither of these ideas is accurate. Prior to the emergence of the disease model, habitual drug use was not generally seen as sinful or criminal. Moreover, the disease model did not grow from scientific discovery. Instead the disease model emerged from a massive social and political movement of the last 200 years that characterized drug use as both evil and sick (Levine, 1978, 1984). This was in turn part of a social reconceptualization of deviance in general over the same period (Foucault, 1979).

In North America, the disease model of addiction was first applied to alcohol use. Prior to the nineteenth century, heavy consumption of alcohol was common and widely accepted by men, women, and children in America. There were conventions and summary punishments to curtail unacceptable behavior (Zinberg, 1984), but alcohol was held in high regard and few people considered habitual drunkenness a great evil or an addictive disease (Levine, 1984:110). However, revolution in thought occurred between about 1780 and 1830. The temperance movement popularized a new, evil/disease concept of drunkenness. As formulated by Benjamin Rush, its principles were that

> distilled liquors were physically toxic, morally destructive and addictive. Regular drinkers . . . ran the serious risk of many diseases . . . they also tended to engage in many forms of antisocial, immoral, and criminal behavior. Further . . . regular drinkers become "addicted" to alcohol . . . in the full contemporary sense of the term: those addicted experienced uncontrollable, overwhelming and irresistible desires for drink. . . . Finally, Rush called this condition a "disease" and recommended total abstinence as the only remedy for the addicted individual (Levine, 1984:110).

These principles contain the key points of the modern disease model with the exception of a genetic predisposition, which was added later when Alcoholics Anonymous reformulated the medical model in the twentieth century. Although many physicians influenced the early temperance movement, it was essentially a popular movement that identified alcohol consumption as the root cause of the burgeoning social deviance that threatened American decorum: "All would be well if only the nation were totally abstinent" (Levine, 1984:111).

The early efforts of the temperance movement were supportive and persuasive, but by the 1850s, as its influence grew, it began to demand universal prohibition of alcohol. By the twentieth century, the temperance movement was dominated by the more militant Anti-Saloon league, which focused on hard-headed lobbying and political pressure tactics. Carry Nation, who organized the illegal physical destruction of saloons on a large scale, became an American celebrity (Taylor, 1966). The targets and methods of political action changed as decades passed, but the disease model provided apparent scientific authority for even greater rhetorical and physical violence. Orford (1985:5) has commented that the nineteenth century view of addiction combined "moral and medical condemnation."

Although the disease model of addiction was first applied to alcohol, it was applied to other drugs when hostility toward them emerged. For example, opium had been widely used for thousands of years before it was "discovered" in the nineteenth century that habitual use was a disease. The disease model was applied to opiate drugs by the 1870s by the German scholar Eduard Levenstein and others (Sonnedecker, 1962, 1963), and gained popularity as pressure for stringent opiate prohibition began to strengthen in England and the United States (Berridge and Edwards, 1981; Musto, 1973). As with alcohol, opium was soon discovered to be the cause of all social problems.

In recent decades the disease model of addiction, the blame for imminent social disintegration, and extraordinarily stringent control measures have been applied to use of marijuana (Jones and Jones, 1977; Nahas, 1979) and cocaine (Gold and Dackis, 1984).

In contrast to the disease model, the adaptive model is an ancient conception (cf. Plato's description of "master passions" in *The Republic,* Lee Translation, 1955:392–395). It is found throughout classical and contemporary literature (e.g., Alexander, 1982; Alexander and Schweighofer, in press) and in everyday discussions of addiction. It does not depict addiction as pathological or evil, but as a natural consequence of human distress.

Drug Control and Humane Values

Currently, the disease model provides a major part of the justification for violent measures against drug traffickers. If drug availability causes addiction, at least in those who are susceptible, and if addiction is a soul-destroying disease, then drug distribution must be curtailed. If drug addiction is not only a disease but an epidemic, then curtailment can become violent without limit—epidemics warrant any measures necessary to protect public health.

Decades ago, such thinking generated a war on drugs, and in the 1980s the war drums are louder than ever. Large numbers of people suspected of distributing drugs have been intimidated, deprived of their jobs, property, crops, and civil rights and subjected to long prison terms. In many countries they are routinely beaten and killed (Epstein, 1977; Trebach, in press). In the present climate of thought, which is suffused with the logic of the disease model, such practices have come to be regarded as normal.

The disease model is not the entire cause of the war on drugs. However, the current harsh and ineffective treatment of drug distributors is easier to justify than past persecutions because the disease model provides a putatively scientific and humane rationale, and this rationale is used incessantly.

The disease model is used to justify harsh and counterproductive measures against users as well as traffickers. The disease model makes it seem justifiable that, for example, users of drugs should be identified through urine testing and deprived of their jobs and/or forced into treatment. Some persons who test positive for amphetamine or cocaine might argue that, under the conditions of fatigue or stress at the time, their work benefited from the drug and that they used it wisely. Such an argument is conceivable from an adaptive viewpoint but is not admissible under a disease model. Using highly addictive drugs is a sign of the contagious disease of drug addiction. Naturally, the user should be fired and/or forced into treatment.

Urine testing is perhaps the most frequent infringement of ordinary rights justified by the disease model, but it is by no means the harshest. Suspected addicts can be incarcerated (i.e., given "compulsory treatment"), denied normal medical and social services, subjected to unnecessarily painful drug withdrawal, or administered summary corporal punishment by the police.

For example, Arnold Trebach (in press:chs. 1 and 2) has extensively documented the story of Fred Collins, an American university student who was forcibly confined and subjected to classical brainwashing techniques including undernourishment (he lost twenty-five pounds), sleep deprivation, twenty-four hour surveillance, deprivation of all outside contact, social humiliation, and threats of extreme physical violence. This treatment for chemical dependence was administered by Straight, Inc., an institution based in Florida with operations in other U.S. cities. Straight, Inc. has been warmly endorsed by Nancy Reagan and other prominent members of the U.S. anti-drug community.

After he eventually escaped, by jumping through a window and eluding his pursuers, Fred Collins sued. Straight, Inc. was convicted of false imprisonment and the jury awarded $220,000 in damages. Straight, Inc.'s legal defense centered on the allegation that Fred Collins was chemically dependent and that stringent actions were necessary to save his life. The jury was convinced by other testimony that he was not a drug addict. In fact, there was no evidence that he was, other than the suspicions of his parents, Straight, Inc.'s dubious diagnosis, and his frank admission of infrequent use of marijuana.

What, however, if Fred Collins *had been* drug addicted? Straight, Inc. is still in operation, and its methods are essentially unchanged. Moreover, even after Fred Collins's suit, its actions have been defended by top-ranking drug experts in the Reagan administration on the grounds that its methods are necessary to control the drug epidemic (Trebach, in press).

The disease model can also be used to justify preventive measures that would be offensive in other contexts. For example, because the disease model identifies a genetic predisposition to addiction as an important part of the cause, it makes sense that people who have alcoholic relatives (or relatives with any other addiction) be forced into preventive treatment, whether they show any signs of addiction themselves or not. It is justifiable to abrogate normal civil rights when the likelihood of contracting a severe disease is certified by medical science. This practice appears to be spreading in the United States (Peele, 1985).

The crucial point is that the disease model provides a logically consistent, putatively scientific justification for cruel, ineffective, and mendacious policies. This connection often goes unrecognized, perhaps because of the genuine goodwill of most of those who endorse the disease model without, I submit, facing its full implications.

From an adaptive viewpoint, punitive measures directed at drug traffickers, users, and users' relatives are inevitably ineffective and counterproductive, for two fundamental reasons. First, people become drug-addicted only if they have failed to maintain adult integration and if addiction is the best substitute adaptation they can muster. Eliminating the drugs that they rely on merely forces such people to choose another substitute adaptation that is likely to be worse for them. From an adaptive viewpoint, the consistent failure of drug prohibition (see Trebach, 1984; Wisotsky, 1983) shows that many people find drug use a better substitute adaptation than other possibilities.

A second reason punitive measures must fail, from an adaptive viewpoint, is that people adopt substitute adaptations only if they have failed to achieve satisfactory adult functioning. People willingly leave substitutes behind when more constructive alternatives become feasible, as demonstrated by the relatively high frequency with which people abandon opiate addiction and alcoholism without treatment (Vaillant, 1983; Waldorf, 1983). Therefore, afflicting them with additional disapproval, guilt, confinement, or refusal of normal supportive services can only exacerbate their sense of failure, and intensify and prolong the addiction.

For these two reasons, the drug control policies that grow from the disease model are intrinsically harmful to people who utilize substitute adaptations, no matter how effectively the policies are executed and no matter how benevolent the people who carry them out.

In the case of people who do not depend on substitute adaptations, prohibitive drug control policies that derive from the disease model can only reduce their options to use drugs reasonably. The opiate drugs, for example, are of great value to the sick, but their use is greatly curtailed because of the fear engendered by the disease model. People in desperate pain have been potentially refused opiate drugs or have denied *themselves* these drugs because of unfounded fears of addiction (Trebach 1982; Zinberg, 1984). Many illicit drugs could be used beneficially if they were more accessible.

Professional Monopoly and Coercion

If addiction is an intractable disease, it requires treatment by professional specialists; if the treatment is not effective, more intensive treatment and more professional control is needed. The system that has emerged from the logic of the disease model is professionalized, expensive, coercive, and ineffective.

There are, of course, some talented professional therapists who can help some of the patients who can pay for their time, but most addicted people in the world do not have access to this quality of treatment. In many parts of Canada and the United States, and more so in the Third World, the disease model logic requires that addiction be treated by professional specialists who are poorly trained and overworked. These specialists are not even available to the bulk of the population. The disease model thus creates a hopeless situation.

From the adaptive viewpoint, coping with failure is *not a disease,* so there is no reason to restrict help to professional specialists. Most people have experienced, at least temporarily, the problems that arise when adult integration is threatened and may therefore understand and help addicted friends and relatives. Some critical cases, of course, may require professional services in the form of organic treatment, sedation, benevolent intimidation, or involuntary commitment. Other addicted people may wish to drop their addiction but may be so tightly knotted in complex rationalizations that professional analysis is required. But most addicted people conduct their dreary lives without need for professional services and many draw away from their addictions without any professional intervention (cf. Schachter, 1982; Vaillant, 1983; Waldorf, 1983).

Disease model logic is often imposed on patients. For example, some professionals refuse services to severe alcoholics until they join Alcoholics Anonymous and become successfully abstinent for several months (Bean-Bayog, 1986b). In effect, such patients are told by their families and friends that they have an incurable disease and that noncompliance with the disease model will prove disastrous. This doctrine is apparently effective with some dangerously excessive drinkers who can adopt the AA philosophy and regimen.

The problem arises when the success of this drastic procedure is taken as justification for imposing the disease model on all addicted people, not just those who are in dire straits and amenable to the disease model's logic (Khantzian, 1985). What, for example, of alcoholic people who are unable to accept the particular ideology and social structure of AA? If their doctor, their family and friends, and AA have all expressed certainty that nonacceptance of disease model doctrine will lead to disaster, but if they cannot comply with the demand, they have been essentially cursed by society under the leadership of its professionals. The disease model in such cases can become a terrible self-fulfilling prophecy.

Even when imposing the disease/AA concept can work, it must be applied sparingly because it is such a drastic treatment. In AA-type programs, the person is told that because of their incurable disease they are "powerless" to control their own destiny without reliance on a higher power (which in effect means indefinite association with AA). Never again can they hope to be independent, powerful, or healthy. This amounts to radical surgery on the self-concept, perhaps the psychological equivalent of an amputation. This is a terrible price unless an addiction is genuinely life-threatening.

The adaptive view is that addicted people are not at all powerless. Rather, they are actively maintaining a substitute adaptation that sustains them in an otherwise drastic situation. Even if the substitute adaptation is failing them, it is a sign that they must try something different, not that they are powerless. Therefore, the adaptive orientation would view addicted people as fully capable of exploring reasonable alternatives.

When its logic is taken one step further, the adaptive orientation becomes a social critique. If conditions are so harsh that significant numbers of people are unable to achieve minimal mature functioning, does it not follow that society needs therapy rather than its individual members? If social life is to be civil and humane, must not more fortunate members of society find a way to mitigate such conditions?

It might seem that the disease model benefits the health professions because it confers responsibility for addiction on physicians and other health workers, but it is a dubious benefit. Some health professionals appear to find the development of large-scale treatment systems appealingly lucrative, but with the responsibility comes the assignment of blame when the treatment fails, as it regularly does. Health professionals lose more than credibility, however.

In this era of war on drugs, any association with illicit drugs and addicts eventually brings a taint. If doctors cannot cure this disease, it is perhaps because they are being hoodwinked by the wily addicts into overprescribing. Or perhaps they are willingly colluding because of the corrosive effects of drugs on everyone's morality in the end. This kind of suspicion, although usually unspoken, is taken seriously. In my city, doctors are routinely visited by undercover policemen, wired for sound, who tell convincing stories of a need for drugs that is plausible and hard to resist. But such prescriptions contravene the *Narcotic Control Act,* under which doctors who write them are charged (Beyerstein and Alexander, 1985). In effect, doctors are coming to be treated like "pushers" by the police. As well, there are proposals that medical professionals should adopt an attitude of vigilant surveillance toward each other. Drugs are accessible and doctors and nurses work under stress. Nobody knows how many are genetically susceptible. By the disease model logic, doctors are due for more scrutiny, suspicion, and regulation than most other segments of society.

Values and Esthetics

The disease model provides a deterministic, probabilistic, mechanical conception of the way human beings react to drugs. Genes, metabolism, and family history assign to each person a degree of susceptibility. If susceptibility is high and the person is exposed to addictive drugs and/or increased stress, it is highly probable that addiction will occur with its consequent ill effects. People are victims of forces beyond their control and must therefore be regulated externally.

The adaptive model paints with warmer hues. People universally struggle to achieve mature self-reliance and social acceptance, but not all succeed. Those who fail are faced with an awful dilemma. Some persist without hope, some find relief in suicide, and some develop substitute adaptations such as addiction that fill the void, at least temporarily. Addicts are conceived as having failed in an essential maturational task, but are nonetheless purposive, creative, resolute, human. Their struggle is one that all adult human beings know, although most have had the good fortune to achieve greater success.

The adaptive model complements values that most people would accept as primary—the importance of strong, independent, happy individuals. The adaptive model envisions people as masters of their own development, with the helpers they choose; people who can choose their virtues and indulgences without excessive supervision; people who can recognize their own excesses and find ways to change them; and people who can expect a welcoming, supportive environment. The disease model suspends these values in the context of the epidemic disease/evil of addiction.

What It Takes to Replace the Disease Model

Scientific Creativity

Kuhn's (1970) concept of the central organizing principle of science, the paradigm, is wonderfully manifold. A paradigm is not just a conceptual framework like the disease and adaptive models but much more. For example, it also includes rules that define proper research techniques and a sense of what findings are important. Most important in the present context, it includes a set of prototypical observations and experimental procedures that powerfully convey the essence of the paradigmatic world view.

Darwin and Mendel did not change history by giving the world unheralded ideas—more, their genius provided science with clear, precise images that made preexisting frameworks powerfully believable. Nature provides images in abundance but not manipulatable scientific ones. Brightly colored birds and profusions of flowers are not enough—Darwin's finches and Mendel's cross-bred peas provided the prototypical observations that transformed frameworks into functioning paradigms.

The task of creating powerful paradigm-defining observations and experiments remains to be accomplished with the adaptive model before the final replacement of the disease model can occur.

Courage

Replacing the disease model requires the courage to give up the promise of easy satisfactions that it offers. For example, it requires giving up the enticing promise that addiction and other forms of deviance can be controlled by application of punitive force and categorical medical treatment. The solution is not as simple as that. For health professionals, the adaptive model means giving up monopoly status on treatment and the unjustified claim of ability to cure a condition that is not a disease. For scientists, it means giving up the simplistic view of an exclusively empirical science and accepting the responsibility for evaluating alternative frameworks by less positivistic framework evaluations. Finally, it means generally giving up the comfortable allegiance to the social structures of the present and facing the need for major changes when too many people fail.

On a more individual level, accepting the adaptive orientation requires the courage to accept the personal responsibility that the disease model disclaims. The disease model asserts that the dread problem of addiction that may afflict my friends, my family, or myself is caused by addictive drugs and by genetic accidents. Help will surely come from pharmacologists who will discover antidotes; doctors who will discover treatments; soldiers, police, and bureaucrats who will stem the flow of pernicious drugs; and geneticists who will look after the next generation. Parents' groups may enlist in the struggle in a disease model framework, but they do not need to worry about the issue of raising healthy, well-integrated children in a violent, chaotic world. Rather, they can take up the conceptually simpler task of protecting their children from pernicious drugs and unseen pushers. This gratuitous self-reassurance, too, must be given up.

Courage may appear a foreign concept in a piece of technical literature.

Such a view, however, reflects on outmoded understanding of science as solely an intellectual game and scientists as only detached technicians. The twentieth-century understanding of history and philosophy of science has liberated scientists from a self-imposed characterization as moral idiots, by showing that they share the responsibility for frameworks that are established on the basis of broad, humane concerns as well as empirical evaluations. That liberating conception provides a way to unblock the progress of scientific understanding when urgent issues must be confronted.

Notes

1. Following Jaffe (1980), *addiction* is used here to mean a harmful, overwhelming involvement with any drug, including alcohol. The reasons for selecting this definition and for preferring addiction to alternative terms like *substance abuse, chemical dependence,* etc., are developed in Alexander and Schweighofer (in press). See also Peele (1985).

2. My colleagues and I have previously contrasted the adaptive orientation to the exposure orientation (Alexander and Hadaway, 1982). The exposure orientation in the previous work is a single causal hypothesis in the more general disease model that is described here. The exposure orientation, in particular, does not include a genetic component and is restricted to opiates. The previous adaptive orientation was a preliminary version of the more articulated adaptive model that is presented here.

3. Some authors who support an adaptive view of addiction do not carry its implications this far. They assume that the adaptiveness of addiction is illusory or only temporary, but this view is better understood as a compromise between the two models (cf. Peele, 1985). My intention here is to apply *adaptive* in a fuller sense.

4. The well-known studies of strain differences in the opiate consumption of mice and rats are of dubious relevance. There is no clear connection between simple consumption of opiates and *addiction,* which is a complex human event involving, by almost any definition, much more than consumption of a substance in large amounts.

5. Conceptualizations of this sort have been called *frameworks of entities* (Carnap, 1952), "epistemes" (Foucault, 1970), "paradigms" (Kuhn, 1970), "the protected hard core of research programmes" (Lakatos, 1978), or "unproblematic background knowledge" (Popper, cited by Lakatos, 1978) or "theories" by other philosophers of science including Feyerabend (1978), Hacking (1983), and William James (1910/1963). I chose the term *frameworks* because paradigms and epistemes are more complex concepts than the two models under consideration here, because the term theories has become ambiguous through diverse usage, and because the others seem too cumbersome.

References

Alexander, B.K. 1982. James M. Barrie and the Expanding Definition of Addiction. *Journal of Drug Issues* 12:397–413.

————. 1984. When Experimental Psychology Is Not Empirical Enough: The Case of the Exposure Orientation. *Canadian Psychology* 25:84–95.

Alexander, B.K., and P.F. Hadaway. 1982. Opiate Addiction: The Case for an Adaptive Orientation. *Psychological Bulletin* 92:367–381.

Alexander, B.K., and A.R.F. Schweighofer. In press. Traditional and Restrictive Meanings of Addiction: A Reappraisal. *Canadian Psychology.*

Bean-Bayog, M. 1986a. Review of "The Meaning of Addiction: Compulsive Experience and Its Interpretation." *New England Journal of Medicine* 314:189–190.

————. 1986b. Address at a symposium of the Psychiatry Department of Cambridge Hospital, Westing Copley Hotel, Boston, MA. March 1.

Berridge, V., and G. Edwards. 1981. *Opium and the People: Opiate Use in Nineteenth Century England.* London, Allan Lane.

Beyerstein, B.L., and B.K. Alexander. 1985. Why Treat Doctors Like Pushers? *Journal of the Canadian Medical Association* 132:337–341.

Brecher, E.M. 1972. *Licit and Illicit Drugs.* Boston: Little, Brown.

Carnap, R. 1952. Empiricism, Semantics, and Ontology. In L. Linsky, ed., *Semantics and the Philosophy of Language.* Urbana, IL: University of Chicago Press.

Chein, I., D.L. Gerard, R.S. Lee, and E. Rosenfeld. 1964. *The Road to H: Narcotics, Delinquency, and Social Policy.* New York: Basic Books.

Courtwright, D.T. 1982. *Dark Paradise: Opiate Addiction in America before 1940.* Cambridge, MA: Harvard University Press.

Epstein, E.J. 1977. *Agency of Fear: Opiates and Political Power in America.* New York: Putnam.

Falk. J.L. 1983. Drug Dependence: Myth or Motive? *Pharmacology, Biochemistry, and Behavior* 19:385–391.

Feyerabend, P. 1978. *Against Method: Outline of an Anarchistic Theory of Knowledge.* London: Verso.

Fingarette, H., and A.F. Hasse. 1979. *Mental Disability and Criminal Responsibility.* Berkeley: University of California Press.

Foucault, M. 1970. *The Order of Things: An Archaeology of the Human Sciences.* London: Tavistock.

————. 1979. *Discipline and Punish: The Birth of the Prison.* New York: Vintage.

Franks, L. 1985. A New Attack on Alcoholism. *New York Times Magazine,* October 20:47–69.

Gold, M.S., and C.A. Dackis. 1984. New Insights and Treatments: Opiate Withdrawal and Cocaine Addiction. *Clinical Therapeutics* 7:6–21.

Gold, M.S., and W.S. Rea. 1983. The Role of Endorphins in Opiate Addiction, Opiate Withdrawal, and Recovery. *Psychiatric Clinics of North America* 6: 489–520.

Goldstein, A. 1979. Heroin Maintenance: A Medical View. A Conversation between a Physician and a Politician. *Journal of Drug Issues* 9:341–347.

Goodwin, D.W. 1979. Alcoholism and Heredity: A Review and Hypothesis. *Archives of General Psychiatry* 36:57–61.

————. 1985. Alcoholism and Genetics: The Sins of the Fathers. *Archives of General Psychiatry* 42:171–174.

Goodwin, D.W., F. Schulsinger, L. Hermansen, S.B. Guze, and G. Winokur. 1973.

Alcohol Problems in Adoptees Raised Apart from Alcoholic Biological Parents. *Archives of General Psychiatry* 28:238–243.

Goodwin, D.W., F. Schulsinger, J. Knop, S. Mednick, and S.B. Guze. 1977. Alcoholism and Depression in Adopted-out Daughters of Alcoholics. *Archives of General Psychiatry* 34:751–755.

Goodwin, D.W., F. Schulsinger, N. Moller, L. Hermansen, G. Winocur, and S.B. Guze. 1974. Drinking Problems in Adopted and Nonadopted Sons of Alcoholics. *Archives of General Psychiatry* 31:164–169.

Hacking, I. 1983. *Representing and Intervening: Introductory Topics in the Philosophy of Natural Science.* Cambridge, Cambridge University Press.

Jaffe, J. 1980. Drug Addiction and Drug Abuse. In A.G. Gilman, L.S. Goodman, and A. Gilman, eds., *Goodman and Gilman's The Pharmacological Basis of Therapeutics.* 6th ed. New York: Macmillan.

James, W. 1910/1963. *Pragmatism and Other Essays.* New York: Washington Square Press.

Jones, H., and H. Jones. 1977. *Sensual Drugs.* Cambridge: Cambridge University Press.

Kaplan, E.H., and H. Wieder. 1974. *Drugs Don't Take People, People Take Drugs.* Secaucus, NJ: Lyle Stuart.

Khantzian, E.J. 1985. Psychotherapeutic Interventions with Substance Abusers: The Clinical Context. *Journal of Substance Abuse Treatment* 2:83–88.

Kuhn, T.S. 1970. *The Structure of Scientific Revolutions.* 2nd ed. Chicago: University of Chicago Press.

Lakatos, I. 1978. *The Methodology of Scientific Research Programmes: Philosophical Papers.* Vol. 1. Cambridge: Cambridge University Press.

Levine, H.G. 1978. The Discovery of Addiction: Changing Conceptions of Habitual Drunkenness in America. *Journal of Studies on Alcohol* 39:143–174.

———. 1984. The Alcohol Problem in America: From Temperance to Alcoholism. *British Journal of Addiction* 79:109–119.

Mayr, E. 1982. *The Growth of Biological Thought: Diversity, Evolution, and Inheritance.* Cambridge, MA: Belknap Press.

Morgan, J.P. 1984. Problems of Mass Screening for Misused Drugs. *Journal of Psychoactive Drugs* 16:305–317.

Murray, R.M., C.A. Clifford, and H.M.D. Gurling. 1983. Twin and Adoption Studies: How Good Is the Evidence for a Genetic Role? In M. Galanter, ed., *Recent Developments in Alcoholism.* Vol. 1. New York: Plenum.

Musto, D.F. 1973. *The American Disease: Origins of Narcotic Control.* New Haven: Yale University Press.

Nahas, G.G. 1979. *Keep off the Grass: A Scientific Enquiry into the Biological Effects of Marijuana.* Oxford: Pergamon Press.

Orford, J. 1985. *Excessive Appetites: A Psychological View of Addictions.* Chichester: Wiley.

Peele, S. 1985. *The Meaning of Addiction: Compulsive Experience and Its Interpretation.* Lexington, MA: Lexington Books.

———. 1986. The Implications and Limitations of Genetic Models of Alcoholism and Other Addictions. *Journal of Studies on Alcohol* 47:63–73.

Plato. c.375 B.C./1955. *The Republic.* Translated by D. Lee. Harmondsworth, England: Penguin.

Reich, W.P., and W.J. Filstead. 1986. The Culture Context of Psychological Approaches to Alcoholism: Should We Contest or Collaborate? *American Psychologist* 41:322–323.

Schachter, S. 1982. Recidivism and Self-Cure of Smoking and Obesity. *American Psychologist* 37:436–444.

Shiffman, S., and T.A. Wills, eds. 1985. *Coping and Substance Use.* Orlando, FL: Academic Press.

Sonnedecker, G. 1962. Emergence of the Concept of Opiate Addiction. *Journal Mondial de Pharmacie* 3:275–290.

———. 1963. Emergence of the Concept of Opiate Addiction. *Journal Mondial de Pharmacie* 1:27–34.

Tarter, R.E., A. I. Alterman, and K.L. Edwards. 1985. Vulnerability to Alcoholism in Men: A Behavior-Genetic Perspective. *Journal of Studies on Alcohol* 46: 329–356.

Taylor, R.L. 1966. *Vessel of Wrath: The Life and Times of Carry Nation.* New York: New American Library.

Trebach, A.S. 1982. *The Heroin Solution.* New Haven: Yale University Press.

———. 1984. Peace without Surrender in the Perpetual Drug War. *Justice Quarterly* 1:125–144.

———. In press. *The War on Us.* New York: Macmillan.

Uttal, W.R. 1978. *The Psychology of Mind.* Hillsdale: NJ: Erlbaum.

Vaillant, G.E. 1983. *The Natural History of Alcoholism: Causes, Patterns and Paths to Recovery.* Cambridge, MA: Harvard University Press.

Waldorf, D. 1983. Natural Recovery from Opiate Addiction: Some Social-Psychological Processes of Untreated Recovery. *Journal of Drug Issues* 13: 237–280.

Wisotsky, S. 1983. Exposing the War on Cocaine: The Futility and Destructiveness of Prohibition. *Wisconsin Law Review* 6:1305–1426.

Zinberg, N.E. 1984. *Drug, Set, and Setting: The Basis for Controlled Intoxicant Use.* New Haven: Yale University Press.

4
Vulnerability to Alcohol and Drug Abuse: A Behavior-Genetic View

Ralph E. Tarter
Kathleen L. Edwards

B y the time the ship docked in Genoa in the spring of 1347, on return from a trading excursion to the Far East, over half the sailors were dead; those who did survive the long voyage rapidly succumbed in the following weeks. So began the Black Plague, which over the next four years was to decimate between 25 to 50 percent of the population of Europe, and for the subsequent 300 years was to wreak havoc on Western civilization. The omnipresence of the infectious agent, Y. *Pestis,* placed the whole population at risk: however, the fact that not all individuals acquired this inevitably fatal disease underscores the variability among individuals with respect to disease susceptibility.

The study of epidemics aptly illustrates that both the susceptibility to develop a disease, as well as the outcome from disease, are variable, ranging from a probability of close to zero (e.g., common cold) to unity (e.g., acquired immune deficiency syndrome). The observation that the vulnerability to develop a given disease is not equally distributed among all individuals in the population suggests that those who develop a particular disease have either an inherited or acquired diathesis or predisposition. Furthermore, casual observation indicates that there must additionally be a facilitating environment for a disease to become manifest in susceptible persons; this could take many forms, ranging from nonspecific stress to specific toxic and infectious agents in the physical and social environments.

Research into the behavioral and psychiatric disorders, especially the substance abuse disorders, has only recently adopted the diathesis-stress model for investigating the etiology and natural history of these conditions. Although empirical inquiry into etiology and the application of clinical interventions have been guided by the diathesis-stress model of psychopathology in the research and treatment of schizophrenia (Moffitt et al., 1983), no systematic effort has, as yet, been made to conceptualize alcoholism and drug abuse within this framework. The following discussion addresses the key theoretical and methodological issues that are pertinent to elucidating the etiology of substance abuse and concludes with a brief description of the relevance of the diathesis-stress model for the prevention and treatment of alcohol and drug abuse.

Conceptual and Methodological Issues

Diathesis-Stress Model of Psychopathology

As noted above, the diathesis-stress model asserts that the etiology of substance abuse cannot be comprehensively understood as a straightforward cause and effect relationship. Rather, there are multiple predisposing organismic characteristics comprising the "causes" that via numerous biological mechanisms, augment the likelihood of a negative outcome. The outcome (e.g., substance abuse) ultimately is determined, however, by facilitating environmental circumstances. Thus, organismic susceptibility may be a necessary, but not a sufficient, condition to produce a pathologic outcome. For example, where alcohol is not available (e.g., fundamentalist Moslem countries), there is no alcoholism, although the genetic propensity (if such truly exists) is present in a segment of the population.

The characteristics of the individual that predispose to an unfavorable outcome are operationally defined as the *vulnerability*. Short stature for the aspiring United States presidental candidate, color blindness for the talented fashion designer, and left-handedness for the skillful polo player readily illustrate in daily life how certain intrinsic individual characteristics adversely impact on the opportunity to be successful. A vulnerability exists, therefore, only in the context of a specific social and physical ecology and particular time in history. For instance, approximately 5,000 people a day were dying in Rome in the second century A.D. from measles, while today (even in persons not vaccinated) the fatality rate is extremely low. Thus, whereas once humans were very susceptible to this disease, today they are essentially invulnerable to its potentially fatal consequences. With reference to substance abuse, the longstanding ambivalence in the United States toward alcohol consumption and drug use has resulted in an assortment of explicit and informal sanctions that in turn influence the per capita consumption level. For example, at the turn of the century, Coca-Cola contained cocaine and was overtly advertised and consumed for its nervous system stimulating properties. Today, there are strong negative attitudes toward cocaine in our society; hence, users tend to be classified as disordered. Also, nicotine use is now (since 1980) potentially diagnosed as a mental disorder (American Psychiatric Association, 1980). The point to be made is that whereas there may be a predisposition to substance use and abuse, this outcome is defined ultimately according to contemporary social values.

Thus, to the extent that a vulnerability is present, it exists at only a particular time and in a specific cultural and physical environment. The multiple forces in the environment impinging on the person so as to exacerbate, as well as protect, the individual and the social environment created by the person's own actions, determines the magnitude of risk for an unfavorable outcome. Even though research has not progressed to this stage, it should be theoretically possible to measure the magnitude of vulnerability and to quantify the environmental parameters so as to estimate the probability of an unfavorable outcome. Hence, although providing the overarching conceptual framework for studying substance abuse etiology, the diathesis-stress model has not yet been applied in research attempting to precisely quantify risk or for implementing prevention and treatment interventions.

Origins of Vulnerability

The susceptibility to an adverse outcome can be either inherited or acquired. With respect to alcoholism, there is emerging evidence pointing to a genetic susceptibility (Cloninger et al., 1981; Goodwin, 1983; Goodwin et al., 1973), although the empirical findings in this regard are not entirely consistent or conclusive (Murray et al., 1983). Recent research suggests that there may also be an acquired vulnerability to an adverse outcome as indicated by a higher prevalence of behavioral deviance in offspring of alcoholics who have a physical handicap (Werner, 1986). Thus, even though the most emphasis to date has been given to the genetic basis of alcoholism vulnerability, it would appear that the predisposition may have, in part at least, a nongenetic basis as well.

Biological Organization

The vulnerability to alcoholism, and possibly also to other drug abuse, may be represented at one or more levels of biologic organization. Research has yielded an impressive and wide array of findings documenting the characteristics of alcoholism vulnerability with respect to morphologic, biochemical, physiologic, neurologic, behavioral, and cognitive processes that are either impaired or deviant in persons at known high risk (see Tarter et al., 1985a for review). Indeed, the cognitions and expectancies about the effects that alcohol will have on the person appear to differ between high- and low-risk individuals (Gabrielli and Plomin, 1985; Newlin, 1985).

The results of the investigations conducted to date, although impressive, have not been integrated into a conceptually coherent framework. With the exception of the behavior genetic theory advanced by Tarter et al. (1985a), little is known of the biologic mechanisms and behavioral propensities that may underlie the risk for alcoholism. For example, antisocial behavior in childhood has been strongly linked to an increased risk for alcoholism in adulthood (McCord and McCord, 1960; Robins, 1966); however, the factors that predispose to deviance are themselves poorly understood at the anatomical, biochemical, physiological, and behavioral levels of analysis.

Sensitivity vs. Specificity

Although a variety of biological and behavioral characteristics have been reported to be associated with the risk for alcoholism, there is, as yet, no study that has identified any particular feature that is specific to only this disorder. Thus, as pointed out by Peele (1986), the issue of specific determinism remains to be addressed. It is possible, indeed even likely, that numerous characteristics that have been ascribed to alcoholism vulnerability also presage other behavioral disorders. Evidence in this regard has been accumulated indicating that there are numerous commonalities among the various disorders of excess (Lang, 1983; Orford, 1985; Peele, 1985), and that there may be a common disposition toward compulsivity for several of these types of conditions (Peele and Brodsky, 1975). Tarter et al. (1985a), in a theoretical analysis of the behavioral diathesis to alcoholism, have argued that there is an aggregation of temperament traits, each having a heritable basis that, depending on sex-role socialization and sociocultural determinants, could result in one of a number of topologically distinct disorders. Among the disorders that appear to share common vulnerability features are borderline personality, antisocial personality, somatization (hysteria), drug abuse, gambling, alcoholism, and bulimia. Whether there are vulnerability characteristics for each of these latter disorders that are distinct and separate from each other is, at present, unknown.

Quantitative and Qualitative
Components of Vulnerability

An important consideration for delineating the parameters of substance abuse vulnerability is that there are a variety of predisposing characteristics, each of which can uniquely and differentially contribute to the risk for ultimately succumbing to an unfavorable outcome. The available evidence strongly indicates that there is no single vulnerability feature that inevitably portends a negative outcome. Rather, the research results suggest that it is the number of vulnerability variables, not a specific variable, that predisposes to a negative outcome (Bry et al., 1982; Newcomb et al., 1986). Restated differently, the evidence does not support the notion of a qualitatively distinct configuration of characteristics (e.g., personality type) as comprising the vulnerability to alcohol or other forms of substance abuse. Instead, it is the number of such characteristics present that appears to best predict outcome. Among the numerous variables that have been identified that presage an adverse outcome are poor school performance, perceived use of drugs by adults, psychological disorders such as depression or sociopathy, low self-esteem, perception of parental drug use, low religious involvement, conflict with parents, sensation seeking, absence of a sense of purpose and reduced social responsibility (Newcomb et al., 1986). Each of these latter variables can account for only a small amount of the variance at outcome, such as quantity, type, and frequency of drug use. Together, employing multivariate statistical procedures, these latter factors can, however, explain a substantially greater amount of the variance on drug use.

In addition, a variety of biological factors have been reported to comprise risk factors for alcohol abuse, including low platelet monoamine oxidase levels (Alexopoulos et al., 1983), neurophysiological abnormalities as measured by the EEG (Pollack et al., 1983), event-related potentials (Begleiter et al., 1984), hormonal reactions (Schuckit et al., 1983), and neurologic abnormalities such as tremor and ataxia (Hegedus et al., 1984). There is also a higher than expected prevalence of left-handed alcoholics (London, 1986), suggesting that brain functional organization may be atypical in persons who are at elevated risk for this condition.

The features cited above aptly illustrate that vulnerability is best understood from a multivariate perspective. For example, a gynic physique in addition to antisocial behavior in adolescence was able in one study to correctly classify 85 percent of subjects at outcome as being either alcoholic or non-alcoholic (Monnelly et al., 1983). In another study, Tarter (1982) found that a history of childhood hyperactivity combined with psychosocial immaturity could explain almost 50 percent of the variance on an alcoholism severity scale. Moreover, there is some indication that alcoholism is more severe in left-handed individuals (Goodwin, 1985). These latter studies underscore the multivariate basis of alcoholism vulnerability, as well as the diversity of influences on alcoholism manifestations with respect to drinking style.

Stability of Vulnerability

The factors that characterize susceptibility to alcohol or drug excess at one point in life may not have the same impact at other times in life. Both the individual and the environment change; consequently, the quality of interaction between the person and the environment determining the decision to use alcohol or drugs changes also. Hence, what comprises a vulnerability factor at one stage in life might not be a vulnerability trait at a different stage. It has been shown, for example, that the factors that predict drinking at age 18 are of little value in predicting drinking behavior by age 31 (Temple and Fillmore, 1986). Also, there is tentative evidence that the percentage of young adults at high risk (sons of alcoholics) who are problem drinkers is not distinguishable from low-risk subjects (Alterman et al., 1986), suggesting problem drinking is not the *sine qua non* of an alcoholism predisposition. In this regard, it is also noteworthy that the consequence of the first alcohol or drug experience influences to some extent future consumption (Haertzen et al., 1983); these reinforcing consequences are themselves determined by the person's age and the social context at the time of the first drug experience.

Cohort Effects

Related to the above issue is the fact that substance use patterns in the general population are not the same across generations. Hence, baseline rates against which problem behaviors are quantified influence the feasibility of detecting vulnerability characteristics, as well as the particular susceptibility features which can be observed. For example, the findings describing the prevalence of alcoholism vulnerability characteristics in a population where the outcome base rate is very low (e.g., during the era of Prohibition) inevitably would yield different results from societies where drinking is more tolerated (e.g., present day). Also, the degree of repressiveness of the society at a given time in history regulates to some extent the particular form and the opportunity to express deviance, factors that presage substance abuse. Thus, because the population base rate is variable with respect to both the type and quantity of substance use, waxing and waning over time, any observed vulnerability characteristic cannot be considered to be an invariant parameter describing the susceptibility to an adverse outcome.

Clinical Heterogeneity

Substance abuse disorders commonly overlap with other psychopathologic conditions. Anxiety, depression, and sociopathy frequently predate the use of alcohol and drugs. Consequently, by studying persons only on the basis of behavioral topography of being a substance abuser may be misleading because the use of such agents may be in actuality a coping reaction to another psycho-pathologic disorder.

Furthermore, there is substantial variability with respect to quantity, frequency, and pattern of substance abuse in the population. Social class, as well as cultural and gender differences, have been frequently reported to be related to substance use topography. Indeed, even the mode of genetic transmission may differ among the population of individuals who exhibit alcohol abuse (Cloninger et al., 1981), suggesting that the particular biological mechanisms and behavioral dimensions of the vulnerability are not the same for all people.

Prodromal Manifestations

One would expect at first glance that individuals at high and low risk could be differentiated from each other according to their use of pharmacologic substances. Indeed, one study (Cloninger et al., 1981) found heavier drinking in high-risk subjects than low-risk subjects. Other studies have not, however, confirmed this association. Goodwin et al. (1973), in an adoption study, while observing a higher prevalence of alcoholism in offspring of alcoholics, also found that there was more heavy drinking and problem behavior in the sons of nonalcoholics. Wechsler and Rohman (1981) noted that heavy drinking was unrelated to parental drinking pattern. Alterman et al. (1986) also reported that the number of days that low-risk college students either drink or drink to a state of intoxication was greater than that of high-risk subjects. Furthermore, the absolute amount of alcohol consumed was higher in the low-risk subjects. The number of associated problem behaviors (47 percent versus 35 percent) also tended to be higher in the low-risk compared to high-risk subjects. Interestingly, despite the lower alcohol consumption level in the high-risk subjects, the number of alcohol-related symptoms of ethanol excess was somewhat greater in this group, although the two groups did not quite differ statistically.

There are at least three important conclusions that can be drawn from the studies reviewed above. First, it would appear that heavy drinking and alcoholism may reflect categorically different phenomena. Second, the vulnerability to alcoholism, measured by the outcome variable of prodromal drinking behavior, may not be detectable in college-age persons. Drinking behavior may thus not comprise a component of the vulnerability at this stage in life. And, third, the problems that emerge consequential to drinking may be more discriminating of high- and low-risk individuals than alcohol consumption per se. Drinking behavior in young adulthood, even if excessive, cannot, therefore, be considered to be invariantly related to future alcoholism.

Subject Selection Criteria

The vulnerability features identified in any study are inevitably circumscribed to the specific sample. Most investigations have capitalized on the familial aggregation of a specific disorder (e.g., alcohol excess). Persons from families with the disorder (high-risk subjects) are contrasted to individuals on some putative variable with persons who do not have a family history (e.g., low-risk subjects) for the disorder in question. This paradigm ignores, however, the fact that many different disorders aggregate within families; thus, whatever characteristic that is detected in the high-risk subjects that differentiates them from low-risk subjects may not be a specific vulnerability feature. For example, impulsivity has often been linked to the risk for alcoholism; however, this complex behavioral propensity is also characteristic of borderline personality, antisocial personality disorder, bulimia, anxiety, and panic disorder. These latter conditions all contain certain common elements such as impulsivity; whether or not this trait is implicated in alcoholism would depend greatly on the type of control group selected in a study. Thus, for example, comparing alcoholic offspring to children of normal parents would suggest that impulsivity may be a predisposing trait, whereas a control group consisting of any of these latter psychopathologic conditions would indicate otherwise.

Vulnerable individuals have also been selected for study based on certain characteristics which, for theoretical reasons, would be expected to presage the disorder under study. Sher and Levenson (1982), for instance, classi-fied subjects according to scores on the MacAndrew Alcoholism Scale of the MMPI. This scale seems to be associated with the risk for alcoholism. However, the behaviors tapped by this scale are not specific to persons with alcoholism but are commonly present as well in individuals who abuse drugs and have other behavioral disorders. Therefore, although this paradigm affords the opportunity to distinguish high from low risk persons according to a predetermined vulnerability parameter, it has not been applied as yet so that characteristics specific to alcoholism or to other drugs can be iden-tified.

The above two subject selection strategies, although revealing distin-guishing characteristics between persons who are at high risk for developing alcoholism from those at low risk, have not been utilized in paradigms that could enable elucidation of characteristics that are *specific* to any single dis-order of excess such as alcoholism, drug abuse, bulimia, gambling, and so forth. It is a very real possibility, therefore, that differences between high-and low-risk subjects reported to date reflect little more than general propensities for deviance present in persons at risk for a range of psychopathological con-ditions. Indeed, controlling for antisocial disorder, Tarter et al. (1985b) found no differences between high- and low-risk children on activity level, a trait that appears to comprise one of the vulnerability features to alcoholism (Alterman and Tarter, 1983). Moreover, it should be pointed out that the decision regarding whether to exclude or include subjects who are exhibiting evidence of problem drinking with subjects who are not exhibiting evidence of problem drinking will substantially influence the results obtained (Sher, 1985).

Conditions of Expression of Vulnerability

Evidence has been accumulating indicating that vulnerability characteristics distinguishing high- from low-risk persons are measurable in both the disposi-tional nondrug state and during an acute drug challenge. A variety of psycho-logical features have been documented in children and adolescents who were tested in the sober condition and subsequently developed problems. How-ever, little is known of drug specific effects that could differentiate such indi-viduals from the population at large. Preliminary evidence has been presented indicating that alcohol metabolism (Schuckit and Rayses, 1979), EEG response (Pollack et al., 1983), ataxia (Schuckit, 1985), and stress dampening (Sher and Levenson, 1982) distinguish vulnerable from control persons, at least with respect to alcoholism. It is also interesting to note that alcohol may have analgesic properties for the alcoholic but not for the social drinker (Cutter et al., 1976). Thus, in addition to dispositional differences, there may also be distinctions between high- and low-risk persons that are circumscribed to the intoxicated or drug state. This further complicates delineating the mechanisms underlying substance abuse vulnerability, especially considering the recent observation that high behavioral activity level is correlated with alcohol's stress reducing effects under only higher doses of ethanol (Sher and Walitzer, 1986).

Role of the Environment

The diathesis-stress model of psychopathology emphasizes the facilitating role of environmental factors in determining an adverse outcome in vulnerable persons. Indeed, for the substance abuse conditions, the environment appears to be a more potent influence affecting outcome than the underlying biological vulnerability. For example, the punishing physiological vasodilation reaction to alcohol experienced by Native Americans would be expected to protect such individuals from excessive consumption of alcohol. However, the alcoholism prevalence is extremely high in this population, suggesting that the environment vis-à-vis social and cultural disorganization, lack of employment opportunity, poverty, and isolation more than offsets whatever protection from alcoholism that may be present biologically. Family, peer, cultural, and demographic factors all impinge on the person to ultimately affect both the likelihood and type of psychopathologic manifestations. The uneven prevalence among various cultural and ethnic groups and between the sexes for the various psychopathological disorders indicates that biological vulnerability is modifiable to ultimately determine the likelihood and type of adverse outcome. A viable question that is raised, therefore, is whether or not there is the same vulnerability for a number of disorders of excess that, depending on environmental and psychosocial factors, leads to topographically distinct outcomes. For instance, Guze (1975) has argued that the overtly disparate psychiatric disorder of hysteria in women and antisocial personality in men may have a common diathesis. The implicated vulnerability is hyperactivity in childhood that, depending on sex-role and development differences between the genders, leads to distinctive expressions of psychopathology. Focusing entirely on the topography of the pathology may thus possibly be a red herring in search for the underlying vulnerability parameters of substance abuse (e.g., alcohol, heroin, nicotine, bulimia, etc.) vulnerability (cf. Orford, 1985; Peele, 1985; Tarter et al., 1985a).

Reconceptualization of Alcohol and Drug Abuse Vulnerability

Current psychiatric taxonomy bestows uniqueness, at least with respect to diagnosis, to the various types of pharmacologic excess (American Psychiatric Association, 1980). These specific disorders, subserved under the general category of Substance Use Disorders, includes alcohol abuse, barbiturate, sedative or hypnotic abuse, opioid abuse, cocaine abuse, amphetamine abuse, phencyclidine (PCP) abuse, hallucinogen abuse, cannabis abuse, and tobacco dependence. However, as shown by Carnody et al. (1985) there is a high degree of concurrent use of alcohol, cigarettes, and caffeine. Amphetamines are the strongest preferred drug of choice after alcohol among alcoholics (Cadoret et al., 1984). Indeed, even casual clinical observation reveals a high prevalence of diverse types of substance use and abuse by alcoholics.

Whether these are discrete conditions as delineated in DSM III is thus arguable. Moreover, there is a familial aggregation among certain of the substance abuse disorders, especially alcohol and opioid abuse (Kosten et al., 1985) and alcohol and benzodiazepene abuse (Vaillant, 1983). Indeed, the polydrug abuser is becoming increasingly typical and is not the exception as the range of mood-altering drugs broadens and their availability increases over time. Whereas in the 1940s alcoholic beverages were the most available mood-altering agents, today there is a plethora of such substances. Indeed, access to sophisticated laboratory equipment for the synthetic manufacture of complex chemicals has ushered in the era of designer drugs for recreational use.

Based on both clinical and empirical observation, it is apparent that there are shared features among individuals who have a propensity to abuse psychoactive substances and who engage in other behaviors of excess. Prior to contemporary psychiatric classification schemes, the word *mania* was the label used to describe and unify topographically disparate disorders that all had in common the element of compulsive excess. Terms such as *kleptomania* (stealing), *pyromania* (fire setting), *adraptomania* (slaves repeatedly trying to escape from the plantation), *nymphomania* (high frequency of female sexual behavior), as well as many others, were proposed and adopted to varying degree by the professional community. Although this terminology and classification of behavior is subject to much criticism, it is addressed here so as to illustrate and highlight the commonalities that are intrinsic to each of these topologically distinct behaviors; namely, their risk taking, and compulsive and potentially self-destructive repetitive qualities.

Could there be a set of behavioral characteristics comprising a general motivational disposition that are associated with the vulnerability to excessive and compulsive behavior? Personality theories in this regard have not been particularly informative, nor has convincing empirical evidence been marshalled to support the notion of an addictive personality. Tarter et al. (1985a) have argued that the vulnerability to alcoholism and other disorders of excess can be fruitfully studied from the perspective of inherited individual differences or temperaments. The number of temperaments having a heritable basis appears to be limited, and, because they are all present to greater or lesser degree in all individuals, this theoretical perspective enables elucidation of the configuration of heritable traits that ultimately could portend the development of the various disorders of excess. Applying the empirically derived temperament dimensions described by Rowe and Plomin (1977), it was shown that persons at risk for alcoholism deviate on such behavioral traits as activity level, emotionality, sociability, soothability, and attention-span persistence. Reaction to food is another temperament trait identified by Rowe and Plomin (1977); however, empirical study of this dimension as a risk factor for alcoholism and other appetite excesses has not been conducted. Specifically, the available information accrued from twin, adoption, family, and longitudinal studies points to a temperament configuration of high emotionality and behavioral activity level, low attention span, low sociability, and low soothability. Because these constitutional characteristics are largely independent from each other and vary in magnitude of expression among individuals, it can be seen that there are a great variety of constellations comprising temperament makeup. Hence, within the general configuration described above, there may be a number of substance abuse predispositions, each of which portends an unfavorable outcome of varying degree. Moreover, it would seem plausible that environmental forces differentially impact on the person, depending on the particular aggregation of temperament traits, so as to ultimately determine the probability and mode of expression of an adverse outcome.

With respect to the methodological and conceptual issues raised previously, the above perspective raises a number of important considerations. First and most obvious, substance abuse may be but one form of compulsive and excessive behavior, the exact type being determined by socialization and environmental opportunity. It is thus proposed that the various manifestations of excessive behavior are functionally equivalent. The upshot of this argument is that vulnerability to a negative outcome may be detected but that the characteristics lack specificity with respect to the various disorders of excess. Second, whereas there may be certain inherited behavioral propensities comprising the vulnerability, the genetic diathesis must be expressed through specific biological pathways. Tarter et al. (in press) have theorized that the behaviors underlying alcoholism vulnerability are subserved by neural systems lying along the frontal-midbrain neuroaxis. These systems regulate the cognitive, effective motivational, and activation processes involved in goal-directed behavior. To date, studies have focused on particular biochemical, physiological, or neurological variables; however, apart from the integrative reviews by Tarter et al. (1985; in press), there has been no attempt to delineate the parameters of substance abuse vulnerability across multiple levels of biological organization.

A third consideration pertains to the origin of the vulnerability. The behavior-genetic approach proposed by Tarter et al. (1985a), although accommodating heritability of the diathesis, places as much or greater importance on nongenetic factors. Only up to 40 to 50 percent of the variance on temperament traits can be accounted for by genetics. Presumably, a plethora of nongenetic factors influence the behavioral (temperament) predispositions, including intrauterine, perinatal, and postnatal events. Fourth, the notion that there may be numerous pathways to a variety of unfavorable outcomes indicates that accurate predictions of risk may not be feasible. The parameters of vulnerability change during the lifespan, the external stressors and available protective influences of the environment also change over time, and the mode of expression of outcome (e.g., gambling, alcohol, drugs, etc.) is contingent on macroenvironment factors that vary from culture to culture. Thus, accurate prediction may not be possible. The indeterminate perspective, although pessimistic with respect to precisely estimating the risk for specific outcomes, does, however, offer the promise of deriving general principles of psychological development and for delineating the mechanisms underlying the motivation for compulsive and excessive behavior. And fifth, there is the possibility, as yet not systematically tested, that treatment strategies that focus on the vulnerabilities underlying the disorder have an enhanced likelihood of being successful. For instance, there is suggestive evidence that boys at risk for alcoholism are impaired in the regulation of behavioral activity level and goal directedness (Tarter et al., 1985a). Treatment of hyperactivity is generally successful with the use of stimulant drugs; these pharmacologic agents have also been shown to be therapeutically effective for alcoholics who meet the criteria of attention deficit disorder residual type (Wood et al., 1976). There is also suggestive evidence indicating that treatment interactions that focus on specific behavioral propensities (e.g., impulsivity, anxiety, social skill deficits, etc.) may be more effective than the nonspecific peer mediated or didactic treatments currently applied. It is reasonable to conjecture that treatments that modify the behaviors that predispose to the outcome problem behavior are most likely to be therapeutically beneficial. Therefore, treatment (and possibly also prevention) strategies can be most effective when directed to the behaviors which predispose to substance abuse. For these reasons, the temperament perspective is especially heuristic for clarifying not only etiology but also for its relevance for practical intervention.

Implications for Prevention and Treatment

The well-established finding that not all individuals in the population are at equal risk to develop problems with alcohol or drugs (or other compulsive and excessive behaviors) suggests that specific procedures could be developed to identify (and treat) those persons deemed to have the vulnerability. For example, a positive family history for such a disorder, combined with a configuration of psychological characteristics, including antisocial tendencies, would appear to be the most accurate current means of detecting the subpopulation that is at heightened risk. This intervention strategy would appear to be more cost-efficient than targeting prevention procedures to the whole population through didactic or other therapeutic formats. Applying interventions that are keyed to the specific behavioral correlates of the vulnerability (e.g., activity dysregulation, impulsivity, poor social skill, etc.), it is likely that the person can be rendered less vulnerable to substance abuse, as well as other forms of deviant behavior.

In a recent examination of the literature, Zucker and Gomberg (1986) identified several specific factors that appear to be associated with an increased likelihood of an adverse outcome. Although addressing the predisposition to alcoholism, the following parameters are noteworthy because they identify particular areas to target prevention intervention.

1. Antisocial behavior in childhood is related to increased risk for alcoholism in adulthood.

2. Poor school achievement and adjustment is associated with an increased risk for alcoholism.

3. High activity level in childhood augments the risk for an alcoholism outcome in adulthood.

4. Poor or superficial interpersonal relationships characterize boys who substantially become alcoholic.

5. Parental conflict and marital discord is more common in the homes of children who grew up to become alcoholic.

6. Inadequate contact and poor parenting is related to increased alcoholism risk in the children.

7. Parents of children who become alcoholic are often poor role models.

Each of the above characteristics is easily detectable and measurable. Singly and in combination they are also amenable to prevention interventions, not only for alcoholism but for other types of substance abuse as well.

The theory that there are commonalities among the various forms of compulsive and excessive behavior also has a number of social policy implications. First, it suggests that policies affecting availability, sale, and distribution of substances substantially determine the incidence and prevalence of the disorders of excess. For example, the prohibition of alcohol in the United States substantially reduced, although did not eliminate, alcohol-related deaths. Liberalizing drug use laws, thereby making such substances more available and accessible, not surprisingly is also associated with higher consumption rates. Legalizing gambling not surprisingly leads to an increase in this behavior in the local population and problems; that is, compulsive gambling also can be expected to increase in a subset of the population. The upshot of this point is that legislative authority can exercise substantial influence on consumption opportunity and pattern, thereby either attenuating or augmenting the risk of an adverse outcome in vulnerable individuals. In effect, therefore, legislative authority responsible for the sale, distribution, and availability of pharmacologic substances can exercise profound impact on the prevalence of disorders involving each substance. The societal need to balance individual freedom (right to access) and social welfare (health and safety) of society's membership, comprises an enduring problem that encompasses diverse ideological positions; consequently, no universally acceptable policy has yet been adopted in any modern society.

The theoretical formulation proposed here thus argues that prevention and treatment will be effective only to the extent that the predisposition or motivation to engage in substance abuse is reduced or eliminated. This, in effect, entails modifying the characteristics comprising the vulnerability. Perhaps because treatment efforts have not specifically focused on the factors underlying the propensity to abuse pharmacologic substances but have instead addressed either clinical epiphenomena (e.g., depression) or have attempted ideological persuasion (e.g., Alcoholics Anonymous), outcome from treatment has been typically unimpressive. Indeed, even where cessation of use of alcohol does occur, substitution of drinking behavior with other forms of compulsive activity often occurs (Vaillant and Milofsky, 1982). Studies in which treatment strategies are directly targeted to the vulnerability, consisting of either pharmacologic or behavioral interventions, have on the other hand yielded encouraging results. It would thus appear highly desirable that considerable effort be given to treatment research that examines the efficacy of directly modifying the biological and behavioral disturbance underlying substance abuse vulnerability.

References

Alexopoulos, G., K. Lieberman, and R. Frances. 1983. Platelet MAO Activity in Alcoholic Patients and Their First-Degree Relatives. *American Journal of Psychiatry* 140:150–154.

Alterman, A., R. Bridges, and R. Tarter. 1986. Drinking Behavior of High Risk College Men: Contradictory Preliminary Findings. *Alcoholism: Clinical and Experimental Research* 10:305–310.

Alterman, A., and R. Tarter. 1983. The Transmission of Psychological Vulnerability: Implications for Alcoholism Etiology. *Journal of Nervous and Mental Disease* 171:147–156.

American Psychiatric Association. 1980. *Diagnostic and Statistical Manual of Mental Disorders*. 3rd ed. Washington, DC: American Psychiatric Association.

Begleiter, H., B. Porjesz, and B. Kissin. 1984. Event-Related Brain Potentials in Children at Risk for Alcoholism. *Science* 225:1493–1496.

Bry, B., P. McKeon, and R. Pandina. 1982. Extent of Drug Use as a Function of Number of Risk Factors. *Journal of Abnormal Psychiatry* 91:273–279.

Cadoret, R., E. Troughton, and R. Widmer. 1984. Clinical Differences between Antisocial and Primary Alcoholics. *Comprehensive Psychiatry* 25:1–8.

Carnody, T., C. Brischetto, J. Matarazzo, R. O'Donnell, and W. Connor. 1985. Co-Occurrent Use of Cigarettes, Alcohol, and Coffee in Healthy, Community Dwelling Men and Women. *Health Psychology* 4:323–335.

Cloninger, R., M. Bohman, and S. Sigvaardson. 1981. Inheritances of Alcohol Abuse: Cross-Fostering Analyses of Adopted Men. *Archives of General Psychiatry* 38: 861–867.

Cutter, H., B. Maloof, N. Kurtz, and W. Jones. 1976. Feeling No Pain: Differential Responses to Pain by Alcoholics and Nonalcoholics before and after Drinking. *Journal of Studies on Alcohol* 37:273–277.

Gabrielli, W., and R. Plomin. 1985. Individual Differences in Anticipation of Alcohol Sensitivity. *Journal of Nervous and Mental Disease* 173:111–114.

Goodwin, D. 1983. Alcoholism. In R. Tarter, ed., *The Child at Psychiatric Risk*. New York: Oxford University Press.

———. 1985. Alcoholism and Genetics. *Archives of General Psychiatry* 42:171–174.

Goodwin, D., F. Schulsinger, L. Hermansen, S. Guze, and G. Winokur. 1973. Alcohol Problems in Adoptees Raised Apart from Alcoholic Biological Parents. *Archives of General Psychiatry* 28:238–243.

Guze, S. 1975. The Validity and Signficance of the Clinical Diagnosis Hysteria (Briquet's Syndrome). *American Journal of Psychiatry* 32:138–141.

Haertzen, C., T. Kocher, and K. Myasato. 1983. Reinforcements from the First Drug Experience Can Predict Later Drug Habits and/or Addiction: Results with Coffee, Cigarettes, Alcohol, Barbiturates, Minor and Major Tranquilizers, Stimulants, Marijuana, Hallucinogens, Heroin, Opium and Cocaine. *Drug and Alcohol Dependence* 11:147–165.

Hegedus, A., R. Tarter, S. Hill, T. Jacob, and N. Winsten. 1984. Static Ataxia: A Possible Marker for Alcoholism. *Alcoholism: Clinical and Experimental Research* 8:580–582.

Kosten, T., B. Rounsaville, and H. Kleber. 1985. Parental Alcoholism in Opioid Addicts. *Journal of Nervous and Mental Disease* 173:461–469.

Lang, A. 1983. Addictive Personality: A Viable Construct? In P. Levison, D. Gerstein and R. Maloff, eds., *Commonalities in Substance Abuse and Habitual Behavior*. Lexington, MA: Lexington Books.

London, W. 1986. Handedness and Alcoholism: A Family History of Left-Handedness. *Alcoholism: Clinical and Experimental Research* 3:357.

McCord, W., and J. McCord. 1960. *Origins of Alcoholism*. Stanford, CA: Stanford University Press.

Moffitt, T., S. Mednick, and R. Cudek. 1983. Methodology of High Risk Research: Longitudinal Approaches. In R. Tarter, ed., *The Child at Psychiatric Risk*. New York: Oxford University Press.

Monnelly, E., E. Harth, and R. Elderkin. 1983. Constitutional Factors Predictive of Alcoholism in a Follow-Up of Delinquent Boys. *Journal of Studies on Alcohol* 44:530–537.

Murray, R., C. Clifford, and H. Gurling. 1983. Twin Adoption Studies: How Good Is the Evidence for a Genetic Role? In M. Galanter, ed., *Recent Developments in Alcoholism*. Vol. 1. New York: Plenum.

Newcomb, M., E. Maddahian, and P. Bentler. 1986. Risk Factors for Drug Use among Adolescents: Concurrent and Longitudinal Analyses. *American Journal of Public Health* 76:525–531.

Newlin, D. 1985. Offspring of Alcoholics have Enhanced Antagonistic Placebo Response. *Journal of Studies on Alcohol* 49:490–494.

Orford, J. 1985. *Excessive Appetites: A Psychological View of Addictions*. New York: Wiley.

Peele, S. 1985. *The Meaning of Addiction*. Lexington, MA: Lexington Books.

———. 1986. The Implications and Limitations of Genetic Models of Alcoholism and Other Addictions. *Journal of Studies on Alcohol* 47:63–73.

Peele, S., and A. Brodsky. 1975. *Love and Addiction*. New York: Taplinger.

Pollack, V., J. Volavka, D. Goodwin, S. Mednick, W. Gabrielli, J. Knop, and F. Schulsinger. 1983. The EEG after Alcohol Administration in Men at Risk for Alcoholism. *Archives of General Psychiatry* 40:857–861.

Robins, L. 1966. *Deviant Children Grow Up. A Sociological and Psychiatric Study of Sociopathic Personality*. Baltimore, MD: Williams and Wilkins.

Rowe, D., and R. Plomin. 1977. Temperament in Early Childhood. *Journal of Personality Assessment* 41:150–156.

Schuckit, M. 1985. Ethanol Induced Changes in Body Sway in Men at High Alcoholism Risk. *Archives of General Psychiatry* 42:375–379.

Schuckit, M., D. Parker, and L. Rossman. 1983. Ethanol-Related Prolactin Responses and Risk for Alcoholism. *Biological Psychiatry* 18:1153–1159.

Schuckit, M., and V. Rayses. 1979. Ethanol Ingestion: Differences in Blood Acetaldehyde Concentrations in Relatives of Alcoholics and Controls. *Science* 203:54–55.

Sher, K. 1985. Excluding Problem Drinkers in High-Risk Studies of Alcoholism: Effect of Screening Criteria on High-Risk Versus Low Risk Comparisons. *Journal of Abnormal Psychology* 94:106–109.

Sher, K.J., and R.W. Levensen. 1982. Risk for Alcoholism and Individual Differences in the Stress-Response-Dampening Effect of Alcohol. *Journal of Abnormal Psychology* 19:350–367.

Sher, K., and K. Walitzer. 1986. Individual Differences in the Stress-Response-Dampening Effect of Alcohol: A Dose-Response Study. *Journal of Abnormal Psychology* 95:159–167.

Tarter, R. 1982. Psychosocial History, Minimal Brain Dysfunction and Differential Drinking Patterns of Male Alcoholics. *Journal of Clinical Psychology* 38:867–873.

Tarter, R., A. Alterman, and K. Edwards. 1985a. Vulnerability to Alcoholism in Men: A Behavior-Genetic Perspective. *Journal of Studies on Alcohol* 46:329–356.

———. In press. Neurobehavioral Theory of Alcoholism Etiology. In C. Chaudron and D. Wilkinson, eds., *Theories of Alcoholism*. Toronto: Addiction Research Foundation.

Tarter, R., A. Hegedus, and J. Gavaler. 1985b. Hyperactivity in Sons of Alcoholics. *Journal of Studies on Alcohol* 46:259–261.

Temple, M., and K. Fillmore. 1986. The Variability of Drinking Patterns and Problems Among Young Men, Age 16–31: A Longitudinal Study. *The International Journal of the Addictions* 20:1595–1620.

Vaillant, G. 1983. *The Natural History of Alcoholism.* Cambridge, MA: Harvard University Press.

Vaillant, G., and E. Milofsky. 1982. Natural History of Male Alcoholism IV: Paths to Recovery. *Archives of General Psychiatry* 39:127–133.

Wechsler, H., and M. Rohman. 1981. Excessive Users of Alcohol Among College Students. *Journal of Studies on Alcohol* 42:149–155.

Werner, E. 1986. Resilient Offspring of Alcoholics: A Longitudinal Study from Birth to Age 18. *Journal of Studies on Alcohol* 47:34–40.

Wood, D., F. Reimherr, P. Wender, and G. Johnson. 1976. Diagnosis and Treatment of Minimal Brain Dysfunction in Adults. *Archives of General Psychiatry* 33:1453–1460.

Zucker, R., and E. Gomberg. 1986. Etiology of Alcoholism Reconsidered: The Case for a Biopsychosocial Process. *American Psychologist* 41:783–793.

5
Anticipation of Pharmacological and Nonpharmacological Events: Classical Conditioning and Addictive Behavior

Shepard Siegel
Marvin D. Krank
Riley E. Hinson

We live in a highly variable external environment, but our survival is dependent on stability of our internal environment. For example, body temperature is maintained within a narrow range despite widely fluctuating ambient temperatures, and heart rate and blood pressure alterations must be tightly controlled despite very variable environmental demands on the relevant organ systems. Sometimes the organism is presented with insults such as those posed by antigenic or chemical agents and must have strategies for dealing with those challenges.

The organism maintains its integrity in the face of such vicissitudes by an elaborate system of homeostatic regulation (see Cannon, 1932). This regulation has typically been conceived as negative-feedback loops; environmentally elicited deviations from optimal functioning elicit responses that attenuate this deviation. The concept of feedback is central to regulatory physiology.

Feedback principles are often incorporated in explanations of the organism's response to a drug. The organism protects itself from disturbances induced by an acute drug administration and deals with chronic drug effects (e.g., development of tolerance) by various compensatory mechanisms. Considerable progress has been made in recent years in the study of the pharmacodynamic and pharmacokinetic processes that provide the basis for such compensation.

The concept of feedback has recently been augmented by the ancillary concept of feedforward: "*Feedforward* means anticipation. It means responding, not to disturbances, but to stimuli that have been associated with disturbances in the past" (Toates, 1979:99). It is now apparent that the understanding of many phenomena of physiological regulation, including drug tolerance, requires an appreciation of feedforward, as well as feedback, principles. That is, the effect of a drug is modulated not only by responses elicited by the drug but also by responses elicited in anticipation of the drug. The experimental study of anticipatory responding was initiated by Pavlov and is called *Pavlovian* (or *classical*) *conditioning*. Such conditioning permits organisms to "make preparatory adjustments for an oncoming stimulus" (Culler, 1938:136).

We will briefly review the evidence that Pavlovian conditioning principles are important for an understanding of pharmacology and further indicate how these principles are also important for understanding several related, nonpharmacological phenomena.

The Pavlovian Conditioning Situation

In the Pavlovian conditioning situation, a contingency is arranged between two stimuli; typically, one stimulus reliably predicts the occurrence of the second stimulus. Using the usual terminology, the second of these paired stimuli is termed the *unconditional stimulus* (UCS). The UCS, as the name implies, is selected because it elicits relevant activities from the outset (i.e., unconditionally), prior to any pairings. Responses elicited by the UCS are termed unconditional responses (UCRs). The stimulus signaling the presentation of the UCS is neutral (i.e., it elicits relevant activity prior to its pairing with the UCR) and is termed the *conditional stimulus* (CS). The CS, as the name implies, becomes capable of eliciting new responses as a function of (i.e., conditional on) its pairing with the unconditional stimulus.

In Pavlov's well-known conditioning research, the CS was a conveniently manipulated exteroceptive stimulus (bell, light, etc.), and the UCS was either food or orally injected dilute acid (both of which elicited a conveniently monitored salivary UCR). After a number of CS-UCS pairings, it was noted that the subject salivated not only in response to the UCS but also in anticipation of the UCS (i.e., in response to the CS). The subject is then said to display a conditional response (CR).

Drugs as UCSs

A wide range of exteroceptive and interoceptive stimuli have been used in Pavlovian conditioning experiments (Razran, 1961). Drugs constitute a particularly interesting class of UCSs. After some number of drug administrations, each administration reliably signaled by a CS, pharmacological CRs can be observed in response to the CS. It was Pavlov who first demonstrated such pharmacological conditioning. He paired a tone with administration of apomorphine. The drug induced restlessness, salivation, and a "disposition to vomit." After several tone-apomorphine pairings, the tone alone "suffced to produce all the active symptoms of the drug, only in a lesser degree." (Pavlov, 1927:35).

Additional research by Krylov (reported by Pavlov, 1927:35–37) indicated that even if there is not an explicit CS (such as an auditory cue), naturally occurring predrug cues (opening the box containing the hypodermic syringe, cropping the fur, etc.) could serve as CSs. In Krylov's experiments, a dog was repeatedly injected with morphine, each injection eliciting a number of responses including copious salivation. After five or six such injections, it was observed that "the preliminaries of injection" (Pavlov, 1927:35) elicited many morphine-like responses, including salivation.

Drug-Compensatory CRs

Most pharmacological conditioning research has been greatly influenced by Pavlov's theory of CR formation. According to this theory, the CR is a replica of the UCR, and, indeed, much drug conditioning work has demonstrated CRs that mimic the drug effect (Siegel, 1985). In contrast, in 1937 Subkov and Zilov reported that dogs with a history of epinephrine administration (each injection eliciting a tachycardiac response) displayed a conditional *brady*cardiac response. Subkov and Zilov cautioned against "the widely accepted view that the external modifications of the conditional reflex must always be identical with the response of the organism to the unconditional stimulus" (Subkov and Zilov, 1937:296). Subsequent research and theory suggest that the characteristics of the pharmacological CR depend very much on the nature and mechanism of the unconditional drug effect (Eikelboom and Stewart, 1982; Mazur and Wagner, 1982). For many effects of many drugs, the CR is an anticipatory compensation; the drug-associated environmental cues elicit responses that are opposite to the drug effect. For example, the subject with a history of morphine administration (and its analgesic consequence) displays a CR of hyperalgesia (Krank et al., 1981; Siegel, 1975b). Similar compensatory-CRs have been reported with respect to the thermic (Siegel, 1978), locomotor (Mucha et al., 1981), behaviorally sedating (Hinson and Siegel, 1984), and gastrointestinal (Raffa et al., 1982) effects of morphine. The CR seen with many monopiate drugs is similarly opposite to the drug effect, e.g., atropine (Mulinos and Lieb, 1929), chlorpromazine (Pihl and Altman, 1971), amphetamnine (Obál, 1966), methyl dopa (Korol and McLaughlin, 1976), lithium chloride (Domjan and Gillan, 1977), haloperidol (King et al., 1978), ethanol (Lê et al., 1979), and caffeine (Rozin et al., 1984).

Drug Compensatory CRs and Tolerance

As indicated above, organisms with a history of drug administration frequently evidence CRs opposite in direction to the drug effect, as revealed by presentation of the usual predrug cues without the usual pharmacological consequences. When these predrug cues *are* followed by the usual pharmacological consequences, the compensatory CR would be expected to attenuate the drug effect. As the association between the environmental CS and the pharmacological UCS is strengthened by repeated pairings, the effect of the drug becomes increasingly attenuated. Such a progressively diminished response to a drug over the course of successive administrations defines tolerance.

Relationship between Conditioning and Nonassociative Interpretations of Tolerance

Most interpretations of tolerance do not acknowledge the importance of learning in the development of tolerance. Rather, they emphasize the role of drug-elicited homeostatic corrections that restore pharmacologically induced physiological disturbances to normal levels. That is, these traditional interpretations stress only feedback mechanisms. Several investigators have indicated the potential adaptive advantage if these homeostatic corrections actually antedate the drug-induced systemic disturbance (e.g., Wikler, 1973). Pavlovian conditioning provides the framework for understanding the contribution of such feedforward processes to tolerance.

Evidence for the Conditioning Analysis of Tolerance

A considerable amount of evidence has accumulated that supports the important contribution that Pavlovian conditioning makes to tolerance. The model has been useful for understanding tolerance to a variety of drugs, including opiates (see review by Siegel, 1983), benzodiazepines (see review by Siegel, 1986), and ethanol (see review by Siegel, 1987). Because much of these data have been extensively reviewed elsewhere, they will be only briefly summarized here.

Environmental Specificity of Tolerance

On the basis of the conditioning analysis, tolerance should not be the inevitable result of repeated drug administration. Rather, it should result from repeated administration in the presence of environmental cues that elicit drug-compensatory CRs because these cues have reliably signaled the central effects of the drug. There are considerable data indicating that there is environmental specificity to tolerance to a variety of effects of many drugs (see Siegel and MacRae, 1984).

The finding that tolerance is more pronounced in the drug administration environment than an alternative environment is rather general. For example, there is environmental-specificity of tolerance to the analgesic effect of morphine in both humans (Ferguson and Mitchell, 1969) and the terrestrial gastropod snail, *Capaea nemoralis* (Kavaliers and Hirst, 1986). Such findings suggest that environmental specificity of tolerance involving classical conditioning may be a general phenomenon having an early evolutionary development and broad phylogenetic continuity from invertebrates through to mammals" (Kavaliers and Hirst, 1986:1201).

Environmental Specificity of Tolerance and Opiate Overdose

The conditioning model of tolerance has been elaborated to account for some instances of overdose in human heroin addicts (Siegel, 1984; Siegel and Ellsworth, 1986; Siegel et al., 1982). Although deaths from overdoses are prevalent (Maurer and Vogel, 1973:101), the mechanisms of many of these deaths are far from clear. Some deaths result from pharmacological overdoses (see Huber, 1974), but often victims die following doses that would not be expected to be fatal for these drug-experienced, and presumably drug-tolerant, individuals (see reviews by Brecher, 1972:101–114; Reed, 1980); indeed, the victims sometimes die following self-administration of a heroin dose that was well tolerated the previous day (Government of Canada, 1973: 314). Some fatalities may result from a synergism between the opiate and other drugs concomitantly administered or from adulterants (especially quinine) in the illicit heroin, but many deaths do not result from such drug interactions (Brecher, 1972; Government of Canada, 1973; Reed, 1980). Thus, it has been suggested that "the term 'overdose' has served to indicate lack of understanding of the true mechanism of death in fatalities directly related to opiate abuse" (Greene et al., 1974:175). Some instances of these enigmatic failures of tolerance may be interpretable by the conditioning analysis. According to this analysis of overdose, an organism is at risk for overdose when the drug is administered in an environment that, for that organism, has not previously been extensively paired with the drug (and thus does not elicit the compensatory pharmacological CR that attenuates the effect of the drug).

Results of a recent experiment support the Pavlovian conditioning interpretation of heroin overdose (Siegel et al., 1982). Rats injected with high doses of heroin in the same environment as that previously associated with the drug were more likely to survive than rats with the identical pharmacological history receiving the final drug administration in an alternative environment.

Interviews with drug addicts who survived a heroin overdose similarly indicate a role for drug-association environmental cues in opiate overdose (Siegel, 1984). The majority of respondents reported that, on the occasion of the overdose, the drug was administered in the context of unusual environmental cues. In addition, a recent case report describes an instance of death from apparent morphine overdose in a patient receiving the drug for relief of pain from pancreatic cancer (Siegel and Ellsworth, 1986). The circumstances of this death from medically prescribed morphine are readily interpretable by the Pavlovian conditioning account of tolerance.

Extinction of Tolerance

Following CR acquisition, presentation of the CS without the UCS causes a descrease in response strength (i.e., "extinction"). If drug tolerance is partially mediated by drug-compensatory CRs, extinction of these CRs should attenuate tolerance. That is, established tolerance should be reversed by placebo administrations. Such extinction has been demonstrated with respect to tolerance to both the analgesic (e.g., Siegel et al., 1980) and lethal (Siegel et al., 1979) effects of morphine, as well as a variety of effects of amphetamine, midazolam (a short-acting benzodiazepine), and the synthetic polynucleotide, poly I:C (see reviews by Dyck et al., 1986; Siegel, in press—a, in press—b).

Another procedure for extinguishing a CS-UCS association is to continue to present both the CS and the UCS, but in an unpaired manner (see Mackintosh, 1974). That is, the subject receives both conditioning stimuli, but the CS does not signal the UCS; rather, the UCS is presented only during intervals between CS presentations. It has been reported that such unpaired presentations attenuate tolerance to the behaviorally sedating effect of morphine in rats (Fanselow and German, 1982). In this experiment, morphine was administered on a number of occasions in the presence of a distinctive environmental cue. When tolerance was established, continued presentation of the drug and cue, but in an explicitly unpaired manner, eliminated tolerance. That is (as expected on the basis of a conditioning analysis of tolerance), despite the fact that morphine-tolerant rats continue to receive morphine, tolerance is reversed if the continued morphine administrations are unpaired with a cue that was initially paired with the drug.

External Inhibition of Tolerance

Pavlov (1927) originally noted that the presentation of a novel, extraneous stimulus disrupts the elicitation of established CRs. Such "external inhibition" has recently been shown to eliminate tolerance to the hypothermic effect of ethanol (Siegel and Sdao—Jarvie, 1986). In this study, rats that were so tolerant to the hypothermic effect of ethanol that they displayed no drug-induced decrease in temperature were presented with a novel stimulus (a flashing strobe light) following ethanol administration. This novel stimulus precipitated a large hypothermic response in these rats. This finding, suggesting that tolerance is subject to external inhibition, is congenial with the conditioning analysis of tolerance (although there are alternative interpretations, see Peris and Cunningham, 1986).

Retardation of Tolerance

A variety of nonpharmacological procedures retard the acquisition of CRs. According to the conditioning interpretation of tolerance, similar procedures should retard the development of tolerance. One technique for attenuating the strength of an association is to repeatedly present the CS alone prior to pairing it with the UCS. The deleterious effect of such preconditioning exposure to the CS has been termed *latent inhibition* (see review by Lubow, 1973). If drug tolerance is mediated, at least in part, by an association between predrug cues and the drug, it would be expected that rats with extensive experience with the administration cues prior to the time that these cues are paired with the drug should be relatively retarded in the acquisition of tolerance (compared to rats with minimal preexposure to these cues), despite the fact that the groups do not differ with respect to their histories of drug administration. Such latent inhibition of tolerance has been reported with respect to the analgesic effect of morphine (Siegel, 1977; Tiffany and Baker, 1981), and the immunostimulatory effect of poly I:C (Dyck et al., 1986).

Another procedure for decreasing the strength of a CS-UCS association is partial (as compared to consistent) reinforcement. That is, if only a portion of the presentation of the CS are paired with the UCS, CR acquisition is retarded (compared to the situation in which all presentations of the CS are paired with the UCS; see Mackintosh, 1974:72). This literature has clear implications for a Pavlovian conditioning account of morphine tolerance: A group in which only a portion of the presentations of the drug administration cues are actually followed by morphine (i.e., a partial reinforcement group) should be slower to acquire tolerance than a group that never has exposure to environmental cues signaling the drug without actually receiving the drug (i.e., a continuous reinforcement group), even when the two groups are equated with respect to all pharmacological parameters. Such a finding has been reported with respect to tolerance to the analgesic, thermic, and anorexigenic effects of morphine (Krank et al., 1984; Siegel, 1977, 1978).

Other Evidence for the Conditioning Analysis of Tolerance

In addition to the research summarized above, results of many other experiments have provided further evidence that Pavlovian conditioning contributes to tolerance to many drugs. These experiments demonstrate that nonpharmacological manipulations of predrug environmental cues affect both CR acquisition and tolerance in a similar manner. For example, tolerance to both morphine (Fanslow and German, 1982; Siegel et al., 1981) and pentobarbital (Hinson and Siegel, 1986) is subject to inhibitory learning. Furthermore, morphine tolerance is subject to sensory preconditioning (Dafters et al., 1983), and can be manipulated by compound conditioning phenomena such as "blocking" (Dafters et al., 1983) and "overshadowing" (Dafters and Bach, 1985; Walter and Riccio, 1983). A full discussion of these findings is beyond the scope of this review, but it should be emphasized that a variety of additional experiments support the conditioning analysis of tolerance.

Pavlovian Conditioning and "Withdrawal Symptoms"

According to most current views, tolerance and withdrawal symptoms are both manifestations of homeostatic mechanisms that correct for pharmacological disturbances—the feedback mechanisms that mediate tolerance (when the drug is administered) are expressed as withdrawal symptoms (when the drug is not administered). It has become increasingly apparent that just as feedforward (as well as feedback) contributes to tolerance, it also contributes to withdrawal symptoms. Thus, some withdrawal symptoms (so-called) are due not to alterations in feedback mechanisms induced by a history of drug administration, but rather to the anticipation of the next drug administration. That is, some drug "withdrawal symptoms" are, more accurately, drug "preparation symptoms"; they result from drug-compensatory CRs.

In discussing the role of compensatory CRs in so-called withdrawal symptoms, it is important to make a distinction between the acute withdrawal reaction seen shortly after the initiation of abstinence (which typically lasts for days or, at most weeks) and the apparently similar symptoms often noted after detoxification is presumably complete (see Hinson and Siegel, 1982). In the latter case it is likely that it is the anticipation of the drug, rather than the drug itself, that is responsible for the symptoms.

> Consider the situation in which the addict expects a drug, but does not receive it; that is, no drug is available, but the addict is in an environment where he or she has frequently used drugs in the past, or it is the time of day when the drug is typically administered, or any of a variety of drug-associated stimuli occur. Research with animals demonstrates that presentation of cues previously associated with drug administration, but now not followed by the drug, results in the occurrence of drug-compensatory CRs. . . . In the situation in which the drug addict expects but does not receive the drug, it would be expected that drug-compensatory CRs would also occur. These CRs

normally counter the pharmacological disruption of functioning which occurs when the anticipated drug is administered. However, since the expected drug is not forthcoming, the CRs may achieve expression as overt physiological reactions, e.g., yawning, running nose, watery eyes, sweating . . . or form the basis for the subjective experience of withdrawal sickness and craving (Hinson and Siegel, 1982:499).

There is a substantial amount of clinical experimental, and epidemiological evidence substantiating the contribution of drug-compensatory CRs to so-called withdrawal symptoms.

Clinical Evidence

Many clinicians have commented on the ability of drug-associated environmental cues to elicit withdrawal symptoms in the long-detoxified former addict. For example, following a long period of enforced drug abstinence in prison, the former convict displays substantial withdrawal distress when he returns to his old neighborhood, rich in drug-associated cues. Addicts asked to describe situations that elicit withdrawal-sickness typically describe circumstances closely associated with drug administration, e.g., being offered some heroin by a friend. Indeed, a frequently reported precursor to post-treatment relapse is confrontation with drug-associated stimuli (summarized in Siegel, 1983).

Similar observations have been made in experimentally addicted animals. For example, there is a description of the behavior of monkeys that were repeatedly injected with morphine in the presence of tape-recorded music (the music, presumably, for the entertainment of the experimenter). This auditory stimulus became capable of eliciting withdrawal distress: "after the animal had been weaned from the drug and maintained drug-free for several months, the experimenter again played the tape-recorded music and the animal showed the following signs: he became restless, had piloerection, yawned, became diuretic, showed rhinorrhea, and again sought out the drug injection" (Ternes, 1977:167–168). As described more fully elsewhere (Siegel, 1983), these symptoms seen in formerly opiate-dependent organisms, as well as "withdrawal symptoms" in general, can be characterized as being opposite in direction to the drug effect.

Common experience confirms the roles of environmental cues in the display of withdrawal distress. Consider the example of cigarette smoking. Individuals attempting to break their nicotine addiction frequently report instances of withdrawal symptoms when confronted with cues that have, in the past, been associated with smoking: the sight of cigarettes, seeing people smoke, the smell of smoke, etc. One may speculate that another example, provided by smokers, of the preparatory nature of so-called withdrawal symptoms involves the glycemic effect of nicotine. Nicotine elevates blood glucose concentration. When the experienced smoker tries to stop smoking, we might expect that cigarette-associated environmental cues would elicit a cigarette-compensatory conditional decrease in blood sugar concentration, in anticipation of the hyperglycemic effect of nicotine usually occurring in the presence of these cues. The hypoglycemic CR is, on this occasion, not modulated by the hyperglycemic effect of nicotine (since the individual is abstaining from cigarettes). Thus, the nicotine addict, in the presence of nicotine-associated cues, might be expected to be hungry. Indeed, excessive eating (and resulting weight gain) is a commonly reported nicotine withdrawal symptom.

Experimental Evidence

Results of many experiments (reviewed in Siegel, 1983) have confirmed the common clinical observation that drug-associated cues can elicit withdrawal symptoms. Generally, these studies have demonstrated that when addicts are confronted with drug-associated stimuli in the laboratory (e.g., the smell of alcohol for an alcoholic, or the injection paraphernalia for the intravenous heroin user), they display substantial symptoms of drug withdrawal (i.e., more than are displayed by nonclinical populations presented with these stimuli).

Some experiments with rats have similarly indicated that drug-associated environmental cues exacerbate withdrawal symptoms (e.g., Hinson and Siegel, 1983). Also, rats addicted to orally consumed morphine, and then denied access to the drug for a considerable period, will subsequently relapse when the drug is again available in accordance with expectations of a conditioning analysis; that is, relapse is most pronounced when the environment of readdiction is most similar to the environment of original addiction (Hinson et al., 1986; Thompson and Ostlund, 1965).

Epidemiological Evidence

On the basis of a conditioning analysis, it would be expected that the prognosis for long-term success of addiction treatment would be greater if, following treatment, the individual returns to an environment other than that in which he or she originally became addicted. This alternative environment, unlike the addiction environment, would not contain a wealth of CSs for compensatory pharmacological CRs. The data concerning relapse in returning United States Vietnam veterans, addicted to heroin while in Vietnam, are congenial with the conditioning model. These men were detoxified, discharged, and returned to the United States—an environment very different than that in which they became addicted. Although a substantial social problem was envisaged (because of the high relapse rate typically seen in treated heroin addicts), relapse was not substantial in this group. These Vietnam veterans displayed a much lower relapse rate than did nonmilitary heroin addicts treated in federal facilities and returned to the same environment in which they were originally addicted (Robins et al., 1975).

There are, of course, many possible reasons why returning, heroin-addicted Vietnam veterans did not display substantial relapse (other than the conditioning rationale offered here). As is the case with correlational data, they are subject to a variety of interpretations. These epidemiological findings, however, are quite parallel with the experimental results concerning relapse in rats (described above) and provide further evidence of the contribution of conditioning to drug dependence.

Noncompensatory Pharmacological CRs

The discussion of the contribution of feedforward processes to tolerance and dependence has emphasized the role of drug-compensatory CRs. In fact, although many drug CRs are opposite to the drug effect, others are not. As previously indicated, Pavlov's (1927) report of pharmacological conditioning described a drug-mimicking CR. He reported an experiment of Krylov, in which a dog was repeatedly injected with morphine (each injection eliciting a number of responses, including copious salivation). After five or six such injections, it was observed that "the preliminaries of injection" (Pavlov, 1927:35) elicited many morphine-like responses, including salivation. Other examples of such drug-like CRs have been described by others (see review by Siegel, 1985).

Determination of Pharmacological
CR Topography

Although both drug-mimicking and drug-mirroring have been noted, the conditions that favor the expression of the two CR forms are not yet entirely clear. However, an important analysis of pharmacological conditioning has been presented by Eikelboom and Stewart (1982) that may elucidate the area. They suggest that there is a fundamental confusion concerning the identification of pharmacological UCSs and UCRs. This confusion arises because the observed effects of drugs, in contrast to the observed effects of most peripherally applied stimuli, may occur without the participation of the central nervous system (CNS).

In the typical (nonpharmacological) Pavlovian conditioning preparation, the UCS is an event with an afferent site of action; that is, the UCS stimulates receptors that initiate activity in the CNS. It is the effects of this CNS activity that constitute the UCR. In such a conditioning situation, the CR usually mimics the UCR. Eikelboom and Stewart (1982) suggest that for those drugs whose effects are mediated in a similar manner (i.e., drugs with an afferent site of action), the CR will similarly mimic the UCR.

In contrast with this situation, however, many chemical UCSs have an *efferent* site of action; the observed drug effect may be due to direct pharmacological stimulation of the effector system. In such cases, it is accurate to consider the drug effect as the UCS (not the UCR), since it elicits (rather than results from) a CNS response. It is this central response to the drug effect that constitutes the UCR. For example, parenterally administered glucose causes a rise in blood glucose concentration, and the CR seen in the animal trained with glucose is a depression in blood glucose concentration (Mityushov, 1954). These results have been presented as examples of a pharmacological CR (hypoglycemia) that mirrors the pharmacological UCR (hyperglycemia) (e.g., Siegel, 1975a). In fact, the hyperglycemia noted following glucose administration is the *UCS* (not the UCR), with this UCS initiating CNS activities that act to compensate for the hyperglycemia; the correctly conceptualized UCR, then, is the CNS-mediated response to the glucose (i.e., homeostatic correlations for the glucose-induced hyperglycemia).

Speaking casually, it is the UCS-elicited activities of the brain that get associated with the CS. These activities may be initiated via direct afferent stimulation, or via efferent stimulation that engages feedback mechanisms to counteract the drug effect. In both cases, according to Eikelboom and Stewart (1982), the CR will mimic the UCR. In the case of pharmacological conditioning, the CR will be in the same direction as the drug effect if the drug has an afferent site of action, and the CR will be opposite in direction to the drug effect if the drug has an efferent site of action. In the case of those drugs with multiple effects, the various components of the CR would be expected either to mimic or to mirror the drug effect, depending on the mechanism by which the effect results.

Drug-Mimicking CRs and Drug Sensitization

In those cases where the pharmacological CR is in the same direction as the drug effect, the net result of the interaction between the anticipatory and central drug effects may be an *augmentation* of the drug effect over the course of successive administrations; that is, there is evidence that "reverse tolerance," or "sensitization," is (like tolerance) partly due to Pavlovian conditioning. Krylov's demonstration of salivary conditioning with morphine suggests that drug-mimicking CRs contribute to drug sensitization: Krylov, in his own description of his work, noted not only a salivary CR but also sensitization of the salivary response to the opiate (Krylov, 1933). In addition, there is considerable evidence that the sensitization that occurs with repeated administration of a variety of stimulant drugs is due to a progressive augmentation of the drug effect by a drug-mimicking CR (Hinson and Poulos, 1981; Post et al., 1980, 1981).

Feedforward and the Immune System

A considerable amount of research has been summarized that attests to the contribution of Pavlovian conditioning to drug tolerance, sensitization, and dependence. That is, understanding of drug effects requires an appreciation not only of the feedback mechanisms that result from demands made on the system by the drug, but also the feedforward systems that are engaged by the anticipation of such demands. Such analyses have also been applied to situations where physiological changes are produced by nonpharmacological means. There are, of course, a variety of nonpharmacological procedures for producing demands on physiological systems. One such procedure involves immunological stimulation. A considerable amount of recent research has evaluated the contribution of Pavlovian conditioning to immunoreactivity.

External Regulation of the Immune System

The complex cellular and biochemical responses of the immune system are responsible for such life-preserving functions as neutralizing toxins, destroying invading bacteria, and counteracting viral infections. Much evidence now suggests that the various cells of the immune system operate within a closely regulated network of communications which includes both the endocrine and nervous systems. Several different lines of evidence support this view. First it has long been known that "psychological" factors such as stress modify the competence of immune responses. Direct links between neuroendocrine events elicited by stress and immune response have been reported (Greenberg et al., 1984; Shavit et al., 1984; Sklar and Anisman, 1981). Moreover, modifications of neurotransmitter functions also modify the magnitude of an immune response (Besedorsky and Sorkin, 1981; Hall and Goldberg, 1981). Finally, evidence is accumulating that the immune response itself is accompanied by feedback responses in endocrine hormone levels, in autonomic neurotransmitter levels in immune organs, and in neural activity in the hypothalamus (Besedorsky and Sorkin, 1981). These observations suggest that, in addition to the *autoregulation* that operates independently within the immune system, the neuroendocrine system imposes a second control process (Besedorsky and Sorkin, 1981; Greenberg et al., 1984). This *external regulation* would allow the immune system to cooperate with other systems of defensive response and would allow for sensitive homeostatic control according to the external demands placed on the organism. Mechanisms for external regulation would also allow for the feedforward regulations of the immune system by Pavlovian conditioning.

Conditioning Within the Immune System

Conditioning of the immune system can be accomplished by pairing an immunologically neutral CS with the UCS, which creates or modifies an immune response. Immunologic CRs are modifications of immune function that occur to the CS only after it has been paired with an immunologic UCS. Studies of conditioning in the immune system have a long history (for a review of the early work, see Ader, 1981). Successful conditioning of immune responses has been reported with several conditioning agents including antigens that activate a specific immune response (e.g., Metal'nikov and Chorine, 1928), drugs that suppress general immune responses (Ader and Cohen, 1985), and drugs that stimulate general immune responses (Dyck et al., 1986). As in drug conditioning studies, immunologic CRs mediate an anticipatory sensitization or tolerance to the UCS. These studies will be briefly reviewed here to characterize the potential role of immunologic CRs in the feedforward regulation of the immune system.

Measurement of Immune Response

The various component responses of the immune system are characterized by the fact that each is initiated by some form of antigenic stimulation by foreign substances. Some common antigens used to measure immunoreactions range from benign cells from other species (e.g., sheep red blood cells, SRBCs) to infectious bacteria (e.g., *Bacillus anthracis*) to cancerous tumors (e.g., SL-5 lymphoma). In conditioning studies of the immune system, antegenic stimulation can serve dual purposes. First, an antigen is normally necessary to stimulate a background activation of the immune system against which CRs can be measured; for example, such background stimulation is necessary to observe any conditioned suppression or enhancement of a normal immune response. The second purpose an antigen may serve in a conditioning study is as the UCS, with activation of immune response serving as the UCR. It is important to differentiate the measurement and the conditioning functions of an antigen when considering the role of conditioning in the regulation of immune function.

Antigens as UCSs

Soviet investigators were the first to demonstrate that the immune system could be modified by learning (see Ader, 1981). These initial studies looked at the effects of a CS signaling the natural antigenic stimulation of the immune system as the UCS. For example, Metal'nikov and Chorine (1926) paired a scratching irritation or thermal stimulation of the skin with intraperitoneal (i.p.) injections of an antigen (tapioca, Bacillus anthracis or *staphylococcus*) in guinea pigs. As a result of this associative training, they observed several sensitization-like changes in the response to the cutaneous CS. For example, i.p. injection of a tapioca emulsion results in a marked increase in the number of polynucleated leukocytes in the peritoneum. Metal'nikov and Chorine (1926) reported that after associative training a small but reliable increase could also be initiated by CS alone presentations.

Metal'nikov and Chorine (1926) also demonstrated the potential adaptive significance of such CRs in the immune system in a study which assessed the role of conditioning in disease resistance. On twelve occasions, three animals received the skin irritation CS paired with an i.p. injection of staphylococcus. Subsequently, two of the three animals were exposed to the CS alone. All three animals then received a lethal injection of *Vibrio cholera*. The two animals that were exposed to the CS after the injection survived the infection, whereas the animal not exposed to the CS died (see also Dolin et al., 1960). Although this study suffers from a lack of adequate control procedures and requires replication, it clearly suggests that signals for antigenic simulation may produce a nonspecific sensitization such that the immune system responds more robustly in the face of a new antigenic challenge. Conditioned enhancement of disease resistance emphasizes the potential importance of feedforward regulation in the immune system in a manner similar to the heroin overdose study discussed earlier (Siegel et al., 1982).

Since these early studies, many different components of immune reactions have been conditioned with antigenic stimulation of the conditioning agent. Gorcyznski et al. (1982), for example, have reported a conditioned enhancement of cytotoxic T-lymphocytes in CBA mice as a result of several skin grafts from C57BL/6J mice. Here the CS was the skin graft procedure itself and the UCS was the presence of alloantigens from the C57BL/6J donor. A conditioned increase in the number cytotoxic T-lymphocytes occurred when these animals were sham grafted. This response extinguished with additional sham grafting experience. Other immunologic responses that have been conditioned with antigen UCSs as the conditioning agent include histamine release (Russell et al., 1984), asthmatic reactions (Dekker et al., 1957; Justesen et al., 1970; Ottenberg et al., 1958), anaphylactic reactions (Dolin et al., 1960), and increased levels of antibody titers (Dolin et al., 1960; Luk'ianenko, 1959; for a review see Ader, 1981).

The pattern of results obtained with antigenic stimulation as the conditioning agent suggests that the CR acquired is a potentiation of the natural defensive reaction normally elicited by that antigen. An antigenic UCS stimulates both specific and general reactions. The specificity of the response is mediated by the biochemical structure of the antigen itself. Antibodies manufactured by the system mirror this structure to permit a selective reaction. In addition to these specific reactions, however, antigens stimulate the release of general neuroendocrine factors that can enhance or inhibit components of the immune system (Besedorsky and Sorkin, 1981). The data from conditioning with antigenic UCSs are consistent with a feedforward initiation of these general responses in anticipation of impending antigenic challenge.

Conditioning with Immunomodulators as UCSs

The likelihood that CRs in the immune system influence general neuroendocrine regulatory mechanisms in a feedforward fashion suggests that, in addition to natural antigenic stimulation, a variety of immunomodulators may be effective conditioning agents. An immunomodulator is a compound which disrupts or enhances the normal functioning of the immune system. Although such a compound may be relatively specific to a subclass of immune function, it would not be antigen specific. Immunomodulators may be divided into two broad classes: immunosuppressants and immunoenhancers. Conditioned immune responses have been reported with both immunosuppressant and immunoenhancement UCSs (Ader and Cohen, 1985; Dyck et al., 1986).

Immunosuppressant UCSs. One very broad immunomodulator is the immunosuppressant drug, cyclophosphamide (Cy). This drug exerts its effects by interfering with basic processes of cell division and reproduction. Because developing immune responses normally rely on the rapid proliferation and growth of lymphocyte cells, Cy dramatically suppresses the response to antigenic stimulation. Regulation of the immune system suggests that Cy would be expected to serve as an effective UCS for a conditioned immune response.

In an impressive series of studies, Ader and Cohen (see review 1985) demonstrated that taste cues paired with Cy acquire the ability to elicit immunosuppression as a CR. In their conditioning group, thirsty animals were given several conditioning trials in which the opportunity to drink a saccharin solution was followed by an injection of Cy. The animal was later challenged with an antigen (usually SRBCs), reexposed to the saccharin solution without Cy, and the development of an antibody response was assayed sometime during the next four to eight days. The effects of conditioning were measured by the effects of the taste cue on SRBC-induced antibody production. Conditioned animals treated in this manner have lower antibody levels than animals in control groups that were (1) not exposed to the Cy, (2) exposed to the Cy that was not paired with the saccharin, or (3) exposed to the Cy that was paired with the saccharin but that were not reexposed to saccharin following inoculation with SRBCs (Ader and Cohen, 1975). This conditioned suppression of antibody production has been replicated under essentially the same conditions by other investigators (i.e., Rogers et al., 1976;

Wayner et al., 1978), with various doses (Ader and Cohen, 1981) and at different times after inoculation (Ader et al., 1982).

Investigators of conditioned immune responses have also found a conditioned compensatory immunoenhancement to signals for Cy (Gorczynski et al., 1984; Krank and MacQueen, 1986; MacQueen and Krank, 1986). Gorczynski et al. (1984) varied the time of day at which initial conditioning sessions began and found that conditioned suppression was acquired by taste cues paired with Cy during the light portion of the diurnal cycle. Conditioning that began during the dark portion of the diurnal cycle resulted in either no CR or a conditioned immunoenhancement. These investigators also reported that animals exposed to chronic stress were likely to develop a conditioned enhancement response rather than a conditioned suppression. They argue that the background level of neuronendocrine hormones is critical to the direction of the CR to a taste cue paired with Cy.

The observation that most conditioning studies of regulatory responses use stimuli other than taste cues suggests an alternative explanation: Cy-induced conditioned suppression may be unique to the use of a taste cue. Other cues, inadvertently present in the conditioning regime, may control CRs different than those CRs elicited by taste cues (e.g., cue to consequence specificity, Garcia and Koelling, 1967). Krank and MacQueen (1986; MacQueen and Krank, 1986) have recently reported that the CR to environmental or drug state cues that signal Cy is a compensatory immunoenhancement. These results suggest that the type of CS used in conditioning with Cy determines the direction of the CR in the immune system. Thus Gorczynski et al.'s (1984) conditioned immunoenhancement under various stress and time of day conditions may have been due to the introduction of differential environmental or internal cues at the time of training.

The possibility that the form of CR to a signal for Cy is determined by either the prevalent neuroendocrine state of the organism (Gorczynksi et al., 1984) or the type of CS present during conditioning (Krank and MacQueen, 1986) makes it difficult to clearly specify the role of such CRs in the feed-forward regulation of the immune system. Nevertheless, several investigators have proposed that processes in the immune system are under homeostatic control (Besedorsky and Sorkin, 1981; Dyck et al., 1986; Greenberg et al., 1984). The homeostatic response to an agent that induces immunosuppression would be a compensatory immunoenhancement. Conditioned immunoenhancement to environmental signals for Cy is consistent with a role for conditioning processes in the homeostatic regulation of immune response (Krank and MacQueen, 1986).

The well-documented conditioned immunosuppression to taste cues signaling Cy (Ader and Cohen, 1985) remains a problem for a homeostatic view of conditioning in the immune system. One way of interpreting these findings within the present framework is to postulate a different form of regulation which recognizes the interdependence of defensive responses of the organism to potential external dangers. Acute external stress, e.g., that induced by footshock, suppresses many functions in the immune system (Greenberg et al., 1984; Monjan, 1981; Shavit et al., 1984; Sklar and Anisman, 1981). Moreover, Sato et al. (1984) have reported a conditioned suppression of antibody production by an auditory cue that had been paired with shock. These observations may indicate that when additional demands to respond to external threats occur resources are allocated to alternative defensive responses away from the immune system. Avoidance responses are also required when the animals are confronted with an aversive taste. The accompanying immunosuppression may represent an allocation of resources to an alternative defensive response.[1] Gorczynski et al.'s (1984) description of behavioral differences between animals that show suppressed antibody levels and animals that do not may reflect the presence of such alternative responses.

Immunoenhancement UCSs. One study has recently reported conditioning of immune responses with the immunoenhancer, polyinosinic polycytidylic acid (Poly I:C), as the UCS (Dyck et al., 1986). Poly I:C is a synthetic polynucleotide that stimulates the production and release of interferon and induces Natural Killer cell (NK) activity in mice. NK activity is an important component of natural tumor resistance and changes in NK activity are reflected in changes in the rate of elimination of specific NK dependent tumors *in vivo* (Greenberg et al., 1984) or tumor cells by spleen extract *in vitro* (Dyck et al., 1986). Following procedures similar to those used to examine the role of conditioning in morphine tolerance, Dyck et al. (1986) demonstrated that tolerance to Poly I:C-induced NK activation is modified by associative manipulations of preinjection cues. They found that presentation of the preinjection cues without Poly I:C after training reduced tolerance that had developed (i.e., extinction occurred) and that presentation of the preinjection cues without Poly I:C before training reduced tolerance development (i.e., latent inhibition occurred). Although direct measurement of the CR was not obtained, these results were interpreted as indicating that preinjection cues elicit a compensatory CR that reduces NK activity in anticipation of Poly I:C stimulation. These observations are consistent with the suggestion that NK activity is under homeostatic control and that disruptions of homeostatic levels of NK activity are subject to feedforward regulation by conditioning.

Summary of Immunological Conditioning

Converging evidence from a variety of sources indicates that the immune system is regulated by a variety of neuroendocrine controls. Conditioning provides the opportunity for feedforward regulation of these controls in the immune system. Conditioned immune responses have been demonstrated with antigenic stimulation, immunosuppressant drugs, and immunoenhancement drugs as UCS. Studies with antigen UCSs consistently suggest that conditioning provides a feedforward potentiation of immune processes. Studies with immunosuppressant and immunoenhancement drugs as UCSs present a more complex picture. Some recent studies (i.e., Dyck et al., 1986; Krank and MacQueen, 1986) suggest that conditioning processes may contribute to the homeostatic regulation of the immune system by reducing the effects of drug-induced disruptions. Other studies (e.g., Ader and Cohen, 1975, 1981) find that conditioning may augment drug-induced disruptions. We have argued that this conditioned augmentation of drug-induced disruption of normal immune function seems to be specific to taste CSs which activate nonimmune defensive responses. These CRs may prevent the recovery of the immune system from the effects of the drug by diverting resources to other defensive responses. This selective allocation of resources may also be viewed as a regulatory response designed to optimize the adaptation of the organism to external threats. Together, demonstrations of conditioned immune responses are consistent with a feedforward regulation of neuroendocrine controls involved in the potentiation of antigenic response, homeostatic counteradjustments to drug-induced disruptions of immune systems, and the allocation of resources to different kinds of defensive responses.

Feedforward and Exercise

One of the most straightforward procedures for producing systematic alterations is exercise, or, more generally, muscular exertion. Regardless of its form, such exertion places demands on many systems: heart rate increases, there is peripheral vasodilation in the musculature primarily involved, energy requirements are increased, and a variety of neuroendocrine changes occur. Anyone who regularly engages in exercise (e.g., aerobics classes) is aware of the "psychological preparation" that precedes such activity. The research summarized below will demonstrate that there is also "physiological preparation" for anticipated physical exertion.

Pavlovian Conditioning of Exertion

One of the earliest studies of the potential role of Pavlovian conditioning in exercise was conducted by Beier (1940). In this experiment, an auditory CS was paired with exercise involving pedaling a bicycle ergometer in human subjects. Responses measured included heart rate, blood pressure, respiration, and pulse rate. In response to exercise on the bicycle ergometer, all these responses showed increases. In order to determine if conditioning occurred,

CR test trials were given in which the CS was presented not followed by the UCS (procedurally identical to the placebo CR test trial discussed earlier with regard to drug and immunological conditioning). All three subjects in the experiment evidenced conditioned increases in blood pressure in response to the CS. There was also evidence of heart rate conditioning, although it was less consistent. One subject demonstrated a conditioned heart rate acceleration that became more pronounced with an increasing number of conditioning trials; however, a second subject showed a biphasic cardiac CR involving deceleration, followed by acceleration, and the third subject showed "conditional cardiac arrhythmia." There was no evidence of conditioning of respiration rate. This study indicates that conditioning may occur when exercise is used as a stimulus to evoke physiological demands, but the nature of the CR's in this situation is unclear.

One principle of Pavlovian conditioning is that the rate of conditioning and magnitude of the CR are positively related to the magnitude of the UCS (Mackintosh, 1974). Peters and Gantt (1951) examined whether this was true when exercise was used to produce the UCS. Their experiment involved three different auditory CSs, each paired with a different degree of muscular exertion (maximal, one-half maximal, or one-sixth maximal) on a hand dynamometer in eleven human subjects. The three intensities of exertion produce different degrees of cardiac acceleration as UCRs. A conditional heart rate acceleration occurred in all cases, and the magnitude of the CR was positively related to the magnitude of the unconditional cardiac response originally produced by the different degrees of exertion.

A number of studies (Rushmer et al., 1960; Antal, 1968; Bolme and Novotny, 1969) have examined conditioned changes in parameters of blood flow in dogs exercising on a treadmill. The study by Bolme and Novotny (1969) is exemplary. In this study nine dogs were trained to exercise on a treadmill. The responses measured included arterial pressure, hind limb blood flow, and heart rate. In response to forced running on the treadmill, dogs exhibited tachycardia, increased arterial pressure, and increased hind limb blood flow. Following two weeks to four months of training, during which each exercise period was signaled by an auditory stimulus, presentation of the CS alone produced the same changes seen in response to exercise itself. Bolme and Novotny (1969) also reported that the magnitude of the conditioned vasodilator response was directly related to the exercise load, a finding in agreement with that of Peters and Gantt (1951) in human subjects. Bolme and Novotny (1969) concluded "that the vasodilator nerves were activated to prepare the animal for the exercise." Antal (1968) reached a similar conclusion: "cortical influences may be expected to play a role in the sense of conditioned reflexes" occurring in anticipation of exercise. Rushmer et al. (1960) indicated the importance of conditioning in these exercise experiments by noting that "in well-trained animals, merely holding the treadmill switch before them is sufficient to induce . . . adjustments which are basically similar to those induced by a subsequent bout of exercise."

Exercise also produces changes in blood levels of several hormones. Whether conditioned hormonal changes are involved in anticipation of exercise has been studied extensively by Mason and colleagues (Mason et al., 1973a, 1973b) and others (Wilkerson et al., 1980). Although these studies differed in some details, they were all similar in that human subjects performed exercise (bicycle ergometer in studies by Mason et al. and treadmill in studies by Wilkerson et al.) at varying work loads with each exercise period signaled by stimuli consisting of the preparations for the exercise and attachment of recording equipment. The measures taken were plasma levels of thyroid-stimulating hormone (Mason et al., 1973a), cortisol, and norepinephrine (Mason et al., 1973b), and testosterone (Wilkerson et al., 1980). All of these measures showed initial increases during a period of exercise. Following training, there were significant elevations in the measures taken in each study during the preexercise period, and in the Wilkerson et al. (1980) study these conditional changes were positively related to the anticipated work load.

Topography of Exercise-Anticipatory Response

In previous discussions of pharmacological and immunological conditioning, it was noted that CRs may either mimic or oppose the drug effect. For example, in the case of conditioned drug responses, the CR opposes the drug action, then tolerance occurs (e.g., Siegel, 1975b) but if the CR mimics the drug action, sensitization occurs (e.g., Hinson and Poulos, 1982). At that time, it was suggested that CRs that oppose a drug action produce "normalization" of physiological responses that are disturbed by the drug. The experiments using muscular exertion described above have consistently reported that the CRs observed apparently mimic the unconditional effect of exercise, thus it would be expected that a phenomenon similar to drug sensitization would be evident. In fact, Wilkerson et al. (1980) describe such sensitization with regard to total plasma testosterone and attribute it to an "an anticipatory response."

An interesting question discussed with regard to conditioning involving drugs was what determines the form of the conditioned response. In the context of that discussion, it was suggested that drug-opposing CRs that underlie tolerance are particularly common because they provide a means of countering the physiological changes induced by drug administration—that is, tolerance is adaptation (Wikler, 1973). However, when physiological changes are produced by muscular exertion, the form of the CR is identical to that produced by the exercise itself, and in fact these changes may be potentiated by conditioning (Wilkerson et al., 1980). Such differences in the form of the

CR may be due to the "site of action" relating to drug-induced compared to exercise-induced physiological changes (cf. Eikelboom and Stewart, 1982). On a more phenomenological level, such differences may be understood from the perspective that adaptation does not always involve apparent normalization (cf. Abrahams et al., 1964; Burchfield et al., 1980; Jakoubek and Gutmann, 1960; Sakellaris and Vernikos-Danellis, 1975). In the case of exercise, muscular requirements for oxygen and nutrients may be met by increased blood flow to the exercising muscles, and there is evidence (see Wilkerson et al., 1980) that plasma testosterone is related to muscular strength and aerobic capacity. The CRs reported in the experiments discussed above may be viewed as "preparatory" in the sense that the animal exhibiting such responses would be better able to sustain muscular activity (Abrahams et al., 1964; Burchfield, 1979; Eliasson et al., 1951; Jakoubek and Gutmann, 1960; Smith and Stebbins, 1965). This analysis suggests that humans and animals are better able to tolerate exercise, at least in part, because of cue-elicited responses (cf. Smith and Stebbins, 1965; Zanchetti et al., 1972). This suggestion leads to several predictions that have yet to be tested with respect to exercise. In animals with a history of cue-exercise pairings, exercise should be better tolerated when the cue is presented than when it is not. This prediction is, of course, identical to that made by the Pavlovian conditioning analysis for drug tolerance. Additionally, research discussed in the section and drug tolerance demonstrated that drug tolerance was not lost simply by withholding the drug; rather a procedure involving repeated presentations of the usual predrug cues not followed by the drug (i.e., extinction was needed to significantly attenuate tolerance). Extending this analysis to exercise, it would be predicted that repeated presentations of preexercise cues not followed by exercise would result in a greater attenuation of "exercise tolerance" than would a similar period in which no exercise was performed. The reader can see that there are several other predictions regarding exercise tolerance that can be made on the basis of research already conducted with respect to drug tolerance (e.g., latent inhibition, partial reinforcement, conditioned inhibition, etc.).

Exercise Anticipation and "Exercise Withdrawal"

In discussing the role of conditioning in drug responses, it was suggested that the elicitation of CRs by the usual predrug cues in the absence of the drug may lead to withdrawal-like symptoms, and that this cue-elicited syndrome may be related to drug-craving and relapse. Extending this analysis to the case of exercise, we would suggest that the occurrence of preexercise cues in the absence of exercise would elicit CRs that may be noticeable to the individual. To what extent such cue-elicited responses play a role in the continuation of exercise programs has not been systematically investigated, but there is much anecdotal evidence that the absence of anticipated exercise leads to subjective experiences, and we would suggest that CRs underlie at least some component of such experiences. If such cue-elicited states contribute to continued involvement with exercise, then it may be appropriate to regard exercise as an addictive substance with some similarities to drugs.

Feedforward and Stress

A wide range of stimuli have been used to produce the state termed stress (e.g., immobilization, cold-water immersion, nociceptive stimuli). A general feature of the state of stress is an alteration of physiological processes, and most analyses of the physiology of stress have emphasized feedback mechanisms to restore these physiological processes to normal levels. There has, however, been considerable research on the role of Pavlovian conditioning in stress (for a recent review, see Burchfield, 1979). In this section, only a few studies from this extensive literature will be highlighted.

Conditioning and Attenuated Corticosterone Response

Pituitary-adrenal function is a common response measured in research on stress-inducing stimuli. In response to a variety of stressful stimuli, rats exhibit an increase in plasma corticosterone (e.g., Burchfield et al., 1980; Mikulaj and Mitro, 1973; Mikulaj and Kvetnansky, 1966; Murgas and Jonec, 1973). Although there is an increased corticosterone response during the short term, with long-term exposure to intermittent stressful stimuli (e.g., forty-two days of immobilization, Mikulaj and Mitro, 1973; three months of cold exposure, Burchfield et al., 1980), this corticosterone response shows tolerance; that is, with repeated exposure, the corticosterone response to presentation of a stressful stimulus is less than it was originally. In addition, this tolerant response is maintained for at least one month (the longest period tested) in the absence of further stress (Mikulaj and Mitro, 1973) and, in this regard, resembles the conditioned tolerant response to drugs described in an earlier section. This attenuated response does not appear to be due to any organic impairment of the secretory or productive capacity of the adrenal cortex (Murgas and Jonec, 1973).

The pattern of attenuated corticosterone response has been attributed to a Pavlovian conditioning process in which corticosterone is secreted in anticipation of stress (i.e., to cues associated with stressful stimuli; Burchfield et al., 1980) thereby lowering the organism's unconditional response to stress. This pattern of conditional responding is assumed to provide an adaptive advantage by "conserving resources while adequately defending the organism against stress" (Burchfield, 1980; see also Mikulaj and Mitro, 1973).

Conditioning and "Stress Overdose"

The adaptive role that such conditioned hormonal responses may play in response to stress is suggested by experiments (Noble, 1942–43; Mikulaj and Kvetnansky, 1966; Murgas and Jonec, 1973) similar to the one involving heroin overdose death described earlier (Siegel, 1984; Siegel and Ellsworth, 1986; Siegel et al., 1982). These experiments used the Noble-Collip device: an open cylinder with internal flanges that has been used to produce stress. The animal is placed inside the cylinder and the drum rotated, the effect being that the animal is lifted by the flanges and then dropped repeatedly. It is possible to administer a lethal "dose" of this treatment to naive animals.

Animals were administered a regime of increasing sublethal doses of rotation over the course of several weeks. Animals were then tested with a lethal dose and it was found that animals given the regime of sublethal doses had "acquired tolerance to . . . a 100 percent lethal dose for non-adapted rats" (Noble, 1942–43; Mikulaj and Kvetnansky, 1966). Furthermore, the survivability was associated with *smaller* adrenal responses in the tolerant rats than in non-adapted rats (Mikulaj and Kvetnansky, 1966; Murgas and Jonec, 1973). Finally, this tolerant response was retained for a period of up to five months, just like the tolerant response to drugs and more traditional CRs. Although no explicit test for the conditional nature of this tolerance to a lethal dose of rotation was given, it is possible that conditioning was involved since the procedures would provide sufficient cues (e.g., Rushmer et al., 1960; Burchfield et al., 1980), conditioning has been demonstrated with respect to diminished adrenal responses to stress, and the response was well retained.

Conclusion

Pavlov realized the importance of anticipatory responding in maintaining the integrity of the organism:

> It is pretty evident that under natural conditions the normal animal must respond not only to stimuli which themselves bring immediate benefit or harm, but also to other physical and chemical agencies—waves of sound, light, and the like—which in themselves only *signal* the approach of these stimuli (Pavlov, 1927:14).

A considerable amount of research has indicated that responding to signals for drugs importantly contributes to drug effects. One reason that this feedforward analysis of drug effects is important is because it provides a common basis for understanding similarities in tolerance and dependence to a variety of biochemically distinctive chemicals. In fact, there is increasing interest in evaluating commonalities between disturbances induced by substance abuse and those induced by other forms of stimulation (see Levison et al., 1983). Pavlovian conditioning principles provide such a commonality (see Donegan et al., 1983).

We have reviewed the evidence that the Pavlovian conditioning of pharmacological responses is relevant to drug tolerance, sensitization, and dependence. In addition, we have suggested that the feedforward processes attributable to such conditioning can importantly extend our understanding in areas that are not primarily pharmacological: immunology, exercise physiology, and stress. Similar analyses may also be relevant to a variety of other areas, such as feeding (see Weingarten, 1985), temperature regulation (see Ollove, 1980) and perceptual processes (see Allan and Siegel, 1986). In summary, it has become increasingly apparent that a complete understanding of physiological regulation requires an appreciation of feedforward, as well as feedback, principles.

Notes

1. Ader and Cohen (1975) argue against this interpretation because LiCl is an effective agent for conditioned taste aversions but does not effectively condition suppression of the response to antigenic stimulation. It should be noted, however, that Sato et al. (1984) found conditioned suppression only in animals with immune systems compromised by irradiation. Conditioned stress effects on antibody production may only be evident in an animal recovering from an already suppressed system (a point suggested by Ader and Cohen, 1985). Cy not only conditions a taste aversion but also compromises the immune system; LiCl only conditions a taste aversion. Thus only Cy-induced but not LiCl-induced taste aversions would be capable of suppressing antibody production. Ader and Bovbjerg's (1982) observation that CS presentations during the interval between the final Cy injection and antigen challenge were particularly effective in reducing the antibody production is consistent with the view that the CR to the taste cue interferes with the recovery of a deficient immune system. Such interference is also consistent with the suggestion that conditioned suppression to taste cues for Cy represents the allocation of resources to an alternative defensive response.

References

Abrahams, V.C., S.M. Hilton, and A.W. Zbrozyna. 1964. The Role of Active Muscle Vasodilation in the Alerting Stage of the Defence Reaction. *Journal of Physiology* 171:189–202.

Ader, R. 1981. The Central Nervous System and Immune Responses: Conditioned Immunopharmacologic Effects. *Advances in Immunology* 1:427–434.

Ader, R., and N. Cohen. 1975. Behaviorally Conditioned Immunosuppression. *Psychosomatic Medicine* 37:333–340.

———. 1981. Conditioned Immunopharmacologic Responses. In R. Ader, ed., *Psychoneuroimmunology*. New York: Academic Press.

————. 1985. CNS-Immune System Interactions: Conditioning Phenomena. *The Behavioral and Brain Sciences* 8:379–394.

Ader, R., N. Cohen, and D. Bovbjerg. 1982. Conditioned Suppression of Humoral Immunity in the Rat. *Journal of Comparative and Physiological Psychology* 96: 517–521.

Allan, L.G., and S. Siegel. 1986. McCullough Effects as Conditioned Responses: Reply to Skowbo. *Psychological Bulletin* 100:388–393.

Antal, J. 1968. Changes in Blood Flow During Exercise in Unanesthetized Animals. In O. Hudlicka, ed., *Circulation in Skeletal Muscle*. New York: Pergamon.

Beier, D.C. 1940. Conditioned Cardiovascular Responses and Suggestions for the Treatment of Cardiac Neurosis. *Journal of Experimental Psychology* 26:311–321.

Besedorsky, H.O., and E. Sorkin. 1981. Immunologic-Neuroendocrine Circuits: Physiologic Approaches. In R. Ader, ed., *Psychoneuroimmunology*. New York: Academic Press.

Bolme, P., and J. Novotny. 1969. Conditional Reflex Activation of the Sympathetic Cholinergic Vasodilator Nerves in the Dog. *Acta Physiological Scandinavica* 77: 58–67.

Brecher, E.M. 1972. *Licit and Illicit Drugs*. Boston: Little, Brown.

Burchfield, S.R. 1979. The Stress Response: A New Perspective. *Psychosomatic Medicine* 41:661–672.

Burchfield, S.R., S.C. Woods, and M.S. Elich. 1980. Pituitary Adrenocortical Response to Chronic Intermittent Stress. *Physiology and Behavior* 24:297–302.

Cannon, W.B. 1932. *The Wisdom of the Body*. New York: Norton.

Culler, E.A. 1938. Recent Advances in Some Concepts of Conditioning. *Psychological Review* 45:134–153.

Dafters, R., and L. Bach. 1985. Absence of Environment-Specificity in Morphine Tolerance Acquired in Nondistinctive Environments: Habituation or Stimulus Overshadowing? *Psychopharmacology* 87:101–106.

Dafters, R., M. Hetherington, and H. McCartney. 1983. Blocking and Sensory Preconditioning Effects in Morphine Analgesic Tolerance: Support for a Pavlovian Conditioning Model of Drug Tolerance. *Quarterly Journal of Experimental Psychology* 35B:1–11.

Dekker, E., H. Pelser, and J. Groen. 1957. Conditioning as a Cause of Asthmatic Attacks: A Laboratory Study. *Journal of Psychosomatic Research* 2:97–108.

Dolin, A.O., V.N. Krylov, V.I. Lukianenko, and B.A. Fklerov. 1960. New Experimental Data on the Conditioned Reflex Production and Suppression of Immune and Allergic Reactions. *Zhurnal Vysshei Nervnoi Deyatelnosti Imeni I.P. Pavlova* 4:108–115.

Domjan, M., and D.J. Gillan. 1977. After-Effects of Lithium-Conditioned Stimuli on Consummatory Behavior. *Journal of Experimental Psychology: Animal Behavior Processes* 3:322–334.

Donegan, N., J. Rodin, C.P. O'Brien, and R.L. Solomon. 1983. A Learning Theory Approach to Commonalities. In P.K. Levison, D.R. Gerstein, and D.R. Maloff, eds., *Commonalities in Substance Abuse and Habitual Behavior*. Lexington, MA: Lexington Books.

Dyck, D.G., A.H. Greenberg, and T.A.G. Osachuk. 1986. Tolerance to Drug-

Induced (Poly I:C) Natural Killer (NK) Cell Activation: Congruence with a Pavlovian Conditioning Model. *Journal of Experimental Psychology: Animal Behavior Processes* 12:25–31.

Eikelboom, R., and J. Stewart. 1982. Conditioning of Drug-Induced Physiological Responses. *Psychological Review* 89:507–528.

Eliasson, S., B. Folkow, P. Lindgren, and B. Uvnas. 1951. Activation of Sympathetic Vasodilator Nerves to the Skeletal Muscles in the Cat by Hypothalamic Stimulation. *Acta Physiological Scandinavica* 23:333–351.

Fanslow, M.S., and C. German. 1982. Explicitly Unpaired Delivery of Morphine and the Test Situation: Extinction and Retardation of Tolerance to the Suppressing Effects of Morphine on Locomotor Activity. *Behavioral and Neural Biology* 35: 231–241.

Ferguson, R.K., and C.L. Mitchell. 1969. Pain as a Factor in the Development of Tolerance to Morphine Analgesia in Man. *Clinical Pharmacology and Therapeutics* 10:372–382.

Garcia, J., and R.A. Koelling. 1967. The Relationship of Cue to Consequence in Avoidance Learning. *Psychonomic Science* 4:123–124.

Gorczynski, R.M., S. Macrae, and M. Kennedy. 1982. Conditioned Immune Response Associated with Allogenic Skin Grafts in Mice. *Journal of Immunology* 129:704–709.

———. 1984. Factors Involved in the Classical Conditioning of Antibody Responses in Mice. In R. Ballieux, J. Fielding and A. L'Abbatte, eds., *Breakdown in Human Adaptation to Stress: Towards a Multidisciplinary Approach.* Boston: Kluwer-Nijhoff.

Government of Canada. 1973. Final Report of the Commission of Inquiry into the Nonmedical Use of Drugs. Ottawa: Information Canada.

Greenberg, A.H., D.G. Dyck, and L.S. Sandler. 1984. Opponent Processes, Neurohormones and Natural Resistance. In B.H. Fox and B.H. Newberry, eds., *Impact of Psychoendocrine Systems in Cancer and Immunity.* Toronto: C.J. Hogrefe.

Greene, M.H., J.L. Luke, and R.L. Dupont. 1974. Opiate "Overdose" Deaths in the District of Columbia I. Heroin-Related Fatalities. *Medical Annals of the District of Columbia* 43:75–181.

Hall, N.R., and A.L. Goldstein. 1981. Neurotransmitters and the Immune System. In R. Ader, ed., *Psychoneuroimmunology.* New York: Academic Press.

Hinson, R.E., and C.X. Poulos. 1981. Sensitization to the Behavioral Effects of Cocaine: Modification by Pavlovian conditioning. *Pharmacology Biochemistry and Behavior* 15:559–562.

Hinson, R.E., and S. Siegel. 1982. Nonpharmacological Bases of Drug Tolerance and Dependence. *Journal of Psychosomatic Research* 26:495–503.

———. 1983. Anticipatory Hyperexcitability and Tolerance to the Narcotizing Effect of Morphine in the Rat. *Behavioral Neuroscience* 97:759–767.

———. 1986. Pavlovian Inhibitory Conditioning and Tolerance to Pentobarbital-Induced Hypothermia in Rats. *Journal of Experimental Psychology: Animal Behavior Processes* 12:363–370.

Hinson, R.E., C.X. Poulos, W. Thomas, and H. Cappell. 1986. Pavlovian Conditioning and Addictive Behavior: Relapse to Oral Self-Adminstration of Morphine. *Behavioral Neuroscience* 100:368–375.

Huber, D.H. 1974. Heroin Deaths—Mystery or Overdose? *Journal of the American Medical Association* 229:689–690.

Jakoubek, B., and E. Gutmann. 1960. Conditioned Metabolic Reactions to Nociceptive Stimulation. *Physiologia Bohemoslovexicia* 9:323–329.

Justesen, D.R., E.W. Braun, R.G. Garrison, and R.B. Pendelton. 1970. Pharmacological Differentiation of Allergic and Classically Conditioned Asthma in the Guinea Pig. *Science* 170:864–866.

Kavaliers, M., and M. Hirst. 1986. Environmental Specificity of Tolerance to Morphine-Induced Analgesia in a Terrestrial Snail: Generalization of the Behavioral Model of Tolerance. *Pharmacology Biochemistry and Behavior* 25:1201–1206.

King. J.J., S.R. Schiff, and W.H. Bridger. 1978. Haloperidol Classical Conditioning: Paradoxical Results. *Society for Neuroscience Abstracts* 4:495.

Korol, B., and L.J. McLaughlin. 1976. A Homeostatic Adaptive Response to Alpha-Methyl-Dopa in Conscious Dogs. *Pavlovian Journal of Biological Science* 11:67–75.

Krank, M.D., and G. MacQueen. 1986. Conditioning in the Immune System: The Effect of Environmental and Taste Cues on the Direction of the Conditioned Response. *Canadian Psychology* 26:328.

Krank, M.D., R.E. Hinson, and S. Siegel. 1981. Conditional Hyperalgesia is Elicited by Environmental Signals of Morphine. *Behavioral and Neural Biology* 32:148–157.

Krank, M.D., R.E. Hinson, and S. Siegel. 1984. The Effect of Partial Reinforcement on Tolerance to Morphine-Induced Analgesia and Weight Loss in the Rat. *Behavioral Neuroscience* 98:79–85.

Krylov, V. 1933. Additional Data on the Study of Conditioned Reflexes on Chemical Stimuli. *Biological Abstracts* 7:871.

Lê, A.D., C.X. Poulos, and H. Cappell. 1979. Conditioned Tolerance to the Hypothermic Effect of Ethyl Alcohol. *Science* 206:1109–1110.

Levison, P.K., D.R. Gerstein, and D.R. Maloff, eds. 1983. *Commonalities in Substance Abuse and Habitual Behavior*. Lexington, MA: Lexington Books.

Lubow, R.E. 1973. Latent Inhibition. *Psychological Bulletin* 79:398–407.

Luk'ianenko, V.I. 1959. The Conditioned Reflex Regulation of Immunological Reactions. *Zhurnal Mikrobiologil, Epidemiologii, i Immunobiologii* 30:53–59.

Mackintosh, N.J. 1974. *The Psychology of Animal Learning*. London: Academic Press.

MacQueen, G., and M.D. Krank. 1986. Conditioning in the Immune System: The Effect of a Drug State Cue (Pentobarbital) on the Response to Antigenic Stimulation. *Canadian Psychology* 26:372.

Mason, J.W., L.H. Hartley, T.A. Kotchen, F.E. Wherry, L.L. Pennington, and L.G. Jones. 1973a. Plasma Thyroid-Stimulating Hormone Response in Anticipation of Muscular Exercise in the Human. *Journal of Clinical Endocrinology and Metabolism* 37:403–406.

Mason, J.W., H. Hartley, T.A. Kotchen, E.H. Mougey, P.T. Ricketts, and L.G. Jones. 1973b. Plasma Cortisol and Norepinephrine Responses in Anticipation of Muscular Exercise. *Psychosomatic Medicine* 35:406–414.

Maurer, D.W., and V.H. Vogel. 1973. *Narcotics and Narcotic Addiction*. Springfield, IL: Charles C. Thomas.

Mazur, J.E., and A.R. Wagner. 1982. An Episodic Model of Associative Learning. In M.L. Commons, R.J. Herrnstein, and A.R. Wagner, eds., *Quantitative Analysis of Behavior: Acquisition.* Vol. 3. Cambridge, MA: Ballinger.

Metal'nikov, S., and V. Chorine. 1926. Role des Reflexes Conditionnels dans l'Immunité. *Annales de l'Institut Pasteur* 40:893–900.

———. 1928. Role des Reflexes Conditionnels dans la Formation des Anticorps. *Comptes Rendus de al Societe Biologie* 102:133–134.

Mikulaj L., and R. Kvetnansky. 1966. Changes in Adrenocortical Activity Prior to and Following Adaptation to Trauma in the Noble-Collip Drum. *Physiologia Bohemoslavaca* 15:439–446.

Mikulaj L., and A. Mitro. 1973. Endocrine Functions During Adaptations to Stress. *Advances in Experimental Medicine and Biology* 33:631–638.

Mityushov, M.I. 1954. Uslovnorleflektornaya Inkretsiya Insulina (the Conditioned-Reflex Incretion of Insulin). *Zhurnal Vysshei Nervnoi Deigtel (Journal of Higher Nervous Activity)* 4:206.

Monjan, A.A. 1981. Stress and Immunologic Competence: Studies in Animals. In R. Ader, ed., *Psychoneuroimmunology.* New York: Academic Press.

Mucha, R.F., C. Volkonsiks, and H. Kalant. 1981. Conditioned Increases in Locomotor Activity Produced with Morphine as an Unconditioned Stimulus, and the Relation of Conditioning to Acute Morphine Effect and Tolerance. *Journal of Comparative and Physiological Psychology* 95:351–362.

Mulinos, M.G., and C.C. Lieb. 1929. Pharmacology of Learning. *American Journal of Physiology* 90:456–457.

Murgas, K., and V. Jonec. 1973. Central Nervous Influence upon the Adrenocortical Reaction During Stress Situations. *Advances in Experimental Medicine and Biology* 33:631–638.

Noble, R.L. 1942–43. The Development of Resistance by Rats and Guinea Pigs to Amounts of Trauma Usually Fatal. *American Journal of Physiology* 138:346–351.

Obál, F. 1966. The Fundamentals of the Central Nervous Control of Vegetative Homeostasis. *Acta Physiologica Academiae Scientiarum Hungaricae* 30:15–29.

Ollove, M.B. 1980. *Anticipatory Thermoregulation in the Rat.* Unpublished Ph.D. Thesis, University of Pennsylvania.

Ottenberg, P., M. Stein, J. Lewis, and C. Hamilton. 1958. Learned Asthma in the Guinea Pig. *Psychosomatic Medicine* 20:395–400.

Pavlov, I.P. 1927. *Conditioned Reflexes.* Translated by G.V. Anrep. London: Oxford University Press.

Peris, J., and C.L. Cunningham. 1986. Handling-Induced Enhancement of Alcohol's Acute Physiological Effects. *Life Sciences* 38:273–279.

Peters, J.E., and W.H. Gantt. 1951. Conditioning of Human Heart Rate to Graded Degrees of Muscular Tension. *Federation Proceedings* 10:104.

Pihl, R.O., and J. Altman. 1971. An Experimental Analysis of the Placebo Effect. *Journal of Clinical Pharmacology* 11:91–95.

Post, R.M., N.R. Contel, and P.W. Gold. 1980. Impaired Behavioral Sensitization to Cocaine in Vasopress in Deficient Rats. *Society for Neuroscience Abstracts* 6:111.

Post, R.M., A Lockfield, K.M. Squillance, and N.R. Centel. 1981. Drug-Environment Interaction: Context Dependency of Cocaine-Induced Behavioral Sensitization. *Life Sciences* 28:755–760.

Raffa, R.B., F. Porreca, A. Cowan, and R.J. Tallarida. 1982. Evidence for the Role of Conditioning in the Development of Tolerance to Morphine-Induced Inhibition of Gastrointestinal Motility in Rats. *Federation Proceedings* 41:1317.

Razran, G. 1961. The Observable Unconscious and the Inferable Conscious in Current Soviet Psychophysiology: Interoceptive Conditioning, Semantic Conditioning and the Orienting Reflex. *Psychological Review* 68:81–147.

Reed, T. 1980. Challenging Some "Common Wisdom" on Drug Abuse. *International Journal of the Addictions* 15:359–373.

Robins, L.N., J.E. Helzer, and D.H. Davis. 1975. Narcotic Use in Southeast Asia and Afterwards. *Archives of General Psychiatry* 32:955–961.

Rogers, M.P., P. Reich, T.B. Strom, and C.B. Carpenter. 1976. Behaviorally Conditioned Immunosuppression: Replication of a Recent Study. *Psychosomatic Medicine* 38:447–451.

Rozin, P., D. Reff, M. Mark, and J. Schull. 1984. Conditioned Responses in Human Tolerance to Caffeine. *Bulletin of the Psychosomatic Society* 22:117–120.

Rushmer, R.F., O.A. Smith, Jr., and E.P. Lasher. 1960. Neural Mechanisms of Cardiac Control During Exertion. *Physiological Reviews* 40:27–34.

Russell, M., K.A. Dark. R.W. Cummins, G. Ellman, E. Callaway, and H.V.S. Peeke. 1984. Learned Histamine Release. *Science* 225:733–734.

Sakellaris, P.C., and J. Vernikos-Danellis. 1975. Increased Rate of Response of the Pituitary-Adrenal System in Rats Adapted to Chronic Stress. *Endocrinology* 97: 597–602.

Sato, K., K.F. Flood, and T. Makinodan. 1984. Influence of Conditioned Psychological Stress on Immunological Recovery in Mice Exposed to Low-Dose X-Irradiation. *Radiation Research* 98:381–388.

Shavit, Y., J.W. Lewis, G.W. Terman, R.P. Gale, and J.C. Liebeskind. 1984. Opioid Peptides Mediate the Suppressive Effect of Stress on Natural Killer Cell Cytotoxicity. *Science* 223:188–190.

Siegel, S. 1975a. Conditioning Insulin Effects. *Journal of Comparative and Physiological Psychology* 89:189–199.

———. 1975b. Evidence from Rats that Morphine Tolerance is a Learned Response. *Journal of Comparative and Physiological Psychology* 89:498–506.

———. 1976. Morphine Analgesic Tolerance: Its Situation Specificity Supports a Pavlovian Conditioning Model. *Science* 193:323–325.

———. 1977. Morphine Tolerance Acquisition as an Associative Process. *Journal of Experimental Psychology: Animal Behavior Processes* 3:1–13.

———. 1978. Tolerance to the Hyperthermic Effect of Morphine in the Rat as a Learned Response. *Journal of Comparative and Physiological Psychology* 92: 1137–1149.

———. 1983. Classical Conditioning, Drug Tolerance, and Drug Dependence. In Y. Israel, F.B. Glaser, H. Kalant, R.E. Popham, W. Schmidt, and R.G. Smart, eds., *Research Advances in Alcohol and Drug Problems*. Vol. 7. New York: Plenum.

———. 1984. Pavlovian Conditioning and Heroin Overdose: Reports by Overdose Victims. *Bulletin of the Psychonomic Society* 22:428–430.

———. 1985. Drug Anticipatory Responses in Animals. In L. White, B. Tursky, and G. Schwartz, eds., *Placebo: Theory, Research, and Mechanisms*. New York: Guilford Press.

————. 1986. Environmental Modulation of Tolerance: Evidence from Benzodiazepine Research. In H.H. Frey, W.P. Koella, W. Fröcher, and H. Meinardi, eds., *Tolerance to Adverse and Beneficial Effects of Antiepileptic Drugs.* New York: Raven Press.

————. 1987. Pavlovian Conditioning and Ethanol Tolerance. In K.O. Lindros, R. Ylikahri, and K. Kiianmaa, eds., *Advances in Biomedical Alcohol Research.* Oxford: Pergamon Press.

Siegel, S., and D. Ellsworth. 1986. Pavlovian Conditioning and Death from Apparent Overdose of Medically Prescribed Morphine: A Case Report. *Bulletin of the Psychonomic Society* 24:278–280.

Siegel, S., and J. MacRae. 1984. Environmental Specificity of Tolerance. *Trends in NeuroScience* 7:140–142.

Siegel, S., and K. Sdao-Jarvie. 1986. Reversal of Ethanol Tolerance by a Novel Stimulus. *Psychopharmacology* 88:258–261.

Siegel, S., R. E. Hinson, and M.D. Krank. 1979. Modulation of Tolerance to the Lethal Effect of Morphine by Extinction. *Behavioral and Neural Biology* 25: 257–262.

Siegel, S., J.E. Sherman, and D. Mitchell. 1980. Extinction of Morphine Analgesic Tolerance. *Learning and Motivation* 11:289–301.

Siegel, S., R.E. Hinson, and M.D. Krank. 1981. Morphine-Induced Attenuation of Morphine Tolerance. *Science* 212:1533–1534.

Siegel, S., R.E. Hinson, M.D. Krank, and J. McCully. 1982. Heroin "Overdose" Death: The Contribution of Drug-Associated Environmental Cues. *Science* 216: 436–437.

Sklar, L.S., and H. Anisman. 1981. Stress and Cancer. *Psychological Bulletin* 89: 369–406.

Smith, D.A., and W.C. Stebbins. 1965. Conditioned Blood Flow and Heart Rate in Monkeys. *Journal of Comparative and Physiological Psychology* 59:432–436.

Subkov, A.A., and G.N. Zilov. 1937. The Role of Conditioned Reflex Adaptation in the Origin of Hyperergic Reactions. *Bulletin de Biologie et de Medecine Experimentale* 4:294–296.

Ternes, J.W. 1977. An Opponent Process Theory of Habitual Behavior with Special Reference to Smoking. In M.E. Jarvick, ed., *Research on Smoking Behavior.* (NIDA Research Monograph 17). Washington, DC: U.S. Government Printing Office.

Thompson, T., and W. Ostlund, Jr. 1965. Susceptibility to Readdiction as a Function of the Addiction and Withdrawal Environments. *Journal of Comparative and Physiological Psychology* 60:388–392.

Tiffany, S.T., and T.B. Baker. 1981. Morphine Tolerance in the Rat: Congruence with a Pavlovian Paradigm. *Journal of Comparative and Physiological Psychology* 95:747–762.

Toates, F.M. 1979. Homeostasis and Drinking. *Behavioral and Brain Sciences* 2:95–139.

Walter, T.A., and D.C. Riccio. 1983. Overshadowing Effects in the Stimulus Control of Morphine Analgesic Tolerance. *Behavioral Neuroscience* 97:658–662.

Wayner, E.A., G.R. Flannery, and G. Singer. 1978. Effects of Taste Aversion Conditioning on the Primary Antibody Response to Sheep Red Blood Cells and *Brucella abortus* in the Albino Rat. *Physiology and Behavior* 21:995–1000.

Wikler, A. 1973. Conditioning of Successive Adaptive Responses to the Initial Effects of Drugs. *Conditional Reflexes* 8:193–210.

Wilkerson, J.E., S.M. Horvath, and B. Gutin. 1980. Plasma Testosterone during Treadmill Exercise. *Journal of Applied Psychology* 49:249–253.

Zanchetti, A., G. Baccelli, G. Mancia, and G.D. Ellison. 1972. Emotion and the Cardiovascular System in the Cat. In *Physiology, Emotion and Psychosomatic Illness* (CIBA Foundation Symposium, New Series No. 8). New York: Elsevier.

Weingarten, H.P. 1985. Stimulus Control of Eating: Implications for a Two-Factor Theory of Hunger. *Appetite* 6:387–401.

6

A Biobehavioral View of
Substance Abuse and Addiction

Ovide F. Pomerleau
Cynthia S. Pomerleau

Introduction

The magnitude of the task of conceptualizing addiction in a way that is both intuitively satisfying and scientifically rigorous has been eloquently expressed by Peele (1985:72) in a recent book on the meaning of addiction:

> A successful addiction model must synthesize pharmacological, experiential, cultural, situational, and personality components in a fluid and seamless description of addictive motivation. It must account for why a drug is more addictive in one society than another, addictive for one individual and not another, and addictive for the same individual at one time and not another. The model must make sense out of the essentially similar behavior that takes place with all compulsive involvements. In addition, the model must adequately describe the cycle of increasing yet dysfunctional reliance on an involvement until the involvement overwhelms other reinforcements available to the individual.

Unfortunately, no formulation exists that can satisfy fully all of these criteria; nor, given the present state of knowledge, would it be possible for us or anyone else to leap to such a formulation. The question, then, becomes one of where to start and how best to deploy finite resources. Our own analysis reflects the conviction that if progress is to be made, priority must be given to questions that can be answered with available scientific technologies. Our discussion will therefore emphasize methodological approaches that involve objective measurement, operational definition of inferential variables, replication, and parametric exploration. Although scientific positivism has tended to deemphasize the subjective or phenomenological aspects of human experience, it is not our intention to deny their reality nor to downplay their importance.[1] Rather than relegating private events to a position outside of science or, obversely, using verbal report as a substitute for the event itself, we hold that subjective phenomena provide useful inferences for *guiding* inquiry. We further observe that recent technological advances offer much promise for scientific resolution: developments in physiological stimulation and measurement using microelectrodes and microcannulae with infra-humans as well as electroencephalography and brain imaging with humans, and in assay techniques such as radioimmunoassay and chromatography, have already pushed the boundaries of objective measurement of events relevant to subjective experience much farther than would have been thought possible a few decades ago. Finally, we believe that an understanding of underlying biobehavioral mechanisms derived from empirical research will be required for adequate management of substance abuse problems, just as knowledge about underlying homeostatic and pathophysiological mechanisms contributed to the development of rational therapies and many of the striking successes of modern medicine.

Toward a Biobehavioral Definition of Addiction

The word *addiction* is singularly difficult to pin down. It has been used to describe a wide variety of behaviors ranging from strong habit to intense compulsion. The task of integrating the diverse phenomena to which the term has been applied, employing a vocabulary that is recognized by both the clinician and substance abuser but is also acceptable to the scientist attempting to develop an animal model or to the social demographer attempting to characterize frequency of use and abuse, is fraught with difficulty.

Over the years, the term *addiction* has come to incorporate certain assumptions and half-truths that confound critical examination. Among the most troublesome is the categorization of the reinforcement of substance administration by two major classes of events—drug-taking to achieve euphoric or favorable effects versus drug-taking to relieve aversive withdrawal effects. The first category constitutes psychological dependence and includes substance use that serves as a coping response—i.e., behavior reinforced by temporary improvements in performance and affect; frequently the behavior is anticipated by reports of craving (desire to consume the substance) and by claims that improvements in affect or performance (self-efficacy) will result from taking the substance. (Depending on setting conditions, as we shall see, the consequences of drug self-administration can serve as either positive or negative reinforcers.) The second category comprises pharmacological dependence and identifies consequences of substance use that have served as the prototype of addiction, incorporating the states of tolerance, withdrawal, and craving (desire for relief from aversive symptoms). (By definition, substance administration to relieve an aversive state of withdrawal constitutes negative reinforcement.)

The distinction stated above is implicit in various characterizations of addiction and dependency both in the lay media and by professionals. The

World Health Organization (1969:6), for example, has defined substance dependence as

> a state, *psychic and sometimes physical,* resulting from the interaction between a living organism and a drug, characterized by behavioral and other responses that always include a compulsion to take the drug on a continuous or periodic basis in order to experience its psychic effects, and sometimes to avoid the discomfort of its absence [italics ours].

This definition is in many ways a useful one. The distinction between substance use to relieve withdrawal and substance use to produce other effects is correct in recognizing that different pathways may be involved in the reinforcement of compulsive drug-taking behavior, a fact with important implications for the development of effective treatment strategies as well as for basic research. Accepted uncritically, however, the distinction has some potential for mischief. A serious shortcoming is that it perpetuates the old specter of mind-body dualism by suggesting that there are unique, non-communicating levels of analysis—psychic and physical. We believe that the proper resolution to this problem lies in the development of technologies that make "private" events more accessible rather than in positing *a priori* boundaries and limits.

An additional problem is that the phrase *physiological dependence* tends to overstate the difficulty of overcoming withrawal (the addict is a helpless victim, physiologically enslaved by the drug); whereas *psychic dependence* tends to understate the difficulty of overcoming other drug effects, such as those that serve as coping responses ("all it takes is a little willpower"). The characteristic endpoints of substance abuse—overwhelming involvement with the substance and its procurement, as well as the high probability of return to a pattern of excessive use after a period of abstinence—should in fact be possible with either psychological or pharmacological dependence, as long as substance administration is sufficiently reinforcing. From this perspective, substance abuse is a continuum in which quantitative differences in response cost, salience of cues associated with substance use, delay of reinforcement, reinforcement magnitude, and availability of alternative reinforcers all play a critical role in determining outcome. The ability of a substance or an activity to produce reinforcing changes in mood or arousal is necessary for producing entrainment that results in addiction and seems to be derived from the capacity to effect changes in neural substrates. Certain habits like gambling can produce such changes and thus may also have dependence-producing or addictive potential (at least in individuals who are susceptible by virtue of social history and biological configuration).

The point is that we must choose and use our words carefully. The concepts of psychological dependence and pharmacological dependence represent distinctions made for purposes of convenience to describe states that vary from situation to situation and within individuals. In some circumstances, psychological and pharmacological dependence seem to be highly correlated; under other conditions, one or the other may predominate. Glib delineations of different "kinds" of addicts are at best premature and at worst erroneous. The problem is not just an academic one, since both treatment and policy decisions can be affected. The outstanding example is Jellinek's (1960:155) "working hypothesis" on alcoholism as a disease, which in the space of a decade went from the status of suggestions for guiding scientific research on putative biochemical and physiological anomalies to that of a central dogma of Alcoholics Anonymous, a highly influential self-help movement (Peele, 1985:27–45; Pomerleau et al., 1976).

For purposes of the present discussion, we propose the following working definition:

> Addiction is the repeated use of a substance and/or a compelling involvement in a behavior that directly or indirectly modifies the internal milieu (as indicated by changes in neurochemical and neuronal activity) in such a way as to produce immediate reinforcement, but whose long-term effects are personally or medically harmful or highly disadvantageous societally.

The virtue of such a definition is that it allows us to use strength of behavior and compulsion[2] as a critical criterion for dependence and to classify addictive phenomena on the basis of the kinds of physiological, biochemical, and subjective changes they produce. A further virtue is that dependence on powerfully reinforced habits such as gambling, overeating, compulsive physical exercise, excessive sexual activity, or even extreme involvement in work does not have to be seen as a separate class of behaviors. Though no drug is ingested, each of these activities can be carried out in a highly compulsive and addictive manner, persisting despite deleterious social, economic, or health consequences. As with drug addicts, "abusers" of these activities report subjective effects that can include intense pleasure during the act or relief following its completion as well as discomfort associated with abstinence. A further similarity is that some of the neuroregulators known to be affected by psychoactive substances such as nicotine, amphetamine, cocaine, and opiates (Iversen and Iversen, 1981; Pomerleau and Pomerleau, 1984; Smith and Lane, 1983) are also affected by intense physical exercise (Carr and Fishman, 1985; Pomerleau et al., 1987), eating behavior and food intake (Morley et al., 1983), performance demand (Williams et al., 1982), and gambling (Wolkowitz, 1985; Wray and Dickerson, 1981). While apparent similarities in effects on neuroregulatory substrates do not prove *ipso facto* that identical reinforcing processes are involved, they do suggest that addictions can be examined productively as members of a class of strongly entrained behaviors involving changes in neurochemical patterns and neural activity rather than as unique, qualitatively different entities.

In this chapter, then, we shall examine addiction from a biobehavioral perspective. The emphasis will be on chemical substance abuse, though other conditions will also be considered. Drawing on well over a decade of clinical and research expérience on cigarette-smoking and nicotine by the first author, we shall focus particular attention on smoking. As an exemplary addiction, smoking happens to have some peculiar merits. The behavioral consistency of the habitual cigarette smoker, the frequency of nicotine self-administration (i.e., a short addictive cycle), the large number of smokers in the population (about one-third of the population still smokes), and the fact that smoking is legal have facilitated human experimentation on smoking without compromising relevance (Pomerleau, 1981). Technological developments, making possible the objective description of smoking using behavioral topography and the quantification of intake using plasma nicotine, have also contributed to recent research productivity. Considering these findings within the larger context of addictive phenomena in general, we shall try to identify some of the factors that must be taken into account in organizing research on substance abuse. We shall also discuss the clinical implications of a biobehavioral perspective.

A Comprehensive Analysis of Smoking Behavior

The intense devotion of smokers to a substance whose subjective effects are subtle and diffuse, whose inherent reinforcing properties have been difficult to demonstrate scientifically, and whose long-term hazards are well-known is perplexing (Pomerleau and Pomerleau, 1986). A number of theorists have attempted to explain the persistence of smoking by characterizing it as an escape/avoidance response to the aversive consequences of nicotine withdrawal (Jarvik, 1977; Russell, 1977; Schachter, 1978). This formulation is essentially a pharmacological dependence model, implying regulation to achieve a minimal level of nicotine intake, tolerance to nicotine, and a defined symptomatology in the absence of the drug. By implication, pleasurable or other reinforcing aspects of nicotine use are discretionary or incidental, as can be seen in the widely used definition of tobacco dependence in the *Diagnostic and Statistical Manual* [DSM III] of the American Psychiatric Association (Spitzer, 1980).

The model is supported by demonstrations in humans and infrahumans of both regulation and tolerance (Gritz, 1980; Henningfield et al., 1985; Pomerleau et al., 1983b). Tobacco withdrawal symptoms have been somewhat more difficult to document and have generally been found to vary from smoker to smoker (Hughes et al., 1984) as well as from environment to environment (Hatsukami et al., 1985); they are relatively mild even at their peak (Hatsukami et al., 1984), compared with those produced by other substances of abuse. Furthermore, because of difficulties in engendering self-administration in animals and variable effects observed for nicotine under different conditions of administration, only recently have investigators been satisfied that the scientific criteria for pharmacological dependence have been met at both the human and animal level (Henningfield et al., 1985; Koop, 1986:144).

Although pharmacological dependence is clearly a factor in the maintenance of smoking, it does not readily account for the difficulties most smokers experience in quitting (Shiffman, 1982). Investigation of situations that cue smoking (Best and Hakstian, 1978; Epstein and Collins, 1977), retrospective examination of factors associated with craving (Myrsten et al., 1977), and analysis of the circumstances surrounding recidivism (Pomerleau et al., 1978; Shiffman, 1982), indicate that stimuli independent of the nicotine-addiction cycle, and therefore unrelated to the time since the last cigarette, reliably increase the probability of smoking. Such stimuli include termination of a meal, coffee drinking, dysphoric states, and cognitive and intellectual demands. Consistent with these observations are reports that many cigarettes are smoked because of perceived improvements in performance, enhancement of pleasure or relaxation, and relief of anxiety (Mausner and Platt, 1971; Pomerleau, 1986). Thus, in contrast to the first cigarette of the day or after an extended period of deprivation, many cigarettes smoked have no clear connection with nicotine deprivation or time since last smoking.

Some of these phenomena can be explained in a straightforward manner within the context of social learning theory[3] (Pomerleau, 1980): Acquisition of the habit is known to occur under conditions of social reinforcement, typically through peer pressure. Initially the inhalation of smoke is aversive, but after practice, habituation and tolerance develop, and the behavior begins to provide sufficient positive reinforcement in its own right to be sustained independently of social reinforcement, generalizing to situations other than the one in which it was originally acquired. With the exception of Kozlowski and Harford's (1976) demonstration that novice smokers who experienced fewer aversive effects from smoking under laboratory conditions were willing to try again at a later time, the problem of initiation has not received much experimental scrutiny.

Discrimination between situations in which smoking is punished socially and those in which it is either attended to neutrally or favorably received constitutes the social learning basis by which various circumstances in daily life (both internal and external) begin to control smoking. Under this formulation, situations such as an empty cigarette pack or an annoying telephone call may, by association with smoking, serve as conditional stimuli (CS) that elicit covert responses such as craving. Craving, then, can be defined as a cognitive manifestation of physiological, biochemical, or behavioral perturbations (respondents) associated with increased likelihood of substance intake (Pomerleau et al., 1983a). The same situations (including both exteroceptive and interoceptive stimuli) can also serve as discriminative stimuli (SDs), setting the occasion for the reinforcement provided by smoking. Stimuli that are preparatory to the act of smoking (e.g., the sight of a cigarette) can thus function as secondary reinforcers for behaviors preceding them (e.g., opening a pack of cigarettes) and also as discriminative stimuli for behaviors that follow them (e.g., lighting a cigarette), forming a chain of responses (smoking ritual). By implication, the successful elimination of the overt act of smoking requires the extinction of many of the conditional stimuli, secondary reinforcers, and discriminatory stimuli that control the habit.

To the extent that smoking is an avoidance/escape response to an aversive state of nicotine withdrawal, stimulus generalization to dysphoric states that resemble the abstinence syndrome, such as anxiety or tension, may provide another means by which these states can serve as discriminative stimuli for smoking. Response generalization, by which the smoking ritual serves as a temporary escape from various aversive situations, may occur as well. Although only a few investigations on the disruption of stimulus control have been conducted in the context of smoking therapy (e.g., Abrams et al., in press), learning and conditioning concepts have been recognized for some time as relevant to the prevention of relapse following treatment for heroin addiction (e.g., O'Brien et al., 1976; Wikler, 1965), problem drinking (Baker et al., 1987; Hodgson and Rankin, 1976), and other substances (Henningfield et al., 1986; Stitzer et al., 1979).

Smoking (nicotine self-administration) can thus be conceptualized as a generalized primary and secondary reinforcer, providing both positive and negative reinforcement over a remarkably wide array of life situations. Smoking is also powerfully entrained because of its ability to provide immediate reinforcement: Nicotine from an inhaled cigarette reaches the brain in seven seconds, twice as fast as intravenous administration. Furthermore, the habit is greatly overlearned: at ten puffs per cigarette, the pack-a-day smoker gets more than 70,000 puffing reinforcements in a year—a frequency unmatched by any other form of drug taking (Russell, 1977). Although most smokers recognize that sustained smoking can lead to a variety of unpleasant consequences, ranging from bronchitis to lung cancer, these aversive consequences are delayed and therefore have less influence over ongoing smoking behavior than immediate consequences—a situation common to a number of substances of abuse. Unlike alcohol and many other dependence-producing substances, however, not only does nicotine *not* impair performance, but it seems to enhance the capacity of normal people to work and to socialize. There are thus few immediate noticeable negative consequences to interfere with entrainment (Jarvik, 1977).

Among the manifestations of stimulus control that are currently receiving renewed attention is craving as an indicator of addictive status and severity of addiction (Kaplan et al., 1985; Monti et al., In press). Tolerance—decreased effect of a drug dose due to repeated administration—has been shown to be the result of a combination of nonassociative factors (i.e., changes in drug metabolism and disposition; Kalant, 1973); and associative factors, which may include both operant elements such as practice under conditions of intoxication (LeBlanc et al., 1976) and respondents that are either compensatory and opposite in direction to the drug's effects (Siegel, 1983) or noncompensatory and drug-similar (Baker and Tiffany, 1985). An important issue under consideration is the relationship between tolerance and craving. Although the presence of a high degree of tolerance might imply intense desire, at present no theory of tolerance adequately accounts for observations that some substance abusers engage in drug-seeking behavior but report no drug urges, while others describe extreme temptation but do not resort to substance use (Tiffany and Baker, 1986). Although these findings clearly apply to the problem of nicotine use and smoking, little systematic research has been conducted to date.

The above line of analysis forms the basis for the majority of behavioral treatment strategies developed. While the analysis has generated a considerable amount of sophisticated research on the role of stimulus control in substance abuse, such conceptualizations have tended to stop at the skin, relegating underlying biological mechanisms to another, more molecular level. We would argue that by extending the analysis to the specification of the substrate for antecedent and consequent reinforcing stimuli, the resulting biobehavioral integration may have greater explanatory power. Not only would a more complete and satisfying explanation of substance abuse emerge, but more efficacious treatment methodologies might result.

Let us examine more closely the pharmacological effects of inhaled nicotine (Pomerleau and Pomerleau, 1984). The drug is known to have direct and indirect actions on several neuroregulatory systems. It acts initially on nicotinic cholinergic receptors, mimicking the effects of acetylcholine at low doses but blocking transmission after initial agonist activity at higher doses. It readily penetrates into brain, where it has been shown to act on central nicotinic cholinergic receptors; a biphasic response paralleling the peripheral pattern of activation superseded by blockade of transmission has been inferred. Nicotine has been shown to increase rates of release and turnover of acetylcholine and the catecholamines (norepinephrine and dopamine) in the brain. It also stimulates the release of a variety of neuromodulatory peptides, including arginine vasopressin, growth hormone, prolactin, adrenocorticotrophic hormone (ACTH), and endogenous opioids such as beta-endorphin. Serotonin (5-hydroxytryptamine) is apparently affected by nicotine as well, although the relationships are not well understood, with reports of decreased turnover in some brain locations and increased activity at other sites.

Of particular relevance to a stimulus control analysis of smoking is that many of the endogenous substances whose synthesis, release, and turnover in the central nervous system are affected by nicotine have been shown, independently of nicotine, to influence behavior and subjective state. Cholinergic mechanisms, for example, seem to play a role in learning and memory, alertness/arousal, and pain inhibition. Norepinephrine pathways are associated with modulation of arousal level, and stimulation of central noradrenergic pathways is associated with improvements in selective attention, increased alertness, enhanced vigilance, and facilitation of rapid information processing. In addition, a number of studies have identified dopaminergic neurons as a critical part of the brain reward mechanism; though its behavioral effects are still not well understood, vasopressin has been implicated in memory consolidation and retrieval. Finally, endogenous opioids have been linked to pain reduction as well as to alleviation of anxiety; they may also have direct rewarding effects.

Because nicotine alters the bioavailability of these neuroregulators, it is plausible to suppose that smokers learn to "use" the drug to regulate or fine-tune the body's normal adaptive mechanisms. In this sense, nicotine might be described as a pharmacological coping response. Table 6–1 shows the range and diversity of the subjective and behavioral consequences that have been reported or demonstrated for smoking. The congruence of these consequences and the psychological effects of the endogenous neuroregulators known to be stimulated by nicotine is remarkable. Table 6–2 summarizes the relationship between reinforcing consequences of smoking and putative neuroregulatory mechanisms. (In those situations in which the presmoking context is neutral or positive and does not involve deprivation or aversive stimulation, the consequences are classified as positive reinforcers; in those situations in which an aversive state or behavioral deficiency can be identified as part of the presmoking context, the consequences meet the definition of negative reinforcement.)

From the above formulation, it follows that dysphoric states like anxiety may prompt smoking because such distress has previously been alleviated by the anxiolytic effects of nicotine-stimulated beta-endorphin release and/or cholinergic activity. Similarly, work or performance demand may trigger smoking because sustained psychomotor performance and alertness have been enhanced in the past by increased cholinergic and/or noradrenergic activity. Taking into account both discriminative stimuli whose functional control over behavior is based on generalization (resemblance) to aversive nicotine withdrawal states and discriminative stimuli that set the occasion for direct reinforcement by nicotine, the number of affective states or performance demands (and their antecedent stimuli) that might cue smoking is potentially very large, providing a plausible explanation for the thorough interweaving of the smoking habit in the fabric of daily life. Many additional

Table 6–1
Commonly Reported Behavioral and Subjective Effects of Smoking

Consequences of smoking in habitual smokers

↑concentration/↑ability to tune out irrelevant stimuli

↑memory (recall)

↑psychomotor performance

↑alertness/↑arousal

↑pleasure/facilitation of pleasure

↓anxiety/↓tension

↓body weight

Consequences of not smoking in habitual smokers

↑anxiety/↑tension

↑irritability/dysphoria

↑craving for cigarettes

↑body weight

↓concentration

↓ability to tune out irrelevant stimuli

↓memory

↓psychomotor performance

↓dullness/anhedonia

Source: Adapted from Pomerleau and Pomerleau (1984).

Table 6–2
Reinforcing Consequences of Smoking and Putative Neuroregulatory Mechanisms

Positive Reinforcement	Negative Reinforcement

Pleasure/enhancement of pleasure
  ↑dopamine
  ↑norepinephrine
  ↑beta-endorphin
	Reduction of anxiety and tension
	  ↑acetylcholine
	  ↑beta-endorphin

Facilitation of task performance
  ↑acetylcholine
  ↑norepinephrine
	Antinociception
	  ↑acetylcholine
	  ↑beta-endorphin

Improvement of memory
  ↑acetylcholine
  ↑norepinephrine
  ↑vasopressin (?)
	Avoidance of weight gain
	  ↑dopamine
	  ↑norepinephrine

	Relief from nicotine withdrawal
	  ↑acetylcholine
	    (↑noncholinergic nicotinic activity)

Source: Adapted from Pomerleau and Pomerleau (1984)

tests of the involvement of specific neuroregulators in the mediation of particular nicotine effects, however, using both agonists and antagonists (e.g., Carruthers, 1976; Stolerman et al., 1973), will be needed to substantiate fully the demonstration of the stimulus control/neuroregulator hypothesis for smoking.

Though the effects of nicotine described above might also be the result of relief of nicotine withdrawal, a series of studies in our laboratory (Fertig et al., 1986; Pomerleau et al., 1984) suggests that, under conditions of minimal deprivation or minimal pharmacological dependence, favorable or adaptive drug effects unrelated to the addiction/withdrawal cycle can be produced by nicotine (Pomerleau, 1986). Specifically, the studies demonstrated nicotine-produced antinociception using a mode of nicotine administration (intranasal snuff) that was unfamiliar to minimally deprived cigarette smokers. The same results were obtained with ex-smokers who had not smoked for at least a year. Because they were no longer nicotine-dependent, ex-smokers were presumed not to be susceptible to relief from nicotine withdrawal. This line of research lends further support to the idea of smoking as a coping response.

The suggestion that reinforcement from nicotine might involve both pleasurable states *and* relief from withdrawal is not without precedent in the literature of addiction. Recent evidence indicates that reinforcement from opiates can also involve both, and that separate neuronal pathways may be implicated: In chronic heroin users, the ability of the drug to terminate withdrawal shows tolerance, but the ability to produce euphoria apparently does not (Kornetsky and Bain, 1983; Meyer and Mirin, 1979). Demonstration of rewarding effects from microinjections of morphine in specific brain areas, without induction of physical dependence or withdrawal (Bozarth and Wise, 1984), suggests a neuroanatomical separation of the euphoric, analgesic, and sedative properties of opiates (Bozarth, 1983). Microinjection techniques may likewise provide a useful method for determining the particulars of nicotine's effects on different neuroregulatory pathways (Kamerling et al., 1982; Wu and Martin, 1983).

An Organizational Scheme for Research on Substance Abuse

The biobehavioral formulation described above grew out of an attempt to explain how smoking is established and maintained (Pomerleau and Pomerleau, 1984). Other substances of abuse may differ in the specifics of their pharmacological action, resulting in different conditions for reinforcement and discriminative control, but they can also be subjected, *mutatis mutandis,* to the same general line of analysis.[4]

Figure 6–1 suggests some of the variables that will need to be considered

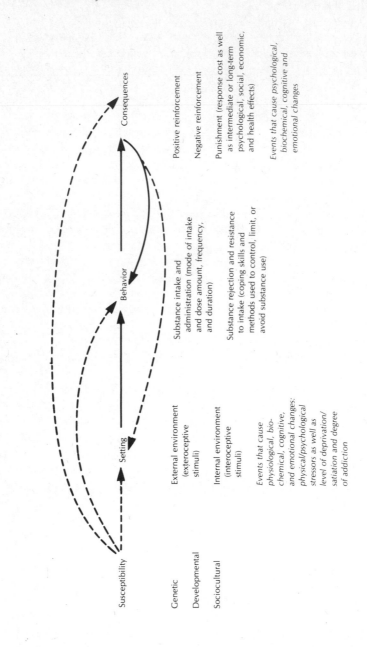

Figure 6–1. Biobehavioral Factors in Substance Abuse

in a balanced explanation of substance abuse. At this point our knowledge of these variables remains fragmented and uneven. Those listed under *Setting* (exteroceptive and interoceptive stimuli) are derived from a general model of human behavior in the Pavlovian and Skinnerian traditions; in combination with the reinforcement factors identified under *Consequences,* they constitute the foundation for behavioral pharmacology (e.g., Goldberg and Stolerman, 1986). Concerning *Behavior,* while some information is available on those activities that define substance taking, very little is known about substance rejection and resistance to intake, especially in relation to response cost and the deleterious psychological, social, economic, and health consequences of substance abuse.

In part due to the lack of agreement about the defining characteristics of substance use prior to a well-established pattern of abuse, what is known about *Susceptibility,* which includes factors such as genetic, developmental, and sociocultural influences, is based almost exclusively on descriptive studies and studies employing questionnaires to examine, retrospectively, the effects of personality traits or of environmental stressors. Some recent animal research, however, suggests interactions between the setting and behavior that may serve to increase susceptibility to the use of psychoactive substances and to the entrainment of certain excessive behaviors. These developments may provide a new method for investigating initiation of substance use prospectively. Events occurring in daily life on an intermittent basis, particularly events eliciting dysphoric or euphoric states (which have been shown to be associated with shifts in central neuroregulator levels; Carlson, 1981:548; Wallace and Singer, 1976) may constitute a sensitization condition that increases the probability of initiation of certain directed "adjunctive" behaviors (e.g., behaviors such as chewing, sipping, inhaling, and even injecting) that constitute the ingestive vehicle for drug taking (Falk et al., 1983; Jeffreys et al., 1979; Singer et al., 1982; Wetherington, 1982). Once started, the use of certain drugs may persist because these substances produce alterations in the internal neurochemical milieu that have reinforcement value in that particular setting (Singer et al., 1982; Weisz and Thompson, 1983).

Schedule-induction has been used to prompt and sustain oral, intravenous, and inhaled self-administration of various substances, including nicotine, cocaine, alcohol, and opiates in animals (Slifer, 1983). At the human level, several demonstrations of schedule-induction involving smoking have been reported (e.g., Cherek, 1982; Wallace and Singer, 1976). Though some reservations have been expressed about whether sufficient information has been accumulated to justify the use of schedule-induced behavior as an adequate model of initiation of substance abuse (Sanger, 1986), the approach shows potential for enabling the dissection of interactions of environmental and pharmacological factors involved in drug-seeking behavior (Jeffreys et al., 1979).

The above discussion invites certain speculations about the evolutionary significance of addictive phenomena. Though there is no obvious selective advantage in susceptibility to addictive substances or behaviors, it is not unreasonable to suppose that addiction represents the ability of these substances or behaviors to tap into biobehavioral mechanisms designed for survival—energy regulation, energy conservation, reproduction, fight-or-flight, etc.—in an earlier and more "natural" environment. Nicotine, for example, has a pharmacological profile that accords ideally with its use as an arousal modulator and hence as a "coping response" in diverse situations, such as performance demand or anxiety states. Other drugs, like heroin, typically do not improve task performance; rather, they may induce an exaggerated or inappropriate version of a physiological response intended for conserving resources in situations where struggle is useless. The abuse of caffeine may begin as an adaptation to the social environment that demands sustained alertness, overriding the body's ninety-minute alertness cycle and ultimately leading to hyperarousal and difficulties in sleeping. Overeating may be simply a normal response appropriate to an environment in which feast-or-famine was a way of life. Thus, modern technology has enabled the identification and refinement of psychoactive and behavior-changing substances, as well as the creation of artificial abundance and wide dispersal, leading to the subversion of responses that were adaptive in a different environmental context.

A full understanding of addictive behavior will require not only explication of the variables subsumed under *Susceptibility, Setting, Behavior,* and *Consequences,* but also functional analyses and systematic experimentation to elucidate larger relationships among these variable-sets. We have attempted in the diagram (figure 6–3) to give some sense of the dynamic interrelationships: Solid arrows indicate critical associations denoting tightly coupled relationships, such as those between behavior and its reinforcing consequences and the effect of those consequences on subsequent behavior; broken arrows indicate correlational and modulational elements. For example, behavioral consequences can change the setting by prompting motor behavior that modifies the external environment or the internal milieu; susceptibility factors can influence not only how the setting is perceived but also how much and what kind of behavior will occur in particular circumstances and how reinforcing the consequences of that behavior will be. In the future, a better understanding of these elements should foster an integrated view of substance abuse: Molecular data on receptor binding, for example, should contribute to an explanation of the molar phenomena of tolerance and withdrawal. Similarly, basic research on drug self-administration in humans and infrahumans should provide the tools by which to generate clinically relevant models of substance abuse. In general, broad overviews of addiction should be able to incorporate microanalyses of specific behavioral, physiological, and biochemical phenomena and vice versa.

Implications for Treatment

A clear implication of the biobehavioral conceptualization is that substance abuse is maintained by a number of critical variables, with complex interactions among susceptibility, setting, the behaviors involving substance intake and resistance, and immediate, intermediate, and delayed reinforcing consequences. Disruption of patterns of behavior that are so overdetermined is likely to require a multifactorial approach. Three broad categories of interventions suggest themselves. The first involves changing the environment to modify the stimulus context that promotes substance abuse or maintains dependence. Techniques ranging from health education to behavior modification/therapy have been available for some time, though further refinement is desirable. Among the problems still needing more attention are prevention and recidivism. For example, supplementing existing skills training and peer group resocialization programs with biobehavioral assessments of susceptibility to the blandishments of substance use might strengthen prevention programs for adolescents (Pomerleau and Pomerleau, 1984). Similarly, a more accurate profile of physiological, behavioral, and subjective reactivity to substances of abuse might strengthen existing cognitively-based relapse prevention programs (Marlatt and Gordon, 1985) for substance users (Baker et al., 1987).

A second category involves a realisitic appraisal of the seductive power of substances that powerfully modulate neuroregulatory functions. The substance-dependent person should not underestimate the disruption that may be caused by excision of an activity that may at various times have served as a stimulus that prompts ongoing behavior (Schuster, 1986), as a coping response for meeting the challenges of daily living (Pomerleau and Pomerleau, 1984), or even as an activity that becomes the organizing principle for living, subverting all other functions (Peele, 1985). Allowance will need to be made for adaptation and time allocated for readjustment and learning of patterns that do not involve artificial dependencies. Variability in clinical outcome and other difficulties encountered in substance substitution programs such as methadone maintenance for heroin addicts and nicotine chewing gum for smokers may result from underestimation of the behavioral adjustments required. Substance blocking or contingent aversion techniques, exemplified by the use of naltrexone for opiate addicts and disulfiram for alcoholics, may have similar limitations. While specific guidelines for the conditioning aspects of such interventions have been promulgated (Wikler, 1976), and an attempt has been made to combine operant and respondent conditioning concepts relating to substance abuse (Wikler, 1975), a more extensive integrative framework is needed to guide therapy. From a biobehavioral perspective, therefore, the use of substitute agonists or antagonists in the absence of a well-defined context for supporting behavior change remediates only part of the problem, as demonstrated in several studies (O'Brien and Greenstein, 1976; Hall et al., 1985). A further implication of a biobehavioral analysis is that more specific and precisely targeted pharmacological substitutes will need to be developed for the restoration of neuroregulatory function subverted by substance dependence (Pomerleau and Pomerleau, 1984); moreover, pharmacological dosing will need to be progressive, with explicit scheduling for eventual reduction and termination, to minimize reliance and provide opportunities for the eventual development of drug- and substance-free behaviors (Hughes and Miller, 1984).

A third category involves the development of adequate short- and long-term behavioral substitutes for substance use. The psychoactive properties of substances of abuse, particularly arousal modulation (increasing or decreasing alertness and emotional involvement), are important attributes. Very little is known about behavioral methods for engendering states that are similar enough in their psychological and neuroregulatory effects to serve as viable substitutes. Deep muscle relaxation (e.g., Jacobson, 1938) or meditation procedures (e.g., Benson, 1975) have been shown to have compelling subjective effects (e.g., Wallace, 1970), but until recently little attention has been devoted to their physiological and neuroregulatory effects (Hoffman et al., 1982). While a number of clinicians have recommended the use of such procedures over the years, there have been only a few clinical trials (e.g., Pechacek, 1986). Physical exercise has powerful effects on neuroregulatory activity, including dramatically increasing circulating catecholamine and endogenous opioid levels (Carr and Fishman, 1985; Pomerleau et al., 1987), and numerous reports indicate favorable affective changes resulting from regular aerobic exercise—benefiting even clinically depressed or clinically anxious populations (Hughes, 1984; Stern and Cleary, 1982). But with few exceptions (Pomerleau et al., 1987), there has been almost no controlled experimentation on physical exercise as a substitute for a substance dependency.

Conclusions

A biobehavioral perspective on substance abuse and addiction is of necessity multidimensional and multifactorial. The principal feature of such a conceptualization is that it provides a framework for examining data from fields as diverse as sociology, psychology, pharmacology, neurology, molecular biology, and biochemistry. An integrative structure is needed for stimulating new hypotheses, guiding research, developing and testing theories, and summarizing the vast amount of information required to do justice to the complexity of addictive phenomena. In its present state of development, the biobehavioral conceptualization may not constitute a "successful" addiction model

(Peele, 1985:72), but, in our opinion, it does offer reasonable hope for eventually reaching a number of objectives. An important feature of the approach is that it does not pretend to knowledge that is not yet available, thereby encouraging future development by facing directly the absence of information and by maintaining rigorous methodological standards for the gathering of evidence.

Among the practical considerations are that the biobehavioral formulation provides a rationale for combining pharmacological interventions with behavioral techniques. Additionally, the approach encourages the tailoring of therapies to individual characteristics and points to particular factors to consider in matching treatment to patient. Looking to the future, a better understanding of underlying mechanisms, particularly the delineation of the substrates involved in the reinforcement of substance abuse, should promote the development of more sophisticated interventions than are currently available. Taken together, these trends should foster the development of rational and more effective approaches to prevention, treatment, and societal management of substance abuse and addiction.

Notes

1. Subjective reports are of interest because they provide some degree of access to private events; they are useful scientifically only to the extent that they can be operationalized and/or corroborated by other relevant measures. As Skinner (1953:278–282) observed, the substitution of the verbal report (from which inferences are made) for the event itself is misleading and may distract and deter scientific inquiry by offering the illusion of explanation. The phenomenology of substance abuse is useful as part of a multifactorial analysis, integrated with behavioral, physiological, and biochemical data. Subjective data may point to the controlling variables governing behavior in a particular context, but they must be treated with great caution when taken out of their multifactorial matrix, in view of the variability in self-awareness and accuracy of self-report and the possibility of biases leading to deliberate or unintentional distortion of verbal statements. Fundamentally, verbal behavior is under the control of contingencies of reinforcement that are not necessarily the same as those that maintain substance administration. This disassociation is dramatically illustrated by the alcoholic in treatment who seeks to please his or her therapists by proclaiming with conviction that he or she no longer desires to drink and who, shortly after discharge, succumbs to the temptation provided by a neighborhood bar, a drinking buddy, or an emotional upset.

2. While the phrase "compulsion to take a drug" is not easy to specify operationally, it does suggest some objectively measurable indices—for example, strength of drug-seeking behavior. As Schuster (1986:357–358) has pointed out in a recent review, response measures such as frequency and resistance to extinction or punishment are germane. In addition, given a choice, a compulsive drug user will select a drug reinforcer over other alternatives. Schuster goes on to state that although sub-

stances differ in reinforcing efficacy, laboratory analysis of drugs as reinforcers has clearly shown that both the frequency of responding maintained by a drug and other measures of response strength are a function of schedule of reinforcement, indicating that "behavioral variables are as important as pharmacologic ones in the development of compulsive drug-seeking behavior."

3. Social learning theory has functioned less as a formal theory of addiction and more as a methodological approach with an associated intervention technology, but it has stimulated research on stimulus control and reinforcement contingencies and has provided a vocabulary that is useful for describing both pharmacological and psychological phenomena relevant to addiction and substance abuse (e.g., Goldberg and Stolerman, 1986). Accordingly, this terminology will be used to describe both associative (learned and conditioned) and nonassociative (pharmacological and neuroendocrine) factors in the sections that follow.

4. Our knowledge of the characters of various substances of abuse is unevenly developed. Some of the pharmacological actions of nicotine and morphine, for example, can be related to agonistic activity at certain receptors, but the cellular actions of ethanol are much more diffuse and have been more difficult to elucidate. Likewise, investigations of conditioning and stimulus control factors in the control of opiate use and in problem drinking go back several decades, whereas experimentation on these factors is much more recent for nicotine, cannabis, and cocaine.

References

Abrams, D.B., P.M. Monti, R.P. Pinto, J.P. Elder, R.A. Brown, and S.I. Jacobus. In press. Psychosocial Stress and Coping in Smokers who Relapse or Quit. *Health Psychology.*

Baker, L.H., N.L. Cooney, and O.F. Pomerleau. 1987. Craving for Alcohol: Theoretical Considerations and Treatment Procedures. In W.M. Cox, ed., *Treatment and Prevention of Alcohol Problems: Resource Manual.* New York: Academic Press.

Baker, T.B., and S.T. Tiffany. 1985. Morphine Tolerance as Habituation. *Psychological Review* 92:78–108.

Benson, H. 1975. *The Relaxation Response.* New York: William Morrow.

Best, J.A., and A.R. Hakstian. 1978. A Situation Specific Model of Smoking Behavior. *Addictive Behaviors* 3:79–82.

Bozarth, M.A. 1983. Opiate Reward Mechanisms Mapped by Intracranial Self-Administration. In J.E. Smith and J.D. Lane, eds., *The Neurobiology of Opiate Reward Processes.* New York: Elsevier Biomedical Press.

Bozarth, M.A., and R.A. Wise. 1984. Anatomically Distinct Opiate Receptor Fields Mediate Reward and Physical Dependence. *Science* 224:516–517.

Carlson, N.R. 1981. *The Physiology of Behavior.* 2nd ed. Boston: Allyn & Bacon.

Carr, D.B., and J.M. Fishman. 1985. Exercise and the Endogenous Opioids. In K. Fotherby and S. Pal, eds., *Exercise Endrocrinology.* New York: De Gruyter.

Carruthers, M. 1976. Modification of the Noradrenaline Related Effects of Smoking by Beta-Blockade. *Psychological Medicine* 6:251–256.

Cherek, D.R. 1982. Schedule-Induced Cigarette Self-Administration. *Pharmacology, Biochemistry, and Behavior* 17:523–527.

Epstein, L., and F. Collins. 1977. The Measurement of Situational Influences of Smoking. *Addictive Behaviors* 2:47–54.

Fertig, J.B., O.F. Pomerleau, and B. Sanders. 1986. Nicotine-Produced Antinociception in Minimally Deprived Smokers and Ex-Smokers. *Addictive Behaviors* 11: 239–248.

Falk, J.L., B. Dews, and C.R. Schuster. 1983. Commonalities in the Environmental Control of Behavior. In P.K. Levison, D.R. Gerstein, and D.R. Maloff, eds., *Commonalities in Substance Abuse and Addictive Behavior*. Lexington, MA: D.C. Heath.

Goldberg, S.R., and I.P. Stolerman, eds. 1986. *Behavioral Analysis of Drug Dependence*. New York: Academic Press.

Gritz, E. 1980. Smoking Behavior and Tobacco Abuse. In N. Mello, ed., *Advances in Substance Abuse*. Greenwich, CT: JAI Press.

Hall, S.M., C. Tunstall, D. Rugg, R.T. Jones, and N. Benowitz. 1985. Nicotine Gum and Behavioral Treatment in Smoking Cessation. *Journal of Consulting and Clinical Psychology* 532:256–258.

Hatsukami, D.K., J.R. Hughes, and R. Pickens. 1984. Tobacco Withdrawal Symptoms: An Experimental Analysis. *Psychopharmacology* 84:231–236.

———. 1985. Characterization of Tobacco Withdrawal: Physiological and Subjective Effects. In J. Grabowski and S.M. Hall, eds., *Pharmacological Adjuncts in Smoking Cessation*. NIDA Monograph 53. Rockville, MD: National Institute on Drug Abuse.

Henningfield, J.E., S.E. Lukas, and G.E. Bigelow. 1986. Human Studies of Drugs as Reinforcers. In J.R. Goldberg and I.P. Stolerman, eds., *Behavioral Analysis of Drug Dependence*. New York: Academic Press.

Henningfield, J.E., K. Miyasato, and D.R. Jasinski. 1985. Abuse Liability and Pharmacodynamic Characteristics of Intravenous and Inhaled Nicotine. *Journal of Pharmacology and Experimental Therapeutics* 234:1–12.

Hodgson, R.S., and H.J. Rankin. 1976. Modification of Excessive Drinking by Cue Exposure. *Behaviour Research and Therapy* 14:305–307.

Hoffman, J.W., H. Benson, P.A. Arns, B.L. Stainbrook, L. Landsberg, J.B. Young, and A. Gill. 1982. Reduced Sympathetic Nervous System Responsivity Associated with the Relaxation Response. *Science* 251:190–192.

Hughes, J.R. 1984. Psychological Effects of Habitual Aerobic Exercise: A Critical Review. *Preventive Medicine* 13:66–78.

Hughes, J.R., and S. Miller. 1984. Nicotine Gum to Help Stop Smoking. *Journal of the American Medical Association* 252:2855–2858.

Hughes, J.R., D.K. Hatsukami, R.W. Pickens, and D.S. Svikis. 1984. Consistency of the Tobacco Withdrawal Syndrome. *Addictive Behaviors* 9:409–412.

Iversen, S.D., and L.L. Iversen. 1981. *Behavioral Pharmacology*. 2nd ed. New York: Oxford University Press.

Jacobson, E. 1938. *Progressive Relaxation*. Chicago: University of Chicago Press.

Jarvik, M. 1977. Biological Factors Underlying the Smoking Habit. In M. Jarvik, J. Cullen, E. Gritz, T. Vogt, and L. West, eds., *Research on Smoking Behavior*. NIDA Research Monograph 17. Rockville, MD: National Institute on Drug Abuse.

Jeffreys, D., T.P.S. Oei, and G. Singer. 1979. A Reconstruction of the Concept of Drug Dependence. *Neuroscience and Biobehavioral Reviews* 3:149–153.

Jellinek, E.M. 1960. *The Disease Concept of Alcoholism*. Highland Park, NJ: Hill-house Press.

Kalant, H. 1973. Biological Models of Alcohol Tolerance and Physical Dependence. In M.M. Gross, ed., *Alcohol Intoxication and Withdrawal: Experimental Studies*. New York: Plenum Press.

Kamerling, S.G., J.W. Wettstein, J.W. Sloan, F.P. Su, and W.R. Martin. 1982. Interaction between Nicotine and Endogenous Opioid Mechanisms in the Un-anesthetized Dog. *Pharmacology Biochemistry and Behavior* 17:733–740.

Kaplan, R.F., N.L. Cooney, L.H. Baker, R.A. Gillespie, R.E. Meyer, and O.F. Pomerleau. 1985. Reactivity to Alcohol-Related Cues: Physiological and Subjective Responses in Alcoholics and Nonproblem Drinkers. *Journal of Studies on Alcohol* 46:267–272.

Koop, C.E., ed. 1986. *The Health Consequences of Using Smokeless Tobacco: A Report of the Advisory Committee to the Surgeon General*. Bethesda, MD: U.S. Public Health Service.

Kornetsky, C., and G. Bain. 1983. Effects of Opiates on Rewarding Brain Stimulation. In J.E. Smith and J.D. Lane, eds., *The Neurobiology of Opiate Reward Processes*. New York: Elsevier Biomedical Press.

Kozlowski, L.T., and M.A. Harford. 1976. On the Significance of Never Using a Drug: An Example from Cigarette Smoking. *Journal of Abnormal Psychology* 85: 433–434.

LeBlanc, A.E., H. Kalant, and R.J. Gibbons. 1976. Acquisition and Loss of Behaviorally Augmented Tolerance to Ethanol in the Rat. *Psychopharmacology* 48: 153–158.

Marlatt, G.A., and J.R. Gordon. 1985. *Relapse Prevention*. New York: Guilford Press.

Mausner, B., and E.S. Platt. 1971. *Smoking: A Behavioral Analysis*. New York: Pergamon Press.

Meyer, R.E., and J.M. Mirin. 1979. *The Heroin Stimulus*. New York: Plenum Press.

Monti, P.M., J.A. Binkoff, D.B. Abrams, W.R. Zwick, T. Nirenberg, and M.R. Liepman. In press. Psychosocial Stress and Coping in Smokers Who Relapse or Quit. *Journal of Abnormal Psychology*.

Morley, J.E., A.S. Levine, G.K. Yim, and M.T. Lowy. 1983. Opioid Modulation of Appetite. *Neuroscience and Biobehavioral Reviews* 7:281–305.

Morrell, E.M., and J.G. Hollandsworth. 1986. Norepinephrine Alterations under Stress Conditions Following the Regular Practice of Mediation. *Psychosomatic Medicine* 48:270–276.

Myrsten, A.L., A. Elgerot, and B. Edgren. 1977. Effects of Abstinence from Tobacco Smoking on Physiological and Psychological Arousal Levels in Habitual Smokers. *Psychosomatic Medicine* 39:25–38.

O'Brien, C.P., R.N. Ehrman, and J.W. Ternes. 1986. Classical Conditioning in Human Opioid Dependence. In S.R. Goldberg and I.P. Stolerman, eds., *Behavioral Analysis of Drug Dependence*. New York: Academic Press.

O'Brien, C.P., and R. Greenstein. 1976. Naltrexone in a Behavioral Treatment Program. In D. Julius and P. Renault, eds., *Narcotic Antagonists: Naltrexone*. NIDA Monograph 9. Rockville, MD: National Institute on Drug Abuse.

Pechacek, T. 1986. Specialized Treatment for Highly Anxious Smokers. Paper presented at the Annual Meeting of the Association for the Advancement of Behavior Therapy, New York City.

Peele, S. 1985. *The Meaning of Addiction: Compulsive Experience and Its Interpretation*. Lexington, MA: Lexington Books.

Pomerleau, O.F. 1980. Why People Smoke: Current Psychobiological Theories. In P. Davidson, ed., *Behavioral Medicine: Changing Health Lifestyles*. New York: Brunner/Mazel.

———. 1981. Underlying Mechanisms in Substance Abuse: Examples from Research on Smoking. *Addictive Behaviors* 6:187–196.

———. 1986. Nicotine as a Psychoactive Drug: Anxiety and Pain Reduction. *Psychopharmacology Bulletin* 22:865–869.

Pomerleau, O.F., D. Adkins, and M. Perschuk. 1978. Predictors of Outcome and Recidivism in Smoking Cessation Treatment. *Addictive Behaviors* 3:65–70.

Pomerleau, O.F., J.B. Fertig, L. Baker, and N. Cooney. 1983a. Reactivity to Alcohol Cues in Alcoholics and Non-Alcoholics: Implications for a Stimulus Control Analysis of Drinking. *Addictive Behaviors* 8:1–10.

Pomerleau, O.F., J.B. Fertig, and S.O. Shanahan. 1983b. Nicotine Dependence in Cigarette Smoking: An Empirically Based, Multivariate Model. *Pharmacology Biochemistry and Behavior* 19:291–299.

Pomerleau, O.F., M. Pertschuk, and J. Stinnett. 1976. A Critical Examination of Some Current Assumptions in the Treatment of Alcoholism. *Journal of Studies on Alcohol* 37:849–867.

Pomerleau, O.F., and C.S. Pomerleau. 1984. Neuroregulators and the Reinforcement of Smoking: Towards a Biobehavioral Explanation. *Neuroscience and Biobehavioral Reviews* 8:503–513.

———. 1986. A Biobehavioral Perspective on Smoking. In T. Ney and A. Gale, eds., *Smoking and Human Behaviour*. Chichester, England: John Wiley & Sons.

Pomerleau, O.F., H.H. Scherzer, N.E. Grunberg, C.S. Pomerleau, J. Judge, J.B. Fertig, and J. Burleson. 1987. The Effects of Acute Exercise on Subsequent Cigarette Smoking. *Journal of Behavioral Medicine* 10:117–127.

Pomerleau, O.F., O.C. Turk, and J.B. Fertig. 1984. The Effects of Smoking on ACTH and Cortisol Secretion. *Life Sciences* 34:57–65.

Russell, M.A.H. 1977. Smoking Problems: An Overview. In M.J. Jarvik, J. Cullen, E. Gritz, T. Vogt, and L. West, eds., *Research on Smoking Behavior*. NIDA Research Monograph 17. Rockville, MD: National Institute on Drug Abuse.

Sanger, D.J. 1986. Drug Taking as Adjunctive Behavior. In J.R. Goldberg and I.P. Stolerman eds., *Behavioral Analysis of Drug Dependence*. New York: Academic Press.

Schachter, S. 1978. Pharmacological and Psychological Determinants of Smoking. *Annals of Internal Medicine* 88:104–114.

Schuster, C.R. 1986. Implications of Laboratory Research for the Treatment of Drug Dependence. In S.R. Goldberg and I.P. Stolerman, eds., *Behavioral Analysis of Drug Dependence*. New York: Academic Press.

Shiffman, S. 1982. Relapse Following Smoking Cessation: A Situational Analysis. *Journal of Consulting and Clinical Psychology* 50:71–86.

Siegel, S. 1983. Classical Conditioning, Drug Tolerance, and Drug Dependence. In R. Smart, F. Glaser, Y. Israel, H. Kalant, R. Popham, and R. Schmidt, eds.,

Research Advances in Alcohol and Drug Problems. New York: Plenum Publishing.

Singer, G., T.P.S. Oei, and M. Wallace. 1982. Schedule-Induced Self-Injection of Drugs. *Neuroscience and Biobehavioral Reviews* 6:77–83.

Skinner, B.F. 1953. *Science and Human Behavior.* New York: Macmillan.

Slifer, B.L. 1983. Schedule-Induction of Nicotine Self-Administration. *Pharmacology Biochemistry and Behavior* 19:1005–1009.

Smith, J.E. and D. Lane, eds. 1983. *The Neurobiology of Opiate Reward Processes.* New York: Elsevier Biomedical Press.

Spitzer, R.L. 1980. *Diagnostic and Statistical Manual.* 3rd ed. Washington, DC: American Psychiatric Association.

Stern, M.J., and P. Cleary. 1982. The National Exercise and Heart Disease Project: Long Term Psychosocial Outcome. *Archives of Internal Medicine* 142:1093–1097.

Stitzer, M.L., G.E. Bigelow, and I. Liebson. 1979. Reinforcement of Drug Abstinence: A Behavioral Approach to Drug Abuse Treatment. In N. Krasnegor, ed., *Behavioral Analysis and Treatment of Substance Abuse.* NIDA Research Monograph 25. Rockville, MD: National Institute on Drug Abuse.

Stolerman, I., T. Goldfarb, R. Fink, and M. Jarvik. 1973. Influencing Cigarette Smoking with Nicotine Antagonists. *Psychopharmacologia* 28:247–259.

Tiffany, S.T., and T.B. Baker. 1986. Tolerance to Alcohol: Psychological Models and Their Application to Alcoholism. *Annals of Behavioral Medicine* 8:7–12.

Wallace, M., and G. Singer. 1976. Adjunctive Behavior and Smoking Induced by a Maze Solving Schedule in Humans. *Physiology and Behavior* 17:849–852.

Wallace, R.K. 1970. *The Physiological Effects of Transcendental Meditation.* Los Angeles: Herbert Herz Co.

Weatherington, C.L. 1982. Is Adjunctive Behavior a Third Class of Behavior? *Neuroscience and Behavioral Reviews* 6:329–350.

Weisz, D.J., and R.F. Thompson. 1983. Endogenous Opioids: Brain Behavior Relations. In P.K. Levison, D.R. Gerstein, and D.R. Maloff, eds., *Commonalities in Substance Abuse and Addictive Behavior.* Lexington, MA: D.C. Heath.

Wikler, A. 1965. Conditioning Factors in Opiate Addiction and Relapse. In D. Wilner and G. Kassenbaum, eds., *Narcotics.* New York: McGraw Hill.

———. 1975. Opioid Antagonists and Deconditioning in Addiction Treatment. In H. Bostrom, T. Larsson, and N. Ljungstedt, eds., *Drug Dependence Treatment and Treatment Evaluation.* Stockholm: Almqvist and Wiksell.

———. 1976. The Theoretical Basis of Narcotic Addiction Treatment with Narcotic Antagonists. In O. Julius and P. Renault, eds., *Narcotic Antagonists: Naltrexone.* NIDA Monograph 9. Rockville, MD: National Institute of Drug Abuse.

Williams, R.B., J.D. Lane, C.M. Kuhn, W. Melosh, A.D. White, and S.M. Schaneberg. 1982. Type A Behavior and Elevated Physiological and Neuroendocrine Responses to Cognitive Tasks. *Science* 218:483–485.

Wolkowitz, O.W., A. Roy, and A.R. Doran. 1985. Pathologic Gambling and Other Risk-Taking Pursuits. *Psychiatric Clinics of North America* 8:311–322.

World Health Organization. 1969. *Technical Report Series,* No. 407. Geneva, Switzerland.

Wray, I., and M.G. Dickerson. 1981. Cessation of High Frequency Gambling and "Withdrawal" Symptoms. *British Journal of Addiction* 76:401–405.

Wu, K.M., and W.R. Martin. 1983. An Analysis of Nicotinic and Opioid Processes in the Medulla Oblongata and Nucleus Ambiguus of the Dog. *Journal of Pharmacology and Experimental Therapeutics* 227:302–307.

7

Common Elements in Youth Drug Abuse: Peer Clusters and Other Psychosocial Factors

E.R. Oetting
Fred Beauvais

Nearly all drug use begins in the preadolescent or adolescent years. Kandel (1978), for example, has shown that it is rare for anyone to try a new drug after age 21, and Oetting and Beauvais (1983) point out that drug acquisition curves, showing how a youth cohort acquires exposure to an illicit drug, begin a negative acceleration around age 16 and probably reach an asymptote soon after that. These findings provide evidence that, even though serious drug problems and alcoholism may emerge later in life, those problems probably had roots reaching back to the adolescent years.

Theories of Drug Use

Why do some young people get unhealthily involved with alcohol and drugs while others do not? In general, there are two types of theories: (1) theories that focus on the effects of drugs, viewing drug use as deriving predominantly from the characteristics or effects of drugs, and (2) theories that focus on the social and psychological causes of drug use.

Drug Effect Theories

Two general types of theories emphasize the effects of drugs; physiologically oriented disease/addiction theories (discussed and effectively countered by Peele, 1985) and the various "gateway" theories that make a major point of the regular progression from one drug to another (Dupont, 1984; Kandel et al., 1978; Mills and Noyes, 1984; O'Donnell and Clayton, 1982). Theoretical models that focus exclusively on the addictive effects of drugs do not adequately explain drug abuse by youth. Nearly all young people, for example, take drugs sporadically and rarely take enough of a given drug to lead to the increased tolerance, withdrawal symptoms, and compulsive use that classically mark addiction (Bejerot, 1980). Furthermore, as Peele (1985) cogently argues, addiction is strongly influenced by social, cultural, and psychological factors.

The gateway theories do not hold up well either, particularly when they suggest that it is the physiological response to one drug that leads a youth to use a more serious drug. The temporal relationships in drug use, for example, are not completely consistent, with one drug serving universally as a "gateway" to use of other drugs, and, in fact, the temporal relationships that do exist can be explained in ways that do not relate to the specific effects of the drugs involved. For example, if we look at a list of drugs as if it were a "menu" and visualize a youth who is interested in taking drugs, what are the first questions that the youth is likely to ask? "What drug can I get? How dangerous is it? What are my friends using? What will my friends think of me if I use it?" and so on. It is easy to see how, in answer to these questions, beer would be chosen easily, marijuana with a bit more difficulty, and heroin very rarely. Whatever orderly progression does exist in the use of drugs is probably highly related to availability and general attitudes toward drugs.

Despite the limitations of theories that view patterns of drug use only as an outcome of taking drugs, it is obvious that taking drugs does influence future drug use. Drugs have psychoactive properties that lead to sensations that can be rewarding, and using drugs can, under some circumstances, lead to a mixture of physiological, social, and psychological dependence. These factors, however, are less important in determining youth drug involvement than psychosocial variables.

Psychological and Social Theories

In general, the psychosocial theories do a better job of describing the underpinnings of drug use by youth. They help explain why drugs are tried in the first place and define the conditions under which continuing and increasing drug use occurs. Numerous research studies show that drug use relates to a wide range of social, cultural, and psychological characteristics. For youth, the social effects from taking drugs are also likely to be more important than the physiological effects. Drugs, for example, can be used as a means of coping with problems to such an extent that the development of more effective coping methods is limited. Taking drugs also places the youth in drug using contexts, where other drugs are more available and there are greater opportunities for other types of deviant behavior. Using drugs can also isolate a youth from the segments of society that might influence that youth in positive ways, for example, from parents and teachers.

Penning and Barnes (1982) reviewed studies of the correlates of marijuana use and showed that drug use is significantly related to a long list of social and psychological variables. The various types of theories draw on subsets of these variables to explain drug abuse. They roughly fall into three groups: social theories, psychological theories, and psychosocial theories.

Social Theories. Social theories such as Parson's structural-functionalism, for instance, explain drug use as a symptom of underlying social problems (Jacobs, 1977; Lukoff, 1980). Another type of social model views alcohol or drug use as a result of acculturation stress in minorities (Graves, 1967; Levy and Kunitz, 1971; Madsen, 1964; May, 1981). Prior to the 1960s, when drug use was identified predominantly with minority ghetto populations, it made considerable sense to view drug use within this framework, but drug use is now a more general phenomenon, reaching every social group and socioeconomic class. It is hard to conceive of a simple model dominated by social disorganization, acculturation, or society's needs that would explain the range of drug involvement now found among young people of all social groups.

Psychological Theories. Psychological theories tend to ignore social factors and to see drug use as meeting personal needs or compensating for personal problems. Among these models, psychodynamic theories suggest that the specific action of the drug fills a very important void in a person's development or life (Gold, 1980; Khantzian, 1980; Spotts and Schontz, 1980, 1984a, 1984b). In some extreme cases, where there is an obsession with a particular drug, psychodynamic models may fit a particular clinical case, but the drug use of most adolescents does not match this pattern because (1) there does not seem to be a dependence on only one type of drug, and, in fact, most drug-involved youth take a variety of different drugs, (2) drugs are used sporadically, not consistently, and (3) drugs are taken primarily in socially defined contexts.

Another psychological approach is to correlate personality traits with drug use. Although drug use does bear some relationship to personality, significant relationships are not found consistently, differences do not always occur in the expected direction, and where correlations are found they usually account only for very small part of the variance in drug use even when they are combined as multivariate predictors. Fisher (1975:36), in a National Institute on Drug Abuse publication, stated "the history of behavioral prediction studies compels us to expect that if marihuana abuse is what we are trying to predict, no personality measures, singly or in linear or nonlinear combination with other personality measures, will yield very high prediction coefficients."

Psychosocial Theories. Psychosocial theories are more successful in describing and predicting drug use. They have the advantage of including both the social environment and characteristics of the person. Jessor and his colleagues have provided the most influential of these theories. (Donovan and Jessor, 1978, 1985; Jessor, Chase, and Donovan, 1980; Jessor, Donovan, and Widmer, 1980; Jessor and Jessor, 1977). Jessor's social learning theory postulates that personality, environment, and behavior are interrelated to develop a state called "problem-behavior proneness." Drug use is one reflection of a tendency to depart from regulatory norms.

Our own model, peer cluster theory, is similar to that of Jessor and his colleagues in that we see a wide range of social and psychological characteristics interacting either to create a potential for drug involvement or to inoculate a youth, protecting that youth from drug use. Jessor, however, while recognizing that peer influences are important, does not place peer relationships in the distinctive and essential position that we believe they deserve. Our peer cluster theory, in contrast to other psychosocial theories, states unequivocally that other variables only set the stage for drug use, that initiation and maintenance of drug use among adolescents is almost entirely a function of peer clusters.

Peer clusters are small groups of people, including a youth's "gang," and also including dyads such as "best friends" and "couples." Within these peer clusters, drug use can play an important role in group membership and identification. In the peer cluster drugs are made available, a youth learns to use drugs, and there is a sharing of beliefs, values, and attitudes and of the rationales for drug use.

We are not alone in our emphasis on peers as a major factor in adolescent drug use. Walters (1980), for example, defined three major adolescent lifestyle types: "rowdies," "straights," and "cools." His model is appealing because we all know these types, but his types are too few and too stereotyped to be useful, and his theory does not point to the critical importance of the small, tight groups that truly define drug use, the peer clusters. Differential association theory (Griffin and Griffin, 1978–79) also points to the importance of peer associations but similarly does not emphasize the critical role of the peer cluster, nor does it detail the specific function of other psychosocial characteristics in determining whether youth will become involved with drug using peer clusters.

Peer cluster theory is not, however, radically different than other psychosocial theories. Nearly all psychosocial theories of drug use seem to be rapidly moving toward a consensus, one that agrees generally, if not in detail, with our model. The following quotations illustrate the awareness, in a wide variety of different theories, of the critical importance of peers.

> The consistently important predictive value of perceived friend's drug use on a person's use should be considered. . . . In terms of prevention, the significance of peer influences in leading persons to use drugs is a strong argument for utilizing peer facilitators in attempting to reduce drug use in groups and neighborhoods (Clayton and Lacy, 1982:664).

Peer related factors are consistently the strongest predictors of subsequent alcohol and marijuana use, even when other factors are controlled (Kandel, 1980:269).

Use of a drug . . . is a decision taking place within a social context of peer influence (Reed, 1980:363).

One of the most promising approaches to understanding the origins of an individual's drug use is examination of drug use by significant others in the individual's life. Numerous studies have demonstrated an association between parent's drug use and that of their adolescent offspring.

Some of these and other studies have also found an even stronger relationship between adolescents' drug use and that of their peers (Apsler and Blackman, 1979:291).

Since involvement with illegal drugs is assumed to begin with the peer group, the fact that by the eleventh grade a majority of these Ss believe, correctly or incorrectly, that their friends are using illegal psychoactive substances constitutes indirect pressure on them. Their perceptions of peer drug use may be inflated, but if this variable is as important as some researchers suggest, it may be the crucial factor in adolescents' drug use (Sorosiak et al., 1976:215).

The peer group clearly has a significantly greater relationship with a college student's marijuana use than does the parent's use of psychoactive drugs and abuse of alcohol (Ellis and Stone, 1979:331).

Peer Cluster Theory

Peer cluster theory begins by postulating a set of psychosocial forces that make some youth particularly susceptible to drug involvement, or that, alternatively, prevent drug involvement. Many of these characteristics are social, part of the youth's environment. Others are internal to the person: personality characteristics, attitudes, and beliefs. These psychosocial factors can interact so that a youth chooses friends who also have problems with social and or personal adjustment. When that happens, drug use is likely. Positive influences from these factors can, on the other hand, lead to building friendships with other youth who have little tendency to get involved with drugs.

The underlying psychosocial factors create the potential for drug use, but that potential is almost always realized through contact with peers, through other young people, siblings, and friends who are approximately the same age as the youth and who have close associations with the youth. When drugs are actually used, it is almost always in a peer context. Peers initiate the youth into drugs. Peers help provide drugs. Peers talk with each other about drugs and model drug using behaviors for each other and in doing so shape attitudes about drugs and drug-using behaviors. A peer cluster consensus is reached about where and when drugs are to be used, about how much to use drugs, and even about how drugs affect you emotionally and how you behave when you take particular drugs. The influence of a peer cluster can also be positive—a group of friends can reject use of alcohol and drugs, and that group will together develop attitudes, values, and rationales that counter the use of drugs and alcohol.

Among adolescents, nearly all drug use occurs with peers, but even when drugs are used alone, it can be a function of the peer cluster. We find, for example, that a youth who uses a drug when alone almost invariably also uses that same drug with peers. The peer cluster also has a direct influence on when and where drugs are used alone. Using a drug when alone is frequently a function of attitudes and beliefs shared within the peer cluster. Ideas about drugs, such as "uppers help you study," or "marijuana will 'cool you out' if you have a fight with your parents," are developed and maintained within the peer cluster. There are, of course, exceptions that occur when a youth becomes obsessed with the action of a particular drug and takes it constantly even when others in the peer cluster do not. These exceptions, however, are very rare. Even heroin users in a ghetto or barrio street gang generally form a small subset within that gang, a peer cluster that is marked by its use of heroin.

Other terms have been used to discuss and define peer relationships, but they do not have the same meaning as *peer cluster*. A *drug lifestyle,* for example, could define a peer cluster, but *lifestyle* is a broad and general term that indicates drugs play a meaningful part in the life of a youth. Two youths could both have a drug-oriented lifestyle, but differ radically in their use of drugs. In contrast, members of a peer cluster usually are very similar in their drug use.

A *peer group* is a general grouping and would include any of the groups that a youth could identify with, for example, the eighth grade or the football team. Unlike these others, the peer cluster is one specific type of peer group. It is small, cohesive, marked by closely shared attitudes and beliefs, and, in the more deviant peer clusters, by shared use of drugs.

Peer pressure also has different connotations. It implies either a general attitude in an entire age cohort toward drugs or implies that an innocent youth is being coerced into taking drugs by a "pusher" or by deviant companions. The youth in a peer cluster is not an innocent victim, but is a part of the cluster, helping shape its attitudes and behaviors, equally a recipient and a source of drug encouragement.

Peer cluster theory grew out of a major effort to understand drug use of both minority and nonminority youth. In the last twelve years, funded by the National Institute on Drug Abuse, we have administered a variety of drug use surveys to more than 15,000 minority youth, mostly Native Americans living on reservations, but including significant numbers of southwestern Hispanic youth (Beauvais et al., 1985a; Chavez et al., in press; Oetting et al., 1980; Oetting and Beauvais, 1985; Oetting and Goldstein, 1979). We have also gathered data on more than 10,000 nonminority youth (Oetting et al., 1984a, 1984b) and several hundred youth in treatment for drug abuse problems (Oetting and Beauvais, in press–a. in press–b).

Although we have some longitudinal data, most of our insights have come from cross-sectional data. Our studies gradually led us to the conviction that the single dominating psychosocial factor in both minority and nonminority drug use was peer influence. Interviews with young people and other literature on youth cliques and gangs led to a conviction that the peer cluster was the major mediating factor in youth drug involvement. Typical examples would be recognized by most drug counselors: (1) Gangs of high school girls experiment together with alcohol and marijuana and use them at parties; (2) a ninth-grade youth with a high tendency for deviance joins a drug using gang and rapidly imitates the drug use of the gang; (3) best friends gradually take up drugs together, getting more and more seriously involved; (4) a boy introduces his girlfriend to drugs and shares drugs with her. Our statistical data also strongly confirm the basic principle that peer clusters mediate drug involvement. We find, for example, that peer drug associations are more highly related to drug use than any other psychosocial variable and, further, that the relationships between other psychosocial characteristics and drug use can be essentially accounted for by their influence on peer drug associations (Oetting and Beauvais, in press a).

Certainly peer cluster theory cannot be considered a fully confirmed position. There are many aspects that need to be examined and tested—for example, our conviction that the peer cluster is a major mechanism for developing and testing personal attitudes, beliefs, and values during adolescent years and that drug use is linked to this more general process. We also believe that the potency of the peer cluster may derive, in part, from the adolescent's move toward independence, the resulting loss of the family as a source of support, values, and role norming, and substitution of the peer cluster to meet these developmental needs. We need much more data to confirm these hypotheses about the dynamics of the peer cluster.

As a model, however, we believe that peer cluster theory has considerable vitality. It fits findings from many research studies and, moreover, explains them. It fits observational data and personal experience about relationships among adolescents. It leads to a very wide range of testable hypotheses. It yields specific implications for prevention, treatment, and research. It describes most clinical cases accurately, and although occasionally peer cluster theory does not seem to apply, the exceptions are rare and the lack of peer cluster involvement seems to mark only the most deviant and the most serious patterns of drug involvement.

Psychosocial Links to Drug Use

Peer cluster theory emphasizes the dominance of peer relationships, but it does not eliminate the need to consider other psychosocial factors. In a way, we have only moved the problem one step back. We still need to know what factors create susceptibility to drug use and thereby encourage involvement with drug using peer clusters. The literature shows that a very large array of psychosocial factors do seem to influence drug involvement.

We have developed short scales to assess many of these variables—scales with reliability generally in the high .70s and .80s, with discriminating cluster structures, and that show significant correlations with drug involvement (Oetting et al., 1984b). We are now building models that look at how these characteristics interact with each other to create the potential for drug involvement. In the next sections, we will discuss these characteristics and will show how we feel that the variables may link together to lead to drug use. The diagrams and discussion may provide some insight into youth drug abuse and suggest prevention, treatment, and research possibilities. For convenience and simplicity, we will separately discuss three different dimensions of variables: socialization characteristics, psychological factors, and environmental and socioeconomic factors.

Socialization Characteristics

There are a number of major socialization links that connect a youth to society and to society's values. They influence the youth in a variety of ways that can have either positive or negative effects. Included are the community, the family, religion, the school, and peers. An added factor for older youth would be work. We have already indicated that the major direct factor in drug use is peers, but how do these other socialization variables interact to make a youth susceptible to peer drug associations? Figure 7–1 presents a model that shows how we believe four of these socialization variables link together.

The model shows family strength as a key and fundamental characteristic countering drug use, radiating its possible effects in many directions: improving school adjustment, enhancing religious identification, creating strong family sanctions against drug use, and having other effects as well. These other characteristics, in turn, reduce the chance that a youth will become involved with peer clusters that use drugs.

The socialization model that we have drawn does not, as yet, include community and work influences. Community effects are related to drug use. They are, however, strongly related to socioeconomic status and will be discussed later in conjunction with that concept. The work environment has an influence on drug use but is not included in the model because we are still

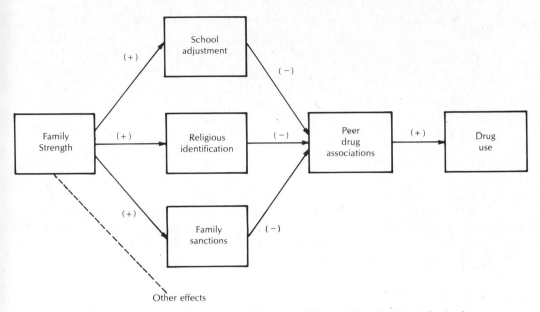

Figure 7–1. Socialization Characteristics and Drug Use: A Hypothetical Path Model

considering how it interacts with other variables. For youth, unfortunately, the effect of work on drug use is likely to be negative. Most of us who value work might assume that a youth who works learns positive work values and the value of effort. If that were true, working youth should avoid drugs, but instead youth who work tend to use drugs more than nonworking youth (Bachman et al., 1980). Although all youth who work do not get drug involved, many working youth do, perhaps only when the following conditions apply: (1) A youth is working because of poor school adjustment, i.e., is a dropout or a part-time student; (2) the working youth is already drug involved, and the money earned allows increased drug purchases; (3) the poor quality of the job that an untrained and inexperienced youth can get leads to associations on the job with other youth and perhaps with young adults who have work adjustment problems and who use drugs.

The Family. Drug use is likely to be higher when a family is not intact, when the youth has not been living with the parents, when family relationships are poor, and when the family does not apply strong sanctions against drug use (Adler and Lotecka, 1973; Blumenfield et al., 1972; Brook et al., 1977; Frumkin et al., 1969; Galli and Stone, 1975; Green et al., 1973; Oetting and Goldstein, 1979; Pandina and Scheule, 1983; Streit et al., 1974; Tec, 1974; Tolone and Dermott, 1975).

A strong family, as we measure it, means that the youth feels that the family cares. Family strength is further increased if the family is intact. Strong family sanctions against drugs are characteristic of strong families and help lead to associations with peers who also have strong sanctions against drugs. The model shows that a strong family also improves the chances for good school adjustment and that high religious identification is more likely to occur when the family is strong. Both of these factors also reduce the chances that a youth will associate with drug using peers. The strong family probably has other effects as well, factors that we have not yet explored.

Family disruption can clearly be a major underlying factor in drug abuse, but the influence is likely to be indirect, through the effect that family problems have on other characteristics. Peer cluster theory suggests that, if family therapy is to have any influence on drug use, it either has to influence peer associations or has to occur early enough so that the improved family adjustment has time to influence school success and other variables that will in turn affect peer drug associations.

Religious Identification. Religious identification of younger children is probably rooted in the family's religious orientation. Later, it seems to become a more individual matter and may be more highly related to religious identification of a youth's peers. The religious youth is less likely to use drugs (Bogg and Hughes, 1973; Brook et al., 1977; Jessor, 1976; Jessor et al., 1973; Rohrbaugh and Jessor, 1975; Turner and Willis, 1984). Peer cluster theory and the model derived from that theory and presented in figure 7–1 suggest that an underlying reason is that the religious youth is likely to build associations with peers who share similar values, who are less deviant, and who do not use drugs.

School Adjustment. There is almost invariably a relatively high relationship between school problems and drug use (Annis and Watson, 1975; Bakal et al., 1975; Brook et al., 1977; Clayton and Voss, 1982; Frumkin et al., 1969; Galli, 1974; Jessor, 1976; Kandel, 1975; Svobodny, 1982). The public perception is that drug use is the cause of school problems, and there is little doubt that a youth who is high on marijuana all day long cannot concentrate enough to do good work in school. But peer cluster theory and figure 7–1 suggest a more indirect relationship may be important—that school problems may predate drug involvement and that difficulties in school adjustment lead to drug use through increasing the chances that a youth will associate with other youth who are drug prone.

Why would school problems increase the chances of peer drug associations? The major factor may be agglutination, the tendency for youth with like values, attitudes and beliefs to seek each other out. Youth who dislike school may have a tendency to form peer clusters. Together, these youth then seek other sources of reinforcement, including deviance and drugs. In contrast, youth who do well in school may form peer clusters with more positive aspects, groups that do not move toward drug use.

The school may, without intending to, encourage this grouping. Through unconscious prejudice, youth with disadvantaged backgrounds, particularly if they are minorities, may be placed together in certain tracks or in remedial classes. Detention, as a punishment, may also bring youth together who have problems. In contrast, successful youth may be brought together in debate, Latin, drama, music, and may associate in certain school clubs or organizations. Peer cluster theory suggests that schools should carefully examine their policies and procedures to determine whether they are unintentionally encouraging the formation of peer clusters that have negative school adjustment and accordingly an increased chance of drug involvement.

Psychological Characteristics

A persistent theory is that youth take drugs because they feel bad and keep taking drugs because drugs mitigate those negative feelings—various personality traits are, therefore, seen as the primary causes of drug use—most often low-self esteem, depression or anxiety. Drug using youth seem to corroborate part of this theory. We find that at least one-third of young drug users say they may take a drug when they are depressed, when they are anxious, or when they are uncomfortable in a social situation.

The next part of the theory, however, does not hold up well. Although there are correlations between personality traits and drug use, those correlations tend to be very small (on the order of .10), and are not always found to be significant (Fisher, 1975; Mirin et al., 1971; Riggs, 1973; Sorosiak et al., 1976; Wingard et al., 1979). At first glance, these findings seem to be contradictory, i.e., youth use drugs because they are depressed, but depressed youth do not necessarily use drugs. All of the findings make sense, however, when we consider that a youth who is not chronically depressed may still get depressed at times, and, if that youth uses drugs, may take a drug when depressed.

The literature and our own findings both show that young people who have low self-esteem and/or who are chronically anxious or depressed are only very slightly more likely to use drugs than other youth. We have, however, found a fairly high correlation between drug use and chronic anger (averaging .25 in various samples). We cannot confirm this finding from other studies because, for some reason, anger has rarely been examined as a factor in drug involvement. Putting together other research and our own findings, figure 7–2 shows how we believe psychological characteristics may link to drug involvement.

Figure 7–2 shows self-esteem as a very fundamental psychological char-

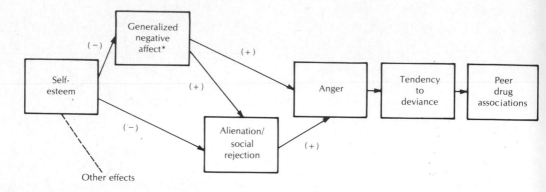

Note: *Anxiety, Depression, Feels blamed, Introversion

Figure 7–2. Psychological Characteristics and Drug Use: A Hypothetical Path Model

acteristic, influencing many other traits. Among those traits, we list general negative affect, including depression, anxiety, feeling blamed, and introversion. We lump them together because, in young people, there are very high correlations among these traits and because the effect on drug use seems to be about the same irrespective of the problem. Whatever the problem, when that problem leads to feelings of social rejection or leads directly to chronic anger, it increases the chances that a youth will tend to deviate and will associate with peers who are also deviant and who use drugs.

In summary, although there are links between personality and drug use, the idea that youth with personality problems take drugs to assuage negative feelings does not hold up well. Many youth do self-medicate with drugs but not necessarily because of chronic personality problems. The traits that are most often viewed as root causes of drug use—self-esteem, depression, and anxiety—are connected only minimally and indirectly to drug involvement. On the other hand, anger, a trait that has not often been studied, seems to be a moderately important correlate of drug use—leading to increased probability of deviance and of associating with drug-using peers.

Socioeconomic and Environmental Characteristics

General population studies do not find a consistent link between socioeconomic status and drug use (Penning and Barnes, 1982; Jessor and Jessor, 1977; Johnston, 1973). These studies, however, focus on middle and upper levels of socioeconomic status and disadvantaged populations are under-represented. Where research is conducted specifically among disadvantaged youth, particularly minority youth, higher rates of drug use are found and can be attributed to the effects of very low socioeconomic status (Beauvais et al., 1985b, Brunswick, 1979; Padilla et al., 1979). It appears that above a certain level of socioeconomic status this factor has little influence on drug use, but it can be a critical factor when socioeconomic status is very low. Prejudice and isolation are also related to disadvantagement so that a number of elements may work together to produce conditions leading to youth drug abuse.

Figure 7–3 presents a partial model showing how these factors might influence drug use. This figure represents our current thinking, but we have not completed as many analyses in this area as we have in the areas of socialization and psychological characteristics so that the model may be logical but the hypotheses are only tentative.

Socioeconomic status of the family, particularly when it is very low, can be a very important and very basic characteristic. It can be shown to affect family strength, which we have already discussed as playing a central role in drug use. Higher socioeconomic status of the family is also directly related to improved school adjustment. The paths from these factors to drug use have already been discussed above.

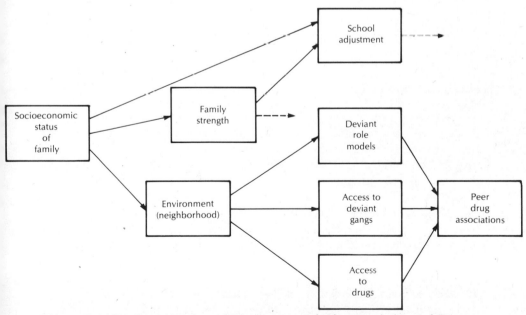

Figure 7–3. Socioeconomic and Environmental Characteristics and Drug Use: A Hypothetical Path Model

Socioeconomic status, however, also influences where a family can live. When the family is poor it is likely to be forced to live in an environment that encourages drug abuse. Figure 7–3 suggests that the worst environments may influence drug use in several ways: (1) They show a youth deviant role models, such as drug-using gang leaders or drug distributors who have money, women, and cars; (2) they provide greater access to drugs; (3) they may even force a youth to join deviant neighborhood gangs.

Although we have not included ethnicity in this model, these effects may be particularly strong when poverty is accompanied by being identified as a minority in a community where groups of minorities live in economically and physically isolated areas such as barrios, ghettos, or Indian reservations (Beauvais et al., 1985b; Brunswick, 1979; Oetting and Goldstein, 1979; Padilla et al., 1979; Simpson and de Barona, 1983). In fact, we believe that socioeconomic status and environment may account for most of the differences between ethnic groups that are typically reported in the literature. Liban and Smart (1982) tend to confirm this in a very important study, showing that the differences in drug use between Anglo and Indian youth disappeared when the Indian youth were matched with Anglos on socioeconomic variables.

Reciprocal Relationships

The path models that we have drawn here are simplified and involve only one direction of influence. These models allow us to discuss the underlying structure, showing the dominant ways that psychosocial characteristics interact to lead to drug abuse. Although this underlying structure is probably reasonably accurate, a complete picture of drug involvement would be much more complex. It would have to involve a whole series of reciprocal relationships. A major factor would be the interactive effects of taking drugs on the characteristics that underlie and lead to drug use. For example, family problems may temporally precede and be an important factor in a youth's choice of drug-oriented friends, but those friends can increase a youth's distance from the family by encouraging rebellion and hostility. Then, as the youth begins to use drugs, drug use can add further to family problems.

Similarly, poor school adjustment can lead to association with peers who have similar problems. The group can then mutually encourage and support negative school attitudes, and the use of drugs can move the group even further from potentially positive associations with teachers and other peers. Despite the existence of these reciprocal relationships, the primary influences are likely to be in the directions we have charted in these figures. Both family and school adjustment problems do tend to precede and set the stage for involvement of a youth with peers who have a penchant for drug abuse.

Summary

The paths to drug abuse that we have charted have certain common patterns. Most important, from the point of view of peer cluster theory, is that they all lead to drug use through their influence on peer drug associations. This central and mediating role of the peer cluster has implications for both treatment and prevention.

Peer cluster theory, for example, indicates that if treatment of an adolescent is to be effective, it must somehow influence the peer cluster—either the peer cluster must be changed or the youth must be isolated from the influence of the peer cluster. Treatments that focus only on the psychodynamics of the individual or on teaching a youth to deal with addiction are going to be blocked by the power of the peer cluster to encourage and maintain a youth's drug use. Inpatient treatments that remove a youth from the peer cluster may work until the youth is returned to the home environment, and therefore to the original drug involved peer cluster.

Prevention programs must also take peer clusters into account. Peer cluster theory suggests that other psychosocial characteristics can be important factors in leading to drug use but that they will influence drug use only through their effect on the kinds of peers that a youth chooses for friends or through creating movement toward drugs within the peer cluster. Prevention programs aimed at correlates of drug use other than peer associations should be modified to assure that whatever changes occur, they will also influence peer clusters. The effects of prevention programs will only be felt if they either lead to a choice of peers who discourage drug use or lead to development of antidrug attitudes within peer clusters.

There is a more subtle common pattern in these paths that may be important. There are some characteristics that seem to be very central, that influence not just one thing, but seem to have an effect on a whole range of other characteristics. The family appears in this role in figure 7–1, self-esteem in figure 7–2, and socioeconomic status in figure 7–3. The influence of these characteristics seems to be pervasive, and therefore important, but at the same time the influence is several steps away from drug use. The suggestion, implicit in these diagrams, is that prevention programs aimed at these characteristics might be highly potent, that they could lead to effects on many other factors that could then influence drug use. At the same time, however, the diagrams show that, until prevention efforts have time to influence these other variables, and these in turn to influence drug use, an effect on drug use is unlikely. By the time a youth is already drug involved, treating drug use by trying to change these characteristics may be ineffective, and even prevention programs aimed at these factors may have to start very early to provide time for their effects to be felt.

A general rule would be that, when involved in treatment, the therapist should work back through the paths, dealing first with the characteristic that is most proximal to drug use, the peer cluster, and then working back to the next levels. By contrast, in prevention the time that is available dictates where a prevention program must start. When dealing with younger children, basic factors such as the family and self-esteem might provide good starting points, and there would be enough time for those fundamental factors to influence school adjustment or anger, which in turn would influence drug orientation of the peer cluster. With older adolescents or young adults, family disruption or low self-esteem may have already had major effects on other variables that occur later in the diagram, and prevention may have to aim at different and more immediate goals.

These paths to drug abuse are correlational effects that are seen across groups of youth. Any individual clinical case is likely to show a unique pattern of psychosocial problems, difficulties that should be considered in trying to understand the young person and plan treatment for that person. Even clients with relatively serious drug problems will not have problems in every area that we have discussed; they do, however, tend to have more problems and more serious problems than less drug-involved people. The one feature that is consistent in every clinical case is the presence of peer-drug associations. The young person's pattern of drug use is matched, almost point by point, by shared drug use with his or her "gang," best friend, and/or boyfriend/girlfriend.

The path models that we have presented here are logical, they are consistent with much of the literature, and they fit well with our own data. They could, however, change radically as we learn more about youth drug abuse. Changes of that kind are expected, and would not challenge the basis of peer cluster theory. Whatever changes occur, however, we are convinced of two fundamental points. First, drug use by youth is best understood as an outcome of psychosocial forces, and not as a result of the physiological effects of drugs. Second, the dominating factor in drug abuse is the peer cluster, and other psychosocial characteristics influence drug use primarily through their effects on peer clusters.

References

Adler, P.T., and L. Lotecka. 1973. Drug Use among High School Students: Patterns and Correlates. *International Journal of the Addictions* 8:537–548.

Annis, H.M., and C. Watson. 1975. Drug Use and School Dropout: A Longitudinal Study. *Canadian Counsellor* 9:155–162.

Apsler, Robert, and C. Blackman. 1979. Adults' Drug Use: Relationship to Perceived Drug Use of Parents, Friends While Growing Up, and Present Friends. *American Journal of Drug and Alcohol Abuse* 6:291–300.

Bachman, J.G., P.M. O'Malley, and L.D. Johnston. 1980. *Correlates of Drug Use, Part I: Selected Measures of Background, Recent Experiences, and Lifestyle Orientations.* Monitoring the Future: Occasional Paper 8. Ann Arbor, MI: Institute For Social Research, University of Michigan.

Bakal, D., S.L. Milstein, and I. Rootman. 1975. Trends in Drug Use Among Rural Students in Alberta: 1971–1974. *Canadian Mental Health* 23:8–9.

Beauvais, F., E.R. Oetting, and R.W. Edwards. 1985a. Trends in the Use of Inhalants Among American Indian Adolescents. *White Cloud Journal* 3(4): 3–11.

———. 1985b. Trends in Drug Use of Indian Adolescents Living on Reservations: 1975–1983. *American Journal of Drug and Alcohol Abuse* 11:209–230.

Bejerot, N. 1980. Addiction to Pleasure: A Biological and Social-Psychological Theory of Addiction. In D.J. Lettieri, M. Sayers, and H.W. Pearson, eds., *Theories on Drug Abuse: Selected Contemporary Perspectives.* NIDA Research Monograph 30. Rockville, MD: National Institute on Drug Abuse.

Blumenfield, M., A.E. Riester, A.C. Serrano, and R.L. Adams. 1972. Marijuana Use in High School Students. *Diseases of the Nervous System* 33(9).

Bogg, R.A., and J. Hughes. 1973. Correlates of Marijuana Usage at a Canadian Technological Institute. *International Journal of the Addictions* 8:489–504.

Brook, J.S., I.F. Lukoff, and M. Whiteman. 1977. Correlates of Marijuana Use as Related to Age, Sex, and Ethnicity. *Yale Journal of Biological Medicine* 50: 383–390.

Brunswick, A. 1979. Black Youths and Drug-Use Behavior. In G.M. Beschner and A.S. Friedman, eds., *Youth Drug Abuse: Problems, Issues and Treatment.* Toronto: D.C. Heath.

Chavez, E., E.R. Oetting, and F. Beauvais. In press. Drug Use by Small Town Mexican-American Youth: A Review and Pilot Study. *Hispanic Journal of Behavioral Sciences.*

Clayton, Richard R., and W.B. Lacy. 1982. Interpersonal Influences on Male Drug Use and Drug Use Intentions. *International Journal of Addiction* 17:655–666.

Clayton, R.R., and H.R. Voss. 1982. *Technical Review on Drug Abuse and Dropouts.* Report on a National Institute on Drug Abuse technical review meeting. Rockville, MD: National Institute on Drug Abuse.

Donovan, J.E., and R. Jessor. 1978. Adolescent Problem Drinking: Psychosocial Correlates in a National Sample Study. *Journal of Studies on Alcohol* 39: 1506–1524.

———. 1985. The Structure of Problem Behavior in Adolescence and Young Adulthood. *Journal of Consulting and Clinical Psychology* 53:890–904.

Dupont, R.L. 1984. *Getting Tough on Gateway Drugs.* Washington, DC: American Psychiatric Press.

Ellis, G.J., and L.H. Stone. 1979. Marijuana Use in College: An Evaluation of a Modeling Explanation. *Youth and Society* 10:323–334.

Fisher, S. 1975. The Quest for Predictors of Marijuana Abuse in Adolescents. In D.J. Lettieri, ed., *Predicting Adolescent Drug Abuse: A Review of Issues, Methods and Correlates.* DHEW Publication No. ADM 76-299. Rockville, MD: National Institute on Drug Abuse.

Frumkin, R.M., R.A. Cowan, and J.R. Davis. 1969. Drug Use in a Midwest Sample of Metropolitan Hinterland High School Students. *Corrective Psychology* 15:8–13.

Galli, N. 1974. Patterns of Student Drug Use. *Journal of Drug Education* 4:237–248.

Galli, N., and D.B. Stone. 1975. Psychological Status of Student Drug Users. *Journal of Drug Education* 5:327–333.

Gold, S.R. 1980. The CAP Control Theory of Drug Abuse. In D.J. Lettieri, M. Sayers, and H.W. Pearson, eds., *Theories on Drug Abuse: Selected Contemporary Perspectives.* NIDA Research Monograph 30. Rockville, MD: National Institute on Drug Abuse.

Graves, T.P. 1967. Psychological Acculturation in a Tri-ethnic Community. *Southwestern Journal of Anthropology* 23:337–350.

Green, M.G., B.F. Blake, and R.T. Zenhausern. 1973. Some Implications of a Survey of Marijuana Usage by Middle Class High School Drug Users. In *Proceedings of the 81st Annual Convention of the American Psychological Association,* 679–680, Montreal, Canada.

Griffin, B.S., and C.T. Griffin. 1978–79. Drug Use and Differential Association. *Drug Forum* 7:1–8.

Jacobs, P.E. 1977. Epidemiology Abuse: Epidemiological and Psychosocial Models. In J. Fishman, ed., *The Bases of Addiction.* Berlin: Bernhard, Dahlen, Konferenzen.

Jessor, R. 1976. Predicting Time of Onset of Marijuana Use: A Developmental Study of High School Youth. *Journal of Consulting and Clinical Psychology* 44:125–134.

Jessor, R., J.D. Chase, and J.E. Donovan. 1980. Psychosocial Correlates of Marijuana Use and Problem Drinking in a National Sample of Adolescents. *American Journal of Public Health* 70:604–613.

Jessor, R., J.E. Donovan, and K. Widmer. 1980. *Psychosocial Factors in Adolescent Alcohol and Drug Use: The 1978 National Sample Study and the 1974–78 Panel Study.* Boulder: University of Colorado, Institute of Behavioral Science.

Jessor, R., and S.L. Jessor. 1977. *Problem Behavior and Psychosocial Development: A Longitudinal Study of Youth.* New York: Academic Press.

Jessor, R., S.L. Jessor, and J. Finney. 1973. A Social Psychology of Marijuana Use: Longitudinal Studies of High School and College Youth. *Journal of Personality and Social Psychology* 26:1–15.

Kandel, D.B. 1975. Reaching the Hard-to-Reach: Illicit Drug Use among High School Absentees. *Addictive Diseases: An International Journal* 1:465–480.

———. 1978. Convergences in Prospective Longitudinal Surveys of Drug Use in Normal Populations. In D.B. Kandel, ed., *Longitudinal Research on Drug Use: Empirical Findings and Methodological Issues.* New York: John Wiley.

———. 1980. Drug and Drinking Behavior among Youth. *Annual Review of Sociology* 6:235–285.

Kandel, D.B., R.C. Kessler, and R.Z. Margulies. 1978. Antecedants of Adolescent Initiation into Stages of Drug Use: A Developmental Analysis. In D.B. Kandel, ed., *Longitudinal Research on Drug Use: Empirical Findings and Methodological Issues.* New York: John Wiley.

Khantzian, E.J. 1980. An Ego/Self Theory of Substance Dependence: A Contemporary Psychoanalytic Perspective. In D.J. Lettieri, M. Sayers, and H.W.

Pearson, eds., *Theories on Drug Abuse: Selected Contemporary Perspectives.* NIDA Research Monograph 30. Rockville, MD: National Institute on Drug Abuse.

Liban, C.B., and R.G. Smart. 1982. Drinking and Drug Use among Ontario Indian Students. *Drug and Alcohol Dependence* 9:161–171.

Levy, J.E., and S.J. Kunitz. 1971. Indian Reservations, Anomie and Social Pathologies. *Southwestern Journal of Anthropology* 27:97–128.

Lukoff, I.F. 1980. Toward a Sociology of Drug Use. In D.J. Lettieri, M. Sayers, and H.W. Pearson, eds., *Theories on Drug Abuse: Selected Contemporary Perspectives.* NIDA Research Monograph 30. Rockville, MD: National Institute on Drug Abuse.

Madsen, W. 1964. The Alcoholic Agringado. *American Anthropologist* 66:355–361.

May, P. 1981. Susceptibility to Substance Abuse among American Indians: Variation across Sociocultural Settings. In *Problems of Drug Dependence.* Research Monograph 41. Rockville, MD: National Institute on Drug Abuse.

Mills, C.J., and H.L. Noyes. 1984. Patterns and Correlates of Initial and Subsequent Drug Use among Adolescents. *Journal of Consulting and Clinical Psychology* 52:231–243.

Mirin, S.M., L.M. Shapiro, R.E. Meyer, R.C. Pillard, and S. Fisher. 1971. Casual versus Heavy Use of Marijuana: A Redefinition of the Marijuana Problem. *American Journal of Psychiatry* 127:1134–1140.

O'Donnell, J.A., and R.R. Clayton. 1982. The Stepping Stone Hypothesis—Marijuana, Heroin, and Causality. *Chemical Dependencies: Behavioral and Biomedical Issues* 4:229–241.

Oetting, E.R., and F. Beauvais. 1983. The Drug Acquisition Curve: A Method for the Analysis and Prediction of Drug Epidemiology. *The International Journal of the Addictions* 18:1115–1129.

———. 1985. Epidemiology and Correlates of Alcohol Use among Indian Adolescents Living on Reservations. Paper presented at Conference on Epidemiology of Alcohol Use and Abuse among U.S. Ethnic Minority Groups, Bethesda, MD, September, National Institute on Alcoholism and Alcohol Abuse.

———. In press–a. Peer Cluster Theory, Socialization Characteristics and Adolescent Drug Use: A Path Analysis. *Journal of Counseling Psychology.*

———. In press–b. Peer Cluster Theory: Drugs and the Adolescent. *Journal of Counseling and Development.*

Oetting, E.R., F. Beauvais, R. Edwards, J. Velarde, and G. Goldstein. 1982. *Drug Use among Native American Youth: Summary of Findings (1975–1981).* Rocky Mountain Behavioral Science Institute, Fort Collins.

Oetting, E.R., F. Beauvais, R. Edwards, and M. Waters. 1984a. *The Drug and Alcohol Assessment System: Book I, Administering and Interpreting the System,* Rocky Mountain Behavioral Science Institute.

———. 1984b. *The Drug and Alcohol Assessment System: Book II, Instrument Development, Reliability and Validity.* Rocky Mountain Behavioral Science Institute.

Oetting, E.R., R. Edwards, G. Goldstein, and V. Garcia-Mason. 1980. Drug Use among Adolescents of Five Southwestern Native American Tribes. *International Journal of the Addictions* 15:439–445.

Oetting, E.R., and G.S. Goldstein. 1979. Drug Use among Native American Adolescents. In G. Beschner and A. Freidman, eds., *Youth Drug Abuse.* Lexington, MA: Lexington Books.

Padilla, E.R., A.M. Padilla, A. Morales, and E.L. Olmedo. 1979. Inhalant, Marijuana, and Alcohol Abuse among Barrio Children and Adolescents. *International Journal of the Addictions* 14:943–964.

Pandina, R.T., and J.A. Schuele. 1983. Psychosocial Correlates of Alcohol and Drug Use of Adolescent Students and Adolescents in Treatment. *Journal of Studies on Alcohol* 44:950–973.

Peele, S. 1985. *The Meaning of Addiction.* Lexington, MA: Lexington Books.

Penning, M., and G. Barnes. 1982. Adolescent Marijuana Use: A Review. *International Journal of the Addictions* 17:749–791.

Reed, T. 1980. Challenging Some "Common Wisdom" on Drug Abuse. *International Journal of the Addictions* 15:359–373.

Riggs, D.E. 1973. Students and Drug Use: A Study of Personality Characteristics and Extent of Drug Using Behavior. *Canadian Counselor* 7:9–15.

Rohrbaugh, J., and R. Jessor. 1975. Religiosity in Youth: A Personal Control against Deviant Behavior. *Journal of Personality* 43:135–155.

Simpson, D.D., and M.S. de Barona. 1983. *Drug Abuse Prevention Programs for High-Risk Youth in Texas.* Behavioral Research Program, Texas A & M University, Texas Department of Community Affairs, Austin, Texas.

Sorosiak, F.M., L.E. Thomas, and F.N. Balet. 1976. Adolescent Drug Use: An Analysis. *Psychological Reports* 38:211–221.

Spotts, J.V., and F.C. Shontz. 1980. A Life Theme Theory of Chronic Drug Abuse. In D.J. Lettieri, M. Sayers, and H.W. Pearson, eds., *Theories on Drug Abuse: Selected Contemporary Perspectives.* NIDA Research Monograph No. 30. Rockville, MD: National Institute on Drug Abuse.

———. 1984a. Drug Induced Ego States. I. Cocaine: Phenomenology and Implications. *International Journal of the Addictions* 19:119–152.

———. 1984b. The Phenomenological Structure of Drug Induced States. II. Barbiturates and Sedative Hypnotics. *International Journal of the Addictions* 19:295–326.

Streit, F., D.L. Halsted, and P.J. Pascale. 1974. Differences among Youth Users and Nonusers of Drugs Based on Their Perceptions of Parental Behavior. *International Journal of the Addictions* 9:749–755.

Svobodny, L.A. 1982. Biographical, Self Concept and Educational Factors among Chemically Dependent Adolescents. *Adolescence* 17:847–853.

Tec, N. 1974. Parent-Child Drug Abuse: Generational Continuity of Adolescent Deviancy? *Adolescence* 9:350–364.

Tolone, W.L., and D. Dermott. 1975. Some Correlates of Drug Use among High School Youth in a Midwestern Rural Community. *International Journal of the Addictions* 10:761–777.

Turner, C.J. and R.J. Willis. 1984. The Relationship between Self-Reported Religiosity and Drug Use by College Students. In S. Eiseman, J. Wingar, and G. Huba, eds., *Drug Abuse: Foundation for a Psychosocial Approach.* Farmingdale, NY: Baywood.

Walters, J.M. 1980. Buzzin': PCP Use in Philadelphia. In H.W. Feldman, M.H. Agar, and G. Beschener, eds., *Angel Dust.* Lexington, MA: D.C. Heath.

Wingard, J.A., G.J. Huba, and P.M. Bentler. 1979. The Relationship of Personality Structure to Patterns of Adolescent Substance Use. *Multivariate Behavioral Research* 14:131–143.

8

On the Possibility of an Addiction-Free Mode of Being

Craig MacAndrew

Ahunter, walking through some woods, came on a sign on which he read the words, "STONE EATING IS FORBIDDEN." His curiosity was stimulated, and he followed a path that led past the sign until he came to a cave at the entrance to which a Sufi was sitting.

The Sufi said to him: "The answer to the question in your mind is that you have never seen a sign prohibiting the eating of stones because there is no need for one. Not to eat stones may be called a common habit.

"Only when the human being is able to avoid other habits, even more destructive than eating stones, will he be able to get beyond his present pitiful state."

In what follows, I want to explore a radical possibility: the possibility of a mode of being that would render one immune to addictive involvements—to "habits, even more destructive than eating stones"—of *any and all sorts.* What, I shall ask, would such a mode of being look like? And what would be required for its attainment?

I shall try to show that these questions are not of recent vintage but have been of abiding human concern. For it was universally recognized by the sages of old that what we now refer to as "the addictive process" is merely an extreme manifestation of a universally bedeviling aspect of human functioning. My aim, then, will be to locate our present understanding of addiction within the context provided by this earlier and broader perspective, and from this, to derive "the possibility of an addiction-free mode of being." I begin my exposition with a procedural aside.

The Veblen Maneuver

When Thorstein Veblen (1921) essayed the notion of sabotage, he began by observing that the term was first used by the French syndicalists to depict their favored adversarial tactic of passive resistance, that it derives from *sabot,* which is French for wooden shoe, and hence that it was intended to call up the image of a slowed, awkward form of movement. In Europe, then, it was readily understood that *sabotage* referred to such things as intentional clumsiness, languor, and general ineptitude. However, when the term was transported to our shores, it took on a sinister coloration. Here, it came to denote such activities as forcible obstruction of movement and of the flow of goods, destruction of product and equipment, incendiarism, and the like. Now, Veblen argued, if one approached the topic of labor/management relations in a spirit of impartiality, he would see that the aim of those who engineered this dubious translation was to discredit U.S. labor's then-fledgling attempts to protect and to enhance its economic interests.

Veblen sought to remove this ideologically inspired bias by redefining the term in such a way that it would be applicable to the activities of *both* sides. Sabotage, he said, is "the conscientious withdrawal of efficiency." How does this definition serve the interest of impartiality? Consider: Throughout the ages, *overproduction* has been understood to mean "production in excess of need," but in an adversarial society such as ours, whose economy is geared to the maximization of profit, this is no longer so. Instead, it has come to mean "production in excess of what can be sold at a reasonable profit," with *reasonable profit* understood to mean the largest possible profit. Now, Veblen argued, when the production process is governed by considerations of profit maximization, it is inevitable that the working capacity of the available productive resources—both human and material—will be used in just as conscientiously inefficient a manner as will the labor power of "the other side." Thus, for instance, such practices as a temporary shortening of the hours of work, temporary layoffs, and temporary plant closings all serve the (conscientiously inefficient) purpose of reducing "supply" in order that "demand" might be satisfied in a maximally profitable fashion. And as time progresses, such business practices come to be viewed by laymen and experts alike as natural, normal, and indubitably reasonable. They become assumptive features of our social reality—a reality that we share, maintain, and enforce as a matter of abiding moral concern.

I shall call Veblen's use of a generic definition to pierce this veil of obviousness *the Veblen maneuver*. It is a maneuver to which I shall eventually resort. But first, let us trace how we have come to our present understanding of the process we call *addictive*.

The Historical Context

The word *addiction* derives from the Latin word *addictus:* "assigned by decree, made over, bound to another, hence attached by restraint or obligation." Eventually it came to denote an attachment to a person or a cause that stemmed from one's own inclination, as, for instance, a disciple's attachment to his teacher or an adherent's attachment to a movement or a cause. Finally, the term has come to signify a strong inclination toward, or a giving oneself over to, *any* interest or pursuit to which one might have become strongly attached. A typical late 1500s' usage is found in one Thomas Lupton's lament that, "The people are so peevishly addicted that they esteeme Wealth over Wisdom." The openness of the term was unquestioned, for it was understood that one might "give oneself over," for example, to poetry, business, or the arts, as well as to such presumably less ennobling activities as drinking, womanizing, or games of chance. Although in succeeding centuries "addiction" took on a more pejorative cast, even into the mid-1800s it could still be employed evenhandedly. Thus, in his *Logic,* John Stuart Mill wrote admiringly of those who "addict themselves to history or science," while in his essay *On Liberty* we find him criticizing "the man who causes grief to his family by addiction to bad habits." It was only with the public's acceptance of the "discovery" of *physiological* addiction (Levine, 1978; MacAndrew, 1969; Szasz, 1974) that the term came to be understood in an all but exclusively invidious sense.

How did this nonempirically based "discovery" take root in the modern mind? By the early nineteenth century, the ideal of progress (Bury, 1932; Nisbet, 1980), which had long since become completely secularized, was broadly equated with a rising level of material consumption; and industrialization was seen as ushering in a new era of unmatched and ever-increasing abundance. Because the labor of the many had to be scrupulously synchronized if industrialization's promised economies of scale were to be realized, the loose discipline that formerly had been exerted on an agricultural populace by the changing of the seasons gradually gave way to the far more exacting requirements of the clock.[1] And because external compulsion was insufficiently precise to orchestrate the punctilious harmonies of thought and action that this new era demanded, control had to be internalized. But it was assumed that this would inevitably occur as people came to a full appreciation of the joys of material aggrandizement and, thusly motivated, freely elected to pursue their self-interests in a properly disciplined manner. With control internalized, and with the free market (Adam Smith's "invisible hand") coordinating the overall design, a beneficent future was assured, or so it was supposed. Such, at any rate, was the intellectual climate during which the seeds of our contemporary understanding of self-control grew and flourished (Foucault, 1975; Weber, 1958). And such was the expectational background against which the "loss" of this much-vaunted human capacity came to be recognized.

But could socially regulated greed ("enlightened self-interest") be relied on to produce in everyone the internalization of control that this new era expected and demanded? As it always had in the past, humanity once again proved to be lumpy. And this lumpiness could not be ignored, for it indicated that something was terribly wrong either with the basic presumption on which the vision of Progress was based, or with those whose lack of control had become evident to all concerned. Indeed, not only did the members of this recalcitrant minority appear to be oblivious to the allurements of material plentitude, many seemed hellbent on self-destruction! Because the most visible portion of this minority consisted of chronic drunkards, it is to them that the reductionist's "explanation" was first applied. How, as I once put the puzzle that the existence of such people presented to common sense (MacAndrew, 1969), are we to *make* sense of the fact that there are people among us who, while seemingly like us in other respects, appear determined to destroy themselves? Enter the reductionists, whose solution goes like this: They continue to drink (and later, by simple extension, "to use") as they do because, unlike the rest of us, they have become physiologically addicted to the substance and hence are incapable of doing otherwise. And what is the empirical warrant for this solution? It is simply that if it *were* in their power to control themselves, they would do so. And, to complete the circle, because they haven't done so, it is obvious that they can't. This solution thus falls into place as a quasi-scientific phrasing of a ploy that compact majorities have always relied on to comprehend those who affront their sense of the appropriate. The general structure of this ploy is: "I'm OK; you're *not* OK!"

With the puzzle thusly "solved," at least for the time being, the public along with its agents and agencies became conditioned to its acceptance. Specialists thrived, clinicians thrived, federal and state bureaucracies devoted to "the problem" thrived, self-help groups thrived, the police thrived, social workers thrived, and courts thrived. Yet, despite all of this increased activity directed to "addicts and their addictions," and despite the many and sometimes munificient payoffs that an increasingly alarmed and attentive society made available,[2] the number of "addicts" has not declined. Instead, in a classically ironic instance of what Max Weber termed "the unforeseen consequences of purposive social action," their number has risen dramatically. Something was very wrong somewhere.

Two Postreductionist Formulations of Addiction

Baldly stated, the problem with all reductionist explanations of addiction is that they are contradicted by the data at every point. I won't attempt to document this assertion here because Peele (e.g., 1985, 1986) and Orford (1985) have recently and convincingly performed this much-needed service. Suffice it to say that the phenomena that reductionist formulations were introduced to explain simply are not the epiphenomena that these formulations suppose them to be. Rather, they are events of human conduct; and as such they can be understood only within, and in terms of, the context that provides them their possibility, viz., the context of the relations between members of a society (e.g., Winch, 1958). Reductionist explanations are thus in error not in this or that particular, but fundamentally and irremediably.

This being so, does it still make sense to segregate certain categories of human activities from others on the grounds that they uniquely possess an "addictive" quality? Both Peele and Orford believe that it does, although they define this quality quite differently. For Orford (1985), whose formulation is by far the more conservative of the two, one can only be addicted to "appetitive" behaviors that (1) are judged to be excessive in some sense and that because of this "excessivity," (2) are accompanied by feelings of conflict and/or are judged by someone (not necessarily the doer) to be morally ambivalent. Orford lists five categories of such appetitive excess: excessive drinking, excessive gambling, excessive drug-taking, excessive eating, and excessive sexuality.[3] Notice, however, where such explicitly culture-bound criteria inexorably lead him: Recognizing that "Excess is not absolute, but is personally and socially defined" and that "Reaction against, or criticism of, appetitive activity is necessary in order for it to be labeled 'addiction,'" he is forced to the view that "Excessive appetitive behaviour is an example of deviance" (1985:321).

For Peele, although "no involvement or object is inherently addictive" (1985:103), "because there are addictive and nonaddictive ways of doing anything" (Peele and Brodsky, 1975:63), "the addiction syndrome can appear with any type of involvement" (Peele, 1985:128). And because, for Peele, the term refers to "compulsive and self-destructive behaviors of all kinds" (1985:2)—the key to its recognition being "its persistence in the face of harmful consequences for the individual" (1985:26)—it is clear that this formulation of addiction encompasses an immeasurably wider range of activities than does Orford's.[4]

Note, however, that although both authors have opted for an enlarged, desomaticized conception of addiction, each in his own way retains the exclusively pathological character of the term with which reductionism had imbued it.

I shall soon return to this point, but before I do, there is one last piece to put into place.

A Conceptual Context

I have found it helpful to anchor my thinking about addiction in a two-space whose ancestry may be traced back at least to the time of Hippocrates and the theory of the four humors (e.g., Roback, 1927). This humoral theory was transformed by Galen into his doctrine of the four temperaments, and in this mode it survived the Middle Ages. In more recent times, the typology was refined by Kant, and Kant's formulation was in turn revised and cast in the form of two bipolar dimensions, first by Ebbinghaus and then by Wundt. These dimensions were again drastically reworked by Eysenck, but although the two-space that is constituted by their intersection is now most commonly associated with Eysenck's well-known dimensional model of personality (e.g., Eysenck, 1947, 1967; Eysenck and Eysenck, 1969), it is on Gray's revision of Eysenck's model (e.g., Gray, 1970, 1981, 1982; Gray et al., 1983), and on an extension of this revision, that I want to focus.

Briefly, what Gray did was to translate Eysenck's dimensions of introversion/extroversion and neuroticism—i.e., hyperemotionality/hypoemotionality—into terms that are more compatible with contemporary learning theory. In this recasting, Eysenck's dimension of neuroticism became a dimension of differential sensitivity to all signals of reinforcement, both appetitive and aversive. Eysenck's dimension of introversion/extroversion became, in turn, a dimension of differential sensitivity to one or the other of these two classes of reinforcement. Thus, an increasing degree of introversion becomes an increasing sensitivity to signals of punishment (including frustrative nonreward); and an increasing degree of extroversion becomes an increasing sensitivity to signals of reward (including nonpunishment). Figure 8–1 contains Gray's representation of this revision.

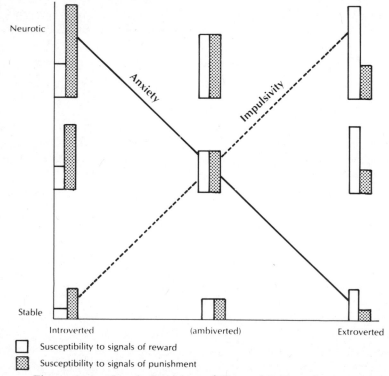

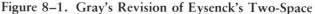

Figure 8–1. Gray's Revision of Eysenck's Two-Space

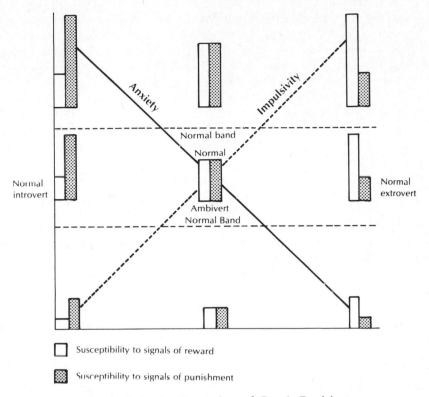

Figure 8–2. An Extension of Gray's Revision

In figure 8–2, I have extended Gray's spatial formulation by raising the normal or stable range from the bottom to the middle of the space.[5] This extension has an important (symmetrical) consequence, for while in figure 8–1 abnormality appears only in the upper band of the space, in figure 8–2 it appears in the lower band as well.

What sort of persons would populate this lower band? Let us first consider the diagonal, which Gray has termed *anxiety* and which runs from the upper left to the lower right. Gray (1982) has presented a very compelling case for the existence of a neurological system (the behavioral inhibition system), whose hyperactive functioning predisposes to anxiety and thus to the development of one or another of the classical neuroses, e.g., phobia, obsession/compulsion, and reactive depression. Now, to what would the *hypo*-activity of this system—the *absence* (or near absence) of anxiety—give rise? It should predispose to the development of primary psychopathy, as Cleckley (1976) has described this condition.[6]

What of the other diagonal that Gray has termed *impulsivity?* The upper right-hand quadrant is the locus of Eysenck's neurotic extrovert—the secondary psychopath, who, like the primary psychopath, is also given to acting on the whim of the moment, but in a more driven fashion, followed by remorse as a consequence. How would the opposite pole of this dimension be defined? Although I have no data that are directly relevant, since, by definition, persons so located are highly self-controlled (the opposite of impulsive) and are very shallow of affect, it would be expected that they would value conformity blindly and would seldom waver in their compliance to their role obligations. For these reasons, they would only rarely become the foci of public attention, and then only when things had gone very wrong in the larger world to which they had uncritically adapted themselves. Because he has become not only visible but notorious, my ideal-typical candidate to represent these normally invisible hyperconformists is Adolf Eichmann.[7]

As for what in figure 8–2 I have labeled the normal band, it is still defined as both Eysenck and Gray have defined it: The normal introvert (broadly construed) on the left, the normal ambivert (broadly construed) in the middle, and the normal extrovert (broadly construed) on the right.

What, finally, of the vertical dimension that bisects this expanded two-space? While in Gray's formulation, it will be recalled, the upper pole depicts the extreme of sensitivity to signals of both reward and punishment and the opposite pole depicts stable ambiversion, a very different formulation emerges when the space is extended. Over the millennia, humans have been characterized as being both "in the world" (as a function of their corporeality) and "of the world" (as a function of their social conditioning). Because an extreme concern with "the world" as the source of both reward and punishment marks the extreme of our "of-the-worldness," and because the opposite pole of this dimension is now defined as a maximum *indifference* to considerations of reward and punishment, this dimension is, in effect, a dimension of differential "of-the-worldness."

This said, I am at last ready to make use of the Veblen maneuver.

The Veblen Maneuver Applied

"It is necessary," said Peele and Brodsky (1975:49), "to transcend the culture-bound, class-bound definition that has enabled us to dismiss addiction as somebody else's problem." This is what I shall now try to do.

I begin with a hypothetical example. Consider Smith, who has made a fortune in recent years by "playing" the options markets. Every day without fail from the moment these markets open and until they close, he is glued to "the tape." And after dutifully observing the day's final transaction, he then spends several additional hours updating, plotting, and analyzing a host of ratios, oscillators, sentiment indicators, moving averages, price-volume charts, point and figure charts, etc. Because he finds all of this infinitely fascinating, the market has become his sole interest and enthusiasm. Now, if Smith were a consistent loser, everyone would classify him as an addict, i.e., a compulsive gambler.[8] But because by stipulation, he has been a big and consistent winner, how are we to regard him—as an addict or as a prudent speculator? While Peele would elect the former characterization and Orford would choose the latter, the point of the example is not that experts sometimes disagree. It is this: Because success in almost any activity ordinarily requires the expenditure of both time and attention capacity, and because these are limited resources, it is typically the case that in order to succeed at one thing, *whatever that thing might be,* one must forfeit the possibility of succeeding at an infinitely large number of other things.

A second example (also hypothetical) will extend this point. Jones, after many years of single-minded persistence, has succeeded in accumulating one of the world's largest collections of matchbook covers. His collection is a source of great personal pride and because of it, at least in those circles in which such collections count, he has become a highly respected personage. And indeed, does Jones's collection really differ in any deep sense from J. Paul Getty's much-admired collection of art works, William Randolph Hearst's much-admired collection of antique furnishings, or (from an only slightly different perspective) Mrs. Marcos's much-criticized collection of shoes? More to the point, is Jones's unceasing quest for ever more matchbook covers really all that different from the myriad of trivial pursuits with which we, in a more cursory fashion, fill the bulk of our waking hours? While Jones' accomplishment is not one that I would want—nor, I should imagine, that you would want—to place on a very high pedestal, who am I to say and, *pari passu,* who are you to say? Is it seemly for a drill press to criticize a lathe because it doesn't make holes in things?

Last year we Americans spent $250 million on suntan lotions (which is up from $210 million the year before). We regularly spend more on the care and maintenance of our hair than we do on our mental health, more on the general grooming of our faces and bodies than we do on books of all kinds,[9] and more on our wardrobes than on practically anything else. Granted that we live in a world of appearances, such expenditure patterns nevertheless strike me as reflecting a rather "obsessive" concern with our *personal* appearances. What is more, at least some of these expenditures appear to be "self-defeating," even on their own terms. This judgment is informed by the following "expert testimony." It seems that as a group, nuns are considered by specialists to have the best complexions; and for this reason, according to the Cosmetics, Toiletries, and Fragrances Association, they are now being used to test new skin products. "What is their beauty secret?" a CTFA spokesman was asked. "They normally don't use cosmetics," he replied (quoted in Litvak, 1980:145).

And when societies give their sanction to the institutionalized expression of our "oddities," farce becomes tragedy. One experiences a shock of recognition on reading the opening lines or Orwell's essay "England, Your England," which were written at the height of the London Blitz (1946:252):

> As I write, highly civilized human beings are flying overhead, trying to kill me. They do not feel any enmity against me as an individual, nor I against them. They are "only doing their duty," as the saying goes.

Thus Dachau, Buchenwald, Treblinka, and the rest; thus Hiroshima, Nagasaki, and the firebombing of Dresden; thus the Gulag and the forced collectivization of Russian and of Chinese agriculture; and thus the doctrine of mutual assured destruction (MAD) on which Pax Hominis Sapientis now precariously rests. But so great are our powers of self-deception that we view such obscenities as exceptions, mere ripples of irrationality on a pervasively tranquil sea of reason. For haven't we been taught that we are the masters of our fate and that what we do, we do "on purpose"?

Very well, but consider that most mundane of occurrences—our passage through a typical day. In a series of wonderfully perspicuous studies of "the routine grounds of everyday activities," Garfinkel (1967:35–75) has shown that this passage proceeds in its usually trouble-free fashion because, and only because, we continuously (but "unconsciously") rely on a vast array of invisible background expectations. Although we are normally unaware even of their existence, when these background expectations are experimentally breached, subjects become acutely aware of the enormous "tolerance" that they have built up for "the commonsense world as (their) social reality." For when those reality-sustaining background expectations cease to operate, the presumedly normal, orderly-appearing character of the world of everyday life disappears; and with this disappearance such "withdrawal symptoms" as anxiety and/or acute anomie arise, as also does a "craving" for the speedy reinstatement of what they had been conditioned to believe was "the way things really are." And I am not using these terms—*tolerance, withdrawal,* and *craving*—in a dilute, only analogical sense. For if we accept that addiction is not a physiological state of affairs, and if we *seriously* examine the arguments of the post–Tractatus Wittgenstein (1953) on the meaning and significance of a "form of life," of Schutz (1962, 1964, 1970; Gurwitch, 1962) on the constitutive phenomenology of everyday life, and of Garfinkel (1967) and his colleagues on reality as a socially managed construction ("ethnomethodology"), we cannot escape the conclusion that in a very real sense we are addicted to our version of social "reality." But behind this, there lurks an even more pervasive addiction. It is to this, our *fundamental* addiction, that I now turn.

In every epoch, Alfred North Whitehead (1948:49) once observed, "There will be some fundamental assumptions which adherents of all the variant systems within the epoch unconsciously presuppose." These assumptions, he continued, "appear so obvious that people do not know what they are assuming because no other way of putting things has ever occurred to them."

What I want to suggest is that just as the assumption of "simple location" has served (until recently) to undergird our lay and professional understanding of the world of nature, the assumption that we are unified, stable, and discrete "selves" has undergirded, and continues to undergird, our lay and professional understanding of the social/psychological world.

This "object self" (Deikman, 1982) that one supposes oneself to be is not, of course, an object. Rather, it is a socially conditioned cognitive construction—literally a self-*concept*—that exists only within an ongoing "stream of consciousness." And because we only rarely think our thoughts—because, that is, most of our thoughts enter and depart our stream of consciousness in an entirely mechanical, unpremeditated fashion—the salient features of this "object" self vary, often radically, from month to month, from day to day, from hour to hour, and sometimes even from minute to minute. Because it only exists within an ongoing stream of consciousness, and because we automatically say *I* and *mine* to every thought, judgment, mood, emotion, fear, and desire that arises within us, this "object" self *is* its every next thought, its every next judgment, its every next mood, its every next emotion, its every next fear, and its every next desire. At any given moment, it *is* whatever happens to be on center stage. And to this multiplicity—this ever-changing pandemonium of ups and downs, of pushes and pulls, of affirmations and negations—we attribute substance, unity, and stability. Because we automatically identify with every next internal happening, we unreflectively suppose that the satisfaction of "its" every desire, the pacification of "its" every fear, the tender concern for "its" every disappointment, the defense of "its" every judgment and belief, and the comfort and beautification of "its" every bodily distress and imperfection are "what life is all about."[10]

This being so, I shall now define what I earlier termed the dimension of differential "of-the-worldness" as a dimension of differential *self-absorption*. In so doing, I am merely saying that to be "of-the-world" is to be oriented to the world on the basis of *self*-interest: and the more that one is so oriented, the more do *self*-ish considerations dominate one's every thought and action.

I am now positioned to assert what I have been leading up to bit by bit: The fundamental addictive *process* is the automatic identification of everything that mechanically arises within one as "oneself." And from this, in a sublime instance of what Whitehead (1948:52) in another context termed the "fallacy of misplaced concreteness," our fundamental addiction to the "object" self is formed. Furthermore, the existence of this, our fundamental, addiction is both the necessary and the sufficient condition for the emergence of all our more specific addictive involvements. Put differently, insofar as *any* given action or activity is *self*-centered, it "feeds" and strengthens one's fundamental addiction; and in so doing it acquires the potential for becoming habitual.

This, then, is the upshot of the application of the Veblen maneuver to the notion of addiction. Let's see if it has fulfilled the task that was stated at the beginning of this section: Addiction is now not just "their" problem, i.e., the problem of the sick or of the morally deficient; it is *our* problem, too. And in its present culture-free rendering, addiction is not just "our" problem, it is a ubiquitously *human* problem!

But, in so broadening addiction's domain of applicability, has the term lost all claim to denotive relevance? Does it now say so much that it says nothing? Recognizing that if there is no alternative, there is no problem, let me put this question in a more interesting way. Are we *fated* to live lives of self-absorption? Certainly, if we remain locked into our conventional formulations of what we are and thus of "what life is all about"—formulations that serve precisely to explicate the couldn't-be-otherwise character of our of-the-worldness—we are indeed so fated. But look again at the vertical bisection of figure 8–2. Self-absorption appears there not as a blanket characterization, but as a dimension along which persons may be ordered in terms of more or less. I submit that just as humanity includes its share of primary psychopaths and of Adolf Eichmanns, it should also include people who are immune to both the blandishments of reward and the fears of punishment. Such people, having transcended the historically conventional view of "what life is all about" and having thereby freed themselves from the incessant concerns and demands of the "object" self, have attained a mode of being in which they are immune to the formation of addictive involvements of any and all sorts.

I want next to suggest that an appreciation of this possibility—the possibility of an addiction-free mode of being—has characterized all of the most revered versions of what it is to be truly human that have appeared throughout the ages.

The Traditional Vision

Peele and Brodsky have suggested that our present vulnerability to addiction can be traced to the fact that "something unequivocally valuable was lost in the transition to the modern age" (1975:143). What was lost, they say, was "an internal self-assurance that came from being in touch with daily life" (1975:143).

I agree that something of utmost importance was lost with the coming of modernity, but what most importantly was lost, I believe, was something more akin to "a sense of the cosmos" and of our place within it. The present desacralized conception of nature and of our (*ex hypothesi*) accidental appearance on the scene is now so firmly entrenched that we find it difficult to imagine that throughout human history and until only the last few centuries, the reigning vision was constructed along very different lines. In the traditional view, human existence was comprehended not only along the horizontal dimension of time and its flow, but also, and more important, in terms of a vertical dimension comprised of graded levels of being. And it was the possibility of raising one's position on this dimension—of raising one's level of being—that gave human existence both its meaning and its purpose.[11]

But with the triumph of science (or more accurately, of *scientism*), this vertical dimension was completely leveled; and with its leveling, both the meaning and the sense of purpose associated with the possibility of vertical movement were lost. One could still zig or zag (for we came to see our existence as occurring, as it were, on a plane), but the possibility of moving up "the great chain of being" was no longer available. The *Sophia Perennis* had become an anachronism. Or had it?

Suppose (and this is not at all an original supposition) that the sages of old on whose existences, utterances, and activities the world's major religions are based were, in fact, highly knowledgeable and preeminently practical teachers of a developmental psychology whose goal was the transformation of human consciousness. Where might this supposition take us?

Ed Shils once remarked that the basic mistake of U.S. radicals was to have believed that they could make a revolution in their spare time. The sages knew better than to take the work connected with inner transformation— with raising one's level of being   as just one activity among many. They were unanimous in contending that this was the *only* human activity that really counted. Thus Guatama Buddha: "Buddhas do but point the way—work out your salvation with diligence." Thus Jalaludin Rumi: "You have a duty to perform. Do anything else, do any number of things, occupy your time fully, and yet, if you do not do this task, all your time will have been wasted." And thus, Christ: "Seek ye *first* the Kingdom of Heaven." Furthermore, although the specific phrasing varied from one teacher to the next, about this quest all were agreed that in order for "Thy Kingdom" to come, "Our Kingdom," i.e., our absorption in the cares and concerns of the "object" self, would first have to go.

As these teachings have come down to us after centuries of institutional accommodation and distortions of transmission, this is now perhaps most clear in the case of Buddhism. "One thing I teach": said Buddha, "suffering and the end of suffering." And what, specifically, did he teach? He taught that life is *dukkha*—i.e., that life is grievously out of balance, and because of this, that it is steeped in suffering. He taught that *tanha*, i.e., a primary focus on the satisfaction of *self*-ish (and thus, separating) desires, is the cause of *dukkha*. And he taught that *dukkha* can only be eliminated by overcoming *tanha*.[12] These are, of course, the first three of the Buddha's Four Noble

Truths. His fourth truth—the Eightfold Path—is a specification of the practices that, Buddhists hold, will lead to the overcoming of *tanha*.

In a distillate of the Hindu perspective as voiced by Ramana Maharshi (1972:19), we find: "Whatever the means, the destruction of the sense of 'I' and 'mine' is the goal, and as these are interdependent, the destruction of either of them causes the destruction of the other."

In Christianity, one need only recall that the "seven deadly sins"—pride, anger, envy, avarice, sloth, gluttony, and lust—are but a list of *self*-ish expressions. Although Christ's public teachings typically took the form of parables,[13] his reaction to the scrupulously law-abiding Pharisees certainly requires no interpretation. Recall that it was because of their pride and vanity that Christ castigated them so savagely.

In this section I have only provided a hint as to the unanimity with which the most revered of all ages but our own have recognized the strength of our fundamental addiction, have warned of its pernicious effect on us, and have taught (each in accordance with the specific characteristics of "time, place, and persons" with which he was confronted) the "way" of its overcoming.

A Reconsideration

In the annals of human history, self-absorption has seldom, if ever, been greater than it now is. And seldom, if ever, have our problems been more numerous or more menacing. As both Weber (1958) and Schumpeter (1942) predicted, and as Hirsch (1976) and Mishan (1967, 1977) have more recently proposed and begun to document, our Western industrial civilization has been living off a steadily eroding, and now rapidly crumbling, legacy of precapitalist social and moral supports.[14] Nisbet (1980:356), in the epilogue to his monumental *History of the Idea of Progress*, puts matters as follows:

> Never in history have periods of culture such as ours lasted for very long. They are destroyed by all the forces which constitute their essence. How can any society or age last very long if it lacks or is steadily losing the minimal requirements for a society—such requirements being the very opposite of the egocentric and hedonistic elements which dominate Western culture today?[15]

If Nisbet's appraisal is correct, and I believe that it is, it would appear that modernity's de facto decision to deny "the possibility of an addiction-free mode of being" and to glorify its opposite, is fatally flawed.

But could we bear to exist in a state of "holy indifference" (St. Francis de Sales), a state no longer governed by *self*-ish concerns? From an ontogenetic perspective, the development of an "object" self is, of course, a vital necessity both for our physical survival and for our sanity. And it remains essential—but not in its present inflated and culturally destructive form. When the sages have insisted, and continue to insist, that we must "die to self," that self must be "annihilated," "destroyed," etc., they were not, and are not, calling for the literal demise of the "object" self, but only that it assume its "rightful," less exalted, place within an infinitely larger scheme of things. In a remarkable, deceptively modest, essay on "the observing self," Deikman (1982) has provided some indication of the sorts of considerations that would perforce replace our reigning *self*-ish concerns, and thereby what such an existence would be like.

But although the spokesmen for the traditional perspective saw (and continue to see) the dethronement of the "object" self as a necessary condition for the achievement of an expanded consciousness, there may well be other, more mundane benefits that would ensue. Deikman (1982:80) reminds us, for instance, that "It is hard to find a neurotic symptom or a human vice that cannot be traced to the desire to possess or the fear of loss." And on the positive side, George Bernard Shaw offers us a clue. In his *Heartbreak House,* Ellie proclaims, "I feel now as if there was nothing I could not do, because I want nothing," to which Captain Shotover enthuses, "That's the only real strength. That's genius. That's better than rum."[16]

There is in this at least a suggestion that were we to "sacrifice" our fundamental addiction, the resulting "withdrawal symptoms" just might be less severe than we would first imagine. It could even be that were we to achieve an addiction-free mode of being, we would not at all "crave" a return to the *status quo ante.*

In Conclusion

I began with a story, and, to keep things in perspective, I shall also close with a story. This story, like its predecessor, may be found in Idries Shah's *The Way of the Sufi.* It is by Jalaludin Rumi, and it is called . . .

The Sheep and the Purse

A man was walking along a road one day, followed by his sheep. A thief went after him, cut the rope that was holding the sheep, and led it away. When the man realized what had happened, he ran all over the place looking for his sheep.

Presently he came to a well where he saw a man apparently in despair. Although he did not know it, it was the thief who had stolen his sheep. He asked him what he was doing, and the thief said. "I have dropped a purse into this well. It contains five hundred silver coins. If you will jump in and get it for me, I will give you a hundred silver pieces."

The man thought, "When one door shuts, a hundred may open. This chance is worth ten times the value of the sheep that I have lost."

So he stripped himself and jumped into the well.

And the thief carried off his clothes.

Notes

1. At the time of American independence, approximately 90% of the nation's able-bodied males were independent land-owning farmers. This percentage has declined dramatically in each subsequent decade and is now well less than one-tenth of this figure.

2. Example: In a little over a decade, the common stock of Comprehensive Care Corporation, which presently controls about 25% of the private sector's inpatient drug-alcohol treatment market, rocketed from a low of $1/16$ to a high of $30^1/8$—a tidy 48,200% increase in share valuation.

3. Orford also suggested (1985:4) that kleptomania and pyromania were suitable candidates for inclusion in his list of addictions. But given his criteria, one wonders how this could be so. Would we say of a serial murderer that at some point in his chain of killings he has become addicted to killing people? Of course not, for we would hold that even the first murder was "one too many," i.e., was "excessive." Then why not also the first theft, and the setting of the first fire?

4. It is interesting that in his "late thoughts," Jung (1961:329) offhandedly anticipated Peele's formulation: "Every form of addiction is bad, no matter whether the narcotic be alcohol or morphine or idealism."

5. Gray himself (1982:458; Gray et al., 1983:188) has suggested that such an extention might be appropriate, but to my knowledge he has not elaborated at any length on this possibility.

6. And, in a criterion-group comparison of the self-depictions of hookers, putative normals, and neurotic outpatients, this is precisely what I have found (paper in preparation).

7. "I obeyed. Regardless of what I was ordered to do I obeyed. Certainly I would have obeyed. I obeyed. I obeyed." So declared Eichmann (1983) while under interrogation by the Israeli police. Hannah Arendt (1976) has convincingly argued that Eichmann was essentially mechanical rather than quintessentially evil. (Thus she subtitles her monograph on Eichmann *A Report on the Banality of Evil.* It is not just that Eichmann obeyed; so, too, for instance, did the vast majority of Milgram's (1975) subjects. It is that when Eichmann obeyed, he did so dispassionately and unquestioningly, year in and year out.

8. For Bergler (1957), who tended to see almost all human foibles in terms of the Freudian dynamic of an "unconscious sense of guilt" giving rise to an "unconscious need for punishment," the distinguishing feature of the *pathological* gambler is that he is motivated by an unconscious wish to lose. So construed, he becomes yet another member of Bergler's motley assemblage of "injustice collectors."

9. Lest you assume (out of occupational bias) that books are an unmitigated "good," consider the fate of 87-year-old Anthony Cima as reported in the *Los Angeles Times* of July 14, 1986, under the caption, "Man's Love of Books Almost Kills Him

in Quake." It seems that Cima shared his 12-foot-square hotel-apartment room with 9,900 hardcover books and a huge accumulation of newspapers and magazines, all of which were stacked from floor to ceiling, leaving room only for his bed and a narrow aisle leading to the door. When the earthquake hit in the early morning hours, the books came tumbling down, seriously injuring Cima and burying him for eleven hours. A spokesman for the San Diego Fire Department reported that it took fire-fighters about twenty minutes just to determine Cima's location within the room and an additional twenty minutes to get him out.

10. Should this depiction strike you as cranky or unduly harsh, I refer you to the following words of St. Teresa of Avila: "I do not require of you to form great and curious considerations in your understanding. I require of you no more than to *look.*"

11. The classic historical treatment of this earlier world view was provided by Lovejoy (1936). Needleman (1976, 1982), Schumacher (1977), and Smith (1977, 1982) are among its better, more recent discussants.

12. Compare this with the judgment contained in the "big book" of Alcoholics Anonymous (Alcoholics Anonymous, 1976:62). "Selfishness—self-centeredness! That, we think, is the root of our troubles . . . the alcoholic is an extreme example of self-will run riot. . . . Above everything, we alcoholics must be rid of this selfishness." As for the important role that the notion of "delusion" plays in Buddhist comprehension, no less an authority than Herbert Guenther (1974:106) says, "In the strictly Buddhist sense of the word, delusion is the conviction of one's own importance."

13. Parables have a threefold function: to reveal, to conceal, and to perpetuate. Nicoll (1984, 1985) has provided interpretations of several of Christ's parables that accord nicely with the present perspective. As for the Christian mystical tradition (Underhill, 1961), the "purification" of self is clearly at the procedural heart of things.

14. Even our age-characterizing faith in the powers of human reason to solve all our problems is beginning to come under informed (rather than merely sentimental) attack (e.g., Ehrenfeld, 1978).

15. When recognition of this "destroying essence" seeps down to the level of "pop" commentary, the result is a wondrous melding of farce and irony. Example: Robert Ringer, the author of *Looking Out for Number One*, has titled his most recent effort, *How You Can Find Happiness during the Collapse of Western Civilization.*

16. I have borrowed this example from Smith (1964:101).

References

Alcoholics Anonymous. 1976. *Alcoholics Anonymous: The Story of How Many Thousands of Men and Women Have Recovered from Alcoholism.* 3rd ed. New York: Alcoholics Anonymous World Services.

Arendt, Hannah. 1976. *Eichmann in Jerusalem: A Report on the Banality of Evil.* New York: Penguin Books.

Bergler, Edmund. 1957. *The Psychology of Gambling.* New York: Hill and Wang.

Bury, J.B. 1932. *The Idea of Progress: An Inquiry into Its Origin and Growth.* New York: Macmillan.

Cleckley, Hervey. 1976. *The Mask of Sanity.* 5th ed. St. Louis: C.V. Mosby.

Deikman, Arthur J. 1982. *The Observing Self*. Boston: Beacon Press.

Ehrenfeld, David. 1978. *The Arrogance of Humanism*. New York: Oxford University Press.

Eichmann, Adolf. 1983. *Eichmann Interrogated: Transcripts from the Archives of the Israeli Police*. New York: Farrar, Straus and Giroux.

Eysenck, Hans J. 1947. *Dimensions of Personality*. London: Routledge & Kegan Paul.

———. 1967. *The Biological Bases of Personality*. Springfield, IL: Charles C. Thomas.

Eysenck, Hans J., and Sybil B.G. Eysenck. 1969. *Personality Structure and Measurement*. London: Routledge & Kegan Paul.

Foucault, Michel. 1975. *Madness and Civilization: A History of Insanity in the Age of Reason*. New York: Vintage.

Garfinkel, Harold. 1967. *Studies in Ethnomethodology*. Englewood Cliffs, NJ: Prentice-Hall.

Gray, Jeffrey A. 1970. The Psychophysiological Basis of Introversion—Extraversion. *Behavior Research and Therapy* 8:249–266.

———. 1981. A Critique of Eysenck's Theory of Personality. In Hans Eysenck, ed., *A Model for Personality*. New York: Springer.

———. 1982. *The Neuropsychology of Anxiety*. New York: Oxford University Press.

Gray, Jeffrey, Susan Owen, and Nicola Davis. 1983. Psychological and Physiological Relations between Anxiety and Impulsivity. In Marvin Zuckerman, ed., *Biological Bases of Sensation Seeking, Impulsivity, and Anxiety*. Hillside, NJ: Lawrence Erlbaum Associates.

Guenther, Herbert V. 1974. *Philosophy and Psychology in the Abhidharma*. 2nd rev. ed. Delhi, India: Motilal Banarsidass.

Gurwitch, Aron. 1962. The Common-Sense World as Social Reality: A Discourse on Alfred Schutz. *Social Research* 29:50–72.

Hirsch, Fred. 1976. *Social Limits to Growth*. Cambridge, MA: Harvard University Press.

Jung, Carl. 1961. *Memories, Dreams, Reflections*. New York: Random House.

Levine, Harry. 1978. The Discovery of Addiction: Changing Conceptions of Habitual Drunkenness in America. *Journal of Studies on Alcohol* 39:143–174.

Litvak, Stuart B. 1980. *Unstress Yourself*. Santa Barbara: Ross-Erikson.

Lovejoy, Arthur O. 1936. *The Great Chain of Being*. Cambridge, MA: Harvard University Press.

MacAndrew, Craig. 1969. On the Notion That Certain Persons Who Are Given to Frequent Drunkenness Suffer from a Disease Called "Alcoholism." In S. Plog and R. Edgerton, eds., *Changing Perspectives in Mental Illness*. New York: Holt, Rinehart & Winston.

Maharshi, Ramana. 1972. *The Spiritual Teaching of Ramana Maharshi*. Boulder, CO: Shambhala.

Milgram, Stanley. 1975. *Obedience to Authority: An Experimental View*. New York: Harper & Row.

Mishan, Edward J. 1967. *The Costs of Economic Growth*. New York: Praeger.

———. 1977. *The Economic Growth Debate: An Assessment*. London: George Allen & Unwin.

Needleman, Jacob. 1976. *A Sense of the Cosmos: The Encounter of Modern Science and Ancient Truth.* New York: Dutton.

———. 1982. *Consciousness and Tradition.* New York: Crossroad.

Nicoll, Maurice. 1984. *The New Man.* Boulder, CO: Shambhala.

———. 1985. *The Mark.* Boston: Shambhala.

Nisbet, Robert J. 1980. *History of the Idea of Progress.* New York: Basic Books.

Orford, Jim. 1985. *Excessive Appetites: A Psychological View of Addictions.* New York: Wiley.

Orwell, George. 1946. England, Your England. In *A Collection of Essays by George Orwell.* New York: Harcourt Brace Jovanovich.

Peele, Stanton. 1985. *The Meaning of Addiction: Compulsive Experience and Its Interpretation.* Lexington, MA: Lexington Books.

———. 1986. The Implications and Limitations of Genetic Models of Alcoholism and Other Addictions. *Journal of Studies on Alcohol* 47:63–73.

Peele, Stanton, with Archie Brodsky. 1975. *Love and Addiction.* New York: Taplinger.

Roback, Abraham A. 1927. *The Psychology of Character.* New York: Harcourt, Brace.

Schumacher, E.F. 1977. *A Guide for the Perplexed.* New York: Harper & Row.

Schumpeter, Joseph. 1942. *Capitalism, Socialism and Democracy.* 3rd ed. New York: Harper.

Schutz, Alfred. 1962. *Collected Papers, Vol. 1. The Problem of Social Reality.* The Hague, Netherlands: Martinus Nijhoff.

———. 1964. *Collected Papers, Vol. 2. Studies in Social Theory.* The Hague, Netherlands: Martinus Nijhoff.

———. 1970. *Reflections on the Problem of Relevance.* New Haven: Yale University Press.

Shah, Idries. 1970. *The Way of the Sufi.* New York: Dutton.

Smith, Huston. 1964. *The Religions of Man.* New York: Harper & Row.

———. 1977. *Forgotten Truth: The Primordial Tradition.* New York: Harper & Row.

———. 1982. *Beyond the Post-Modern Mind.* New York: Crossroad.

Szasz, Thomas. 1974. *Ceremonial Chemistry.* Garden City, NY: Anchor Press.

Underhill, Evelyn. 1961. *Mysticism: A Study in the Nature and Development of Man's Spiritual Consciousness.* New York: Dutton.

Veblen, Thorstein. 1921. *The Engineers and the Price System.* New York: Viking Press.

Weber, Max. 1958. *The Protestant Ethic and the Spirit of Capitalism.* New York: Scribners.

Whitehead, Alfred N. 1948. *Science in the Modern World.* New York: Macmillan.

Winch, Peter. 1958. *The Idea of a Social Science.* New York: Humanities Press.

Wittgenstein, Ludwig. 1953. *Philosophical Investigations.* New York: Macmillan.

9

Guilt Is Soluble in Alcohol:
An Ego Analytic View

John McFadden

Introduction

Freud's (1923) discovery of unconscious guilt led to a paradigm shift in his theory and practice, and the author of psychoanalysis' standard clinical texts, Fenichel (1941, 1945), designated the new model "ego analysis."[1] In this view, guilt or self-punishment is the essential source of psychological-behavioral dysfunction, including substance abuse such as alcoholism. This is in part because, as a leading social-learning theorist made clear, "there is no greater punishment than self-contempt" (Bandura, 1977:154). According to psychoanalytic cultural analysis, as represented by Stein (1985), guilt is pervasively reinforced in technologically advanced societies. In varying degrees, pain induction is entrenched in socially approved moralistic belief systems as the cure (rather than the cause) of many dysfunctions, especially alcohol- and drug-related antisocial personality disorders.

Vaillant (1983), expressing both disease and social-learning views, argued against conventional psychoanalytic explanations of alcoholism. Although the conventional id analysis and ego psychology theories focus on infantile impulses instead of guilt, they are similar enough that Vaillant's contentions against them serve as clarifying contrasts to the ego analytic view.[2] The first of Vaillant's two main arguments is based on longitudinal studies of alcoholics, both his own research and others' (e.g., Jones, 1968; Kammeier et al., 1973). These studies show that excessive dependence and/or other conventional symptoms of mental illness cannot account for substance abuse, because these factors are not evident either before or after many sufferers' abuse careers. This rationale rests on the assumptions that psychologically normal people are immune to serious emotional-behavioral problems. Both this premise and the longitudinal rationale support the disease theorists' view—that only the physiological distortions wrought by biochemical factors can account for many alcoholics' destructive behavior, including their excessive drinking. The ego analytic counterargument is established by a reinterpretation of Vaillant's (1983) case history of James O'Neill, a compulsive gambler and alcoholic, who had been assessed psychologically healthy during his early adulthood. This reinterpretation will show that O'Neill's transition from normal functioning to antisocial behavioral and emotional patterns was most likely caused by an intensification of his deep guilt.[3]

Although Vaillant grants that "the superego is notoriously 'soluble' in ethanol" (1983:77), he believes that social learning theory explains this phenomenon better than conventional psychodynamic theories, and he relies mainly on Marlatt's (1978, in press) concept of "maladaptive expectancies" to make this second major point. According to this idea, sufferers are conditioned by social influences to expect a positive outcome from excessive consumption, and this powerfully reinforced expectation compels them to overindulge despite increasingly negative outcomes from their drinking. Contrary to this view, the ego analyst argues that negative emotional outcomes of excessive consumption are adaptive because they ward off self-negating thoughts that are even less tolerable than the guilt experienced during and after inebriation.

The ego analytic treatment alternative contrasts with the unwitting induction of self-punishment by disease theorists and cognitive behaviorists. Both Vaillant and Marlatt recommend indoctrinating specific views of addiction, a technique that depends on the infallibility of the professional's vision and instructions. Given its infallibility, if the indoctrination does not produce the desired behavior sufferers can conclude only that they are at fault; their posttreatment failures further confirm clients' pretreatment suspicions that they are fundamentally irrational or irresponsible. In other words, the therapist's norms induce self-negation. Fenichel, on the other hand, attempts only nonauthoritarian challenges to the sufferer's self-blaming thoughts. By helping the client to work through the extensive and emotionally loaded opinions and facts that form the bases for each self-accusing thought, the analyst and client achieve "a gradual alteration of the superego" (1941:180). That is, correcting for the implication of an inner entity by virtue of thorough and reasonably objective reflection, a moralistic system of self-evaluation and self-control is partially supplanted by a nonjudgmental one. Thus, the pain of punishment is reduced enough that sufferers no longer require escape through alcohol.

The Foundations of an Ego Analytic View of Alcoholism

Freud's opinion that unconscious guilt is "the most powerful of all obstacles to recovery" from virtually all psychological-behavioral problems (1923:228) leads to a conclusion contrary to Vaillant's assumption that psychologically healthy people are immune to severe emotional problems. Freud laid the foundation for the conclusion that an intensification of unconscious guilt explains the transitions from normalcy through obsessiveness and / or depression and then to antisocial behavior with the following important corollaries:

> The normal man is not only far more immoral than he believes but also far more moral than he has any idea of. (1923:230)

> Even ordinary normal morality has a harshly restraining, cruelly prohibiting quality. (p. 232)

> The reproaches of conscience in certain forms of obsessional neurosis are just as painful and tormenting . . . [as the reproaches in depression]. (p. 231)

> It was a surprise to find that exacerbation of this Ucs [unconscious] sense of guilt could turn people into criminals. But it is undoubtedly a fact. In many criminals, especially youthful ones, it is possible to detect a very powerful sense of guilt which existed before the crime, and is not therefore the result of it but its motive. (p. 230)

In other words, obsessives and, contrary to commonsense opinion, normal people and even sociopaths are afflicted by harsh guilt feelings. Normal people are vulnerable to an intensification of self-blame, which can account for their subsequent alcohol-related, sociopathic behavior. Fenichel clearly suggested this explanation of the ordinary person's transformation into an antisocial personality when he said that "after a 'normal' superego has been established, subsequent circumstances create a contradictory 'parasitic' double of this superego" (1945:504). In other words, as the subsequent analysis of Vaillant's case history will demonstrate, the average person's self-hating reactions to the inevitable disappointments of life can literally drive the person to drink and eventually force him or her to believe that he or she is basically immoral.

Moralistic versus Moral and Psychological Thinking

Without benefit of Freud's idea that guilt can be a sufficient motive for sociopathy, it would be difficult to discern the influence of unconscious guilt in any socially deviant person. This is especially true when the antisocial person was considered normal prior to drinking alcoholically. This difficulty is only partly accounted for by the fact that such people repress guilt and anxiety. Of greater significance, ego analytic cultural analysis discloses that the widespread belief that guilt is a valid tool for preventing antisocial behavior powerfully reinforces guilt as a means of control and distracts observers from the clues to a guilt-ridden personality. As Freud said, the morality of normal people has a "harshly restraining, cruelly prohibiting quality" on themselves and their views of others.

Both Freud's use of the term *morality* and ordinary usage imply a confusion of moralistic with moral and psychological reasoning, and this further muddles attempts to understand his basic insight. In fact, prior to 1973, Webster's dictionary did not include the word *moralistic,* and a more precise and better developed definition is needed. Moralistic thinkers confuse the problem of setting standards of conduct with the psychological task of explaining behavior and prescribing corrective interventions. The hallmarks of a moralistic explanation are that it attributes destructive behavior to an immoral agent or process of irresponsibility in the sufferer and to a weak system of self-control. In this vein, classical depth analysts and neo-Freudian ego psychologists have argued that antisocial impulses and a weak ego explain deviance.[4] According to this moralistic reasoning, the person who violates standards of conduct *is* irresponsible and weak. Moreover, people such as rapists who evoke our deepest outrage *are* evil or animalistic. The perpetrator's internal pressures are discounted. Thus, moralistic explanations are reductionistic.

In the moralistic approach, change is accomplished by various forms of indoctrination that depend more on the seductiveness of simplistic slogans than on reason. Specific prescriptions for right behavior and correct thinking are applied uniformly to complex situations without allowing for individual differences, particularly the differential reactions of clients to the indoctrination. In other words, like the moralistic explanation, the prescription is inevitably reductionistic, especially when it is applied to individual cases. Far worse, this method of change induces self-punishment, and the extreme forms actually prescribe guilt feelings. For instance, in a book popular in the Alcoholics Anonymous (AA) community, Milam (1983:152) argued that the alcoholic who has been through "truly effective treatment" should be subjected to a moral imperative to behave better.

A combination of moralistic, moral, and psychological reasoning influence the psychologically normal person. It is typical for empathic people to believe that they apply ethical and psychological thinking to all but the most extreme moral violations. Moralistic thinking and the use of guilt do intensify in direct relation to the severity of the transgression. As normal people drift toward sociopathic behavior patterns, they are warned with increasing intensity that they will be punished and feel extreme guilt if they continue to slide. Even if primarily nonjudgmental people are not subjected to such aversive experiences, the threat of severe punishment functions as an anxiety-provoking sentinel, appearing for instance in dreams of immoral behavior. Contrary to their beliefs about themselves, even psychologically healthy people routinely lapse into moralistic thinking in relation to minor issues. Many normal parents instruct rather than objectively discuss when confronted with a violation of relatively unimportant behavioral standards, such as correct table manners. Even those who are most intent on being nonjudgmental are routinely subjected to the vicissitudes of arbitrary and narrow explanations of and prescriptions for their behavior.

In addition to the aversive quality of guilt, it is especially difficult to sustain a nonmoralistic view because the moralistic perspective prevails in technologically advanced society as a whole and, to a lesser extent, in our mental health system, particularly regarding antisocial behavior. Narrow explanations of complex problems creep into psychiatry under the guise of diagnostic labels that used to be designated "character disorders" and are now referred to as "personality disorders." The fact that similar subcategories—i.e., antisocial personality disorder, conduct disorder, etc.—are retained under the new heading is a clue that our thinking has not changed much since Judeo-Christian culture first divided experience into right and wrong and pursued an approach to life that relies heavily on corporal punishment, of which guilt is the psychological equivalent.

In the American Psychiatric Association's (1980) *Diagnostic and Statistical Manual* (DSM-III), the old moralistic logic prevails. The belief that a weak conscience translates into irresponsible behavior is reflected in descriptions such as, "fails to resist impulses to steal" (p. 294), "failure to accept social norms with respect to unlawful behavior" (p. 321), and, most important, "persistence of behavior patterns even under circumstances in which more self-assertive and effective behavior is possible" (p. 329). This last description implies that such people could behave more effectively if only they would choose to. In other words, the idea that antisocial persons are psychologically trapped is not reflected in DSM-III, and the internal suffering they endure is only briefly mentioned. The major focus in contemporary diagnostics of sociopaths is on behavior and morals, not whole psychological experiences. On the other hand, well-behaved obsessives are described in more empathic and psychological terms. A major diagnostic criterion of the obsessive compulsive disorder is that "the obsessions or compulsions are a significant source of distress to the individual or interfere with social or role functioning" (p. 235). For the obsessive, "senseless or repugnant" (p. 235) thoughts account for failures of social and role functioning, whereas the effect of the antisocial person's troubling inner experiences on his or her behavior is discounted.

The DSM-III's implication that a "failure to accept social norms" explains antisocial behavior is set in the context of similar moralistic ideas that undergird major social institutions. For instance, our system of justice maintains that all but the most strangely motivated behavior issues from criminal intent rather than from psychological torment. Models of achievement and well-being on the professional athletic field and in business offices promote the belief that failure stems from inner weakness. Along the same lines, popular religionists also assert that those who act irresponsibly are evil.

In the alcoholism field, the moralizer's confusion of behavior with its causes is described by Stan Shaw, who maintains that

> the fashionable jargon of "impaired control" and "priming" is exactly the same as "craving," and "loss of control" in this crucial respect—the *experience* of wanting more alcoholic drink—is taken to be *the reason itself* why more drinking occurs (1985:36).

In other words, just as the moralistic thinker maintains that a person who behaves irresponsibly is a bad person, some conventional theorists think that alcoholics are impelled to drink by an inner agent of craving. Blind to the power of guilt, these theorists focus mainly on the influence of reinforcement. The pervasiveness and rigidity of these guilt-inducing and circular explanations of behavior are what led Stein (1985:228), a psychoanalytically oriented medical anthropologist, to conclude that, in the alcoholism field, "despite our best intentions, the moralistic model prevails over the seemingly moderating or humanizing influence of the medical model."

A Critique of Vaillant and Marlatt

Vaillant (1983) assailed McCord and McCord's (1960) prospective research and other studies that argue for psychodynamic causation of substance abuse. These retrospective studies (Blum 1966; Tahka, 1966) claimed that, prior to onset, alcoholics were controlled by emotional problems, such as sociopathy, low self-esteem, egocentricity, anxiety, emotional insecurity, and latent homosexuality. McCord and McCord's psychiatric theory was that the alcoholic's "character is organized around a quest for dependency" (1960: 156). According to Vaillant, subsequent prospective studies by Jones (1968), Kammeier et al. (1973), and Vaillant (1980) countered McCord and McCord's remaining psychodynamic explanation by showing that excessive dependency did not precede alcoholism. This research is then adduced by Vaillant in support of the disease theory, which maintains that the psychological-behavioral aberrations experienced by abusers are biochemically induced.

Vaillant (1983:90–95) illustrated this argument against emotional causation of alcoholism through his analysis of the case history of James O'Neill, a severely afflicted alcoholic and compulsive gambler. O'Neill was assessed as having been psychologically healthy prior to his twelve-year drinking career and as becoming sociopathic only after the onset of alcoholism. Vaillant used data from O'Neill's pre- and postmorbid periods to make his case that

O'Neill was not impelled by psychiatric difficulties. Vaillant concluded his analysis with his own observations of O'Neill after O'Neill became abstinent.

The research staff of the longitudinal college study in which O'Neill was a subject categorized O'Neill "'in the unqualified group in terms of ethical character'" (Vaillant, 1983:90). On the basis of a blind reading of clinical data gathered when O'Neill was age 18, including several psychiatric interviews, psychological tests, and an interview with his parents, a child psychiatrist wrote the following summary:

> His parents were reliable, consistent, obsessive, devoted parents. They were relatively understanding; their expectations appear to have been more non-verbal than explicit. No alcoholism was reported. Warmth, thoughtfulness and devotion to the home were some of the comments. The subject spoke of going to his father first with any problems, and of being closer to his mother than to his father. His peer relations were reported to have been good, and little or no conflict with his parents was reported (Vaillant, 1983:92).

The psychiatrist predicted that

> the young student would develop into an obsessional, hard-working, non-alcoholic citizen. . . . He would probably marry and be relatively straight with his children. He would probably expect high standards from them (Vaillant, 1983:90).

His success at age 23 in achieving his own high ethical standards was confirmed by his commanding officer, who commented that O'Neill gave "superior attention to duty" (Vaillant, 1983:93). Whereas Vaillant missed the significance of these and other clues to harsh self-evaluations, an ego analyst would have used these symptoms to predict O'Neill's vulnerability to subsequent alcohol abuse. O'Neill's perfectionism was also discounted in subsequent psychological evaluations. As a condition of application for a graduate school grant, O'Neill was analyzed by psychologists independent of both his college and the college-study staffs. They ranked him in the top third in terms of psychological health in a group that was previously categorized by the college study staff as being in the top third of the total sample.

From an ego analyst's perspective, a series of events ignored by Vaillant are obvious historical clues to the self-castigation that led to O'Neill's antisocial behavior. The history taken by the college study staff reveals that O'Neill's

> drinking and gambling began . . . when he became depressed because he did not do well on his Ph.D. generals and was refused entrance into a fellowship organization. The patient at this time began to drink during the day, and to miss teaching appointments (Vaillant, 1983:91).

It is likely that O'Neill began to drink alcoholically in an effort to ward off harsh self-recriminations that were prompted by his career failures. Also, this sort of man—one who paid superior attention to duty—would be likely to suffer an intensification of self-blame in response to his drinking behavior. The ego analyst would suspect that a vicious cycle of drinking and then berating himself for it would be set in motion.

Eventually, this escalating internal harangue would culminate in the kind of "psychopathic" behavior that was noted by psychiatrists twelve years after O'Neill's early career failures. This result would be expected regardless of whether O'Neill used mind-altering substances or not. Like any nonalcoholic sociopath, O'Neill became trapped in a complex pattern of irresponsible behavior—in his case, thievery, sexual infidelities, and gambling—for which he experienced no remorse. Even the death of his mother, to whom he had been particularly close prior to his alcoholic drinking, evoked no self-reproach. From an ego analyst's viewpoint, his lack of remorse—or, more precisely, his repression of remorse—would be likely to occur not as the result of drinking but because he could not tolerate the painfulness of this guilt. By this time, his moralistic case against himself would have been unbearably extensive and severe.

The experience of beleaguered sufferers like O'Neill is one of being brainwashed by themselves and society—under penalty of inner and external punishment—to believe that they are, at root, sociopathic. Damning self-accusations that are typical of normal young adults engaged in arguments—such as, "You don't care about anyone but yourself," or "If you continue to act irresponsibly then you must be irresponsible to the core"—become increasingly convincing. These accusations are especially believable given the sufferer's deviant behavior and his or her immersion in moralistic thinking. As the vicious cycle of drinking and then berating him/herself reaches intolerable proportions, condemnations such as, "You're a psychopath," signal a categorical change in self-image. This last professionally sanctioned epithet was actually accepted by O'Neill when, as Vaillant reported

> his [O'Neill's] pattern of drinking, sexual infidelity, gambling and irresponsible borrowing led him to recognize from his reading that it adds up to diagnosis of psychopathic personality—especially since he has experienced no remorse about it (Vaillant, 1983:91).

In other words, O'Neill's harsh reaction to his failures and to his ways of escaping inner punishment gradually forced him to think and act as an antisocial person who had only pretended to be normal.

As noted earlier, Fenichel explains that "after a 'normal' superego has been established subsequent circumstances create a contradictory 'parasitic' double of this superego" (1945:504). As a consequence of extreme guilt that has been evoked by ordinary mistakes and failures, an antisocial belief system and self-concept tyrannizes the sufferer's consciousness. Instead of being good and trying to disown inner experiences that seem bad, the sufferer acts bad and tries to disown hope and concern. These positive expressions are warded off because they evoke the extreme counterclaims that he or she had experienced before he or she retreated into the relatively untroubled inner world of the sociopath. Ironically, in a later section, Vaillant inadvertently lent support to this ego analytic explanation of O'Neill's sociopathy in his unexplained comment that O'Neill's "shame had facilitated his denial of his disease for two decades" (p. 94).

Vaillant reported that O'Neill joined AA, stopped drinking, and subsequently returned to psychological health. The main supporting evidence—other than O'Neill's sobriety—for this evaluation is that O'Neill had

> sublimated his interest in gambling by becoming a consultant to the Governor of Massachusetts in setting up the state lottery . . . ; in other words, with the remission of alcoholism, O'Neill's ego functioning had matured. Instead of acting out his compulsive gambling, he had harnessed that interest in a socially and personally constructive way (Vaillant, 1983:94).

Vaillant added his own direct observations of O'Neill to help make his point.

> Although he avoided eye contact, however, there was a serious awareness of me as a person and I always felt he was talking to me. He behaved like a cross between a diffident professor and a newly released prisoner of war, rather than like a person truly frightened of contact.
>
> I never got the feeling that O'Neill was cold or self-absorbed (Vaillant, 1983:94).

In sum, to Vaillant, O'Neill—as well as any individual could—represented those alcoholics who are not motivated to drink by psychiatric problems.

Ironically, an observation that Vaillant himself made provides a basis for challenging his positive, post-morbid diagnosis of O'Neill. After O'Neill returned to sobriety, he asserted his intense belief in the value of a harsh conscience. Vaillant quoted him as saying, "I think that I will the taking up of a drink. I have a great deal of shame and guilt and remorse and think that's healthy" (1983:94). Vaillant confirmed this self-evaluation, observing after O'Neill's recovery, "if anything, he suffered from hypertrophy, not agenesis, of the conscience" (Vaillant, 1983:94).

Vaillant's argument against psychodynamic theories relied heavily on the ideas of cognitive behaviorism. For example, Marlatt (1978, in press) maintained that those who drink alcoholically are conditioned by social influences to expect that alcohol will relieve them of self-criticism, or guilt. It is this conditioned expectation of psychological relief that motivates excessive consumption. This expectation is proved maladaptive by the negative mood that occurs after the sufferer imbibes too much alcohol and by the vicious cycle of overindulgence and intensification of guilt that ensues. While agreeing that self-castigation and drinking constitute a vicious cycle, ego analysts argue that this involvement is essentially the effect of self-punishment and moralistic thinking in general, whereas maladaptive expectancies and irrationality per se are only contributing factors.

Marlatt explained that sufferers' expectation of relief from guilt is powerfully reinforced by cognitive mediators. That is, sufferers learn to associate the relief of guilt with a variety of alcohol-related cues, such as advertisements that picture ordinary people drinking and feeling cheerful. Socially sanctioned occasions for drinking can create a "disinhibition effect," or a reinforcement of more carefree behavior and mood than are usually socially permitted. Marlatt (in press) explained that the rewards are great for those who drink to escape guilt:

> There is a double payoff for the drinker who shows a disinhibition effect after drinking: (a) the person is able to indulge in an activity (e.g., aggressive or sexual responding) associated with immediate gratification; and (b) the person is able to avoid or be exonerated from delayed negative reactions (such as guilt or social disapproval) by "disclaiming authorship" for the disinhibited behavior.

Marlatt maintained that the expectancy of relief of negative states such as guilt is maladaptive because this powerful expectation traps the drinker in a vicious cycle: "The disequilibrium experienced after one drinking occasion sets the stage for repeated use as an attempt to restore" a positive mood, and "any short-term relief is quickly dispelled by the delayed negative effects which in turn give rise to another attempt to gain relief." Marlatt concluded that "the addicted individual is thus caught in a trap of his or her own making: the expected solution (more drugs) exacerbates the initial problem" (Marlatt, in press).

Marlatt's position begs the question of guilt's causative contribution to addiction and alcoholism. Based on Festinger's (1957, 1964) theory of cognitive dissonance, Marlatt (1978:297) commented that guilt is the consequence of

> a cognitive dissonance effect wherein the occurrence of the previously restricted behavior is dissonant with the cognitive definition of oneself as abstinent. Cognitive dissonance is experienced as a conflict state, and underlies what most people would define as guilt for having "given in to temptation."

In other words, guilt also is a learned experience. Marlatt (1978:298) further explicated that "dissonance is experienced as a negative emotional drive state and can serve as a motivating force to engage in behaviors which serve to reduce dissonance." This formulation is remarkably similar to the ego analyst's view that guilt motivates excessive consumption. But the similarity ends when Marlatt argued that both guilt itself and addiction are explained solely by the addicted person's maladaptive, or irrational, thinking. In focusing on maladaptive expectancy, Marlatt (1978) reduced the scope of aversive factors he considers to the particular negative experiences reported by the subject after drinking.[5] In contrast, the ego analyst points to a series of unconscious self-hating thoughts in a causal chain of such inner experiences. That is, relatively minor guilt feelings can preoccupy sufferers and thereby help to ward off even less tolerable self-blame (Fenichel, 1941: 172).[6] This principle implies the addiction-related idea that excessive consumption is adaptive despite the negative outcomes produced by it.

In the ego analytic view, excessive drinkers sense, but cannot articulate, the impression that the negative outcome of drinking is preferable to the experience of being sober or only mildly intoxicated. The negative outcome itself can serve to ward off less tolerable inner experiences. This self-protective process appears regularly in the clinical experience of the ego analyst. For example, Bill, an alcoholic with a personality profile similar to O'Neill's, used an idea that is much like Marlatt's to castigate himself. He said, "Wasn't I a fool for getting drunk last night? I should've known better. Now, my wife is furious and my body feels miserable." Then, in a flood of bewilderment and self-recrimination, he instructed himself: "When am I going to learn that I'm just going to feel worse when I drink too much?" While Marlatt focused narrowly on these behaviorally oriented cognitions, the ego analyst assumes that these thoughts help ward off literally intolerable self-hate and that this is a reasonable motivation for drinking to excess.

For example, what typically emerges in cases like Bill's is that the sufferer is afraid that his relationship with his wife has become unstable. This threat to his sense of well-being comes to mind when he has free time at home, and he cannot tolerate the thought of it. He also suffers from the self-castigating opinion that he is primarily to blame for the problems in his relationship. Add to this profound self-criticism the fact that he has little if any skill in addressing these difficulties, and the composite inner circumstances begin to demonstrate that his lapse into drunkenness is a reasonable defense. In other words, his drinking makes sense because it is the only way he knows to handle the feelings that trap him. At the same time, he and his wife are likely to fend off their disturbing marital dissatisfaction by focusing on their relatively limited conflicts surrounding his drinking and his behavior while drunk. Their conflicts about his drinking distract them from the more disruptive incompatibilities they are motivated to ignore.

In sum, the unexplicated logic of the drinker is as follows: "If I quit altogether or drink only moderately I will endure more emotional anguish and pain-inducing crises than I do when I drink too much." This view is captured by the bumpersticker pronouncement, "Drugs are okay; it's reality I can't stand."

Differences in Treatment

The ego analytic clinical style is indicated in Fenichel's main practical suggestion, to analyze on the side of the ego (1941:171), i.e., to help sufferers change their inner realities by making sense of the behaviors that they tend to castigate themselves for. The point of this interpretative strategy is to relieve the sufferer of the painful self-condemnations that motivate excessive consumption and to establish a more tolerant and viable self-relationship. This practice contrasts with the aim of medical or behavioristic approaches like those of Vaillant and Marlatt, which rely on indoctrination into one point of view or another—a technique that encourages obedience to the authority of others.

Vaillant and Marlatt both rely heavily on slogans in treatment such as, "There is one thing [drinking] I cannot do" (Vaillant, 1983:290); or "ONE DRINK DOES NOT MEAN A DRUNK!" (Marlatt, 1978:309). As these slogans imply, the two recommend different goals. Vaillant is committed to total abstinence, whereas Marlatt permits clients to strive for either controlled drinking or abstinence. Also, Marlatt is much more interested in the specifics of particular risk situations, and he provides elaborate instructions based on a view of psychological and environmental pressures that is far more intricate than Vaillant's.

Vaillant (1983:288) actually argued directly against "pondering the sociological and psychodynamic complexities of alcoholism":

> We must change the person's belief system and then maintain that change. Time and time again, both evangelists and behavior therapists have demonstrated that if you can but win their hearts and minds, their habits will follow. In other words, if we can but combine the best placebo effects of acupuncture, Lourdes, or Christian Science with the best attitude change inherent in the evangelical conversion experience, we may be on our way to an effective alcoholism program.

In the same vein, he recommended the "systematic *indoctrination* and *repetition* using mass media and *opportunity for identification* through peer support programs" [Vaillant's italics] that are proposed by John Farquhar and his colleagues in their work with coronary patients (1978:288).

From an ego analytic clinical perspective, the most useful instruction given by Marlatt is included in a list of things to remember and do if a slip occurs. Marlatt instructed, "There is no reason why you have to give in to these [self-blaming] feelings and take another drink" (1978:308). This instruction overlooks the pervasive and emotionally compelling character of guilt and moralistic thinking. Also, like all therapeutic indoctrinations, it induces the state it attempts to eliminate. The instruction is self-contradictory in that it places the sufferer in a negative relationship to his or her self-negations. Stated differently, Marlatt instructed the sufferer to judge his judgments rather than neutralize or disarm them in the context of an open-minded discussion of both sides of each self-negating thought. Clients who still feel guilty after reminding themselves of Marlatt's axiom have no way of explaining continuing guilt feelings other than by appealing to Marlatt's implicit view that they are irrational. If there is "no reason" to feel guilty, those who fail to eliminate self-blame from consciousness can conclude only that they are stupid or, depending on the frequency of the "irrational" thoughts, insane.

Stein (1985) pointed out the global negative consequence of indoctrination, particularly the Alcoholics Anonymous variety that Vaillant and others recommend:

> The return to sobriety is in fact a restitutional syndrome. Treatment spells victory for the superego. To be rehabilitated is to become drunk on dryness. Therapy is successful even when a dour, bitter "dry drunk" has completely supplanted a flamboyant wet one. (p. 227)

O'Neill's postmorbid functioning—his harsh self-attitude and his involvement in setting up a lottery—is an example of the restitutional syndrome. Although this and other less bitter but still problematic outcomes of treatment based on the disease theory seem preferable to continued alcoholic drinking, cases such as O'Neill's suggest the likelihood that the offspring of restituted alcoholics will be at risk for a guilt-ridden personality. It is possible to obtain less ambiguous results in ego analytic therapy and in a comprehensive treatment program that is built on the ego analytic principle of nonjudgmental and collaborative discussion of both sides of self-hating thoughts.

The logic of this position is that to gain access to the more intolerable self-hating thoughts that actually motivate excessive consumption it is necessary to work carefully through a chain of defensive, self-castigating reactions. Or, as Fenichel puts it, "interpretation begins on the defense side" (1941:171) in order to achieve "a gradual alteration of the superego" (p. 180), or inner authority. The therapist attempts to make sense of the defenses that the client thinks are nonsensical or that he finds inadequate.

To illustrate this kind of interpretation, which is the sole technique of ego analysis, Fenichel (1941:323) tells a story about a lecturer who was railing against what he considered to be standard psychoanalytic technique.

He told of an acquaintance who was being analyzed and who, though fifty years of age, wished still to learn ice skating. This man practiced skating on lonely mountain lakes surrounded by steep walls of rock. His analyst tried to convince him that he made this choice of place out of a longing for his mother's womb. In actuality, said the lecturer, this fifty-year-old gentleman wanted merely to escape spectators in less lonely places who would have laughed at his attempts to learn skating. This critic is absolutely right.

In this way, rather than demonstrate how foolish defensiveness is—an evaluation that already burdens the client—the ego analyst attempts to uncover its reasonableness. Successive defenses and castigations of them are, in turn, carefully neutralized by the analyst's empathic interpretations.

The following case vignette, which is adapted from McFadden and Peterson (1986), illustrates the ego analyst's technique of making sense of a typical alcoholic's defensiveness. In what was intended to be a one-shot phone conversation with a nonjudgmental confidant, an "alcoholic" said, "I hate the thought of counseling because I can't stand talking about myself. I'm calling only so I can tell my wife I tried. Then maybe I can get her off my back."

At this point, the behavioristic theorist might be tempted to "break" through the sufferer's defense against the thought of counseling by pressuring the caller with the negative consequences of not talking and/or the positive rewards of coming for treatment. The ego analyst, on the other hand, deduces the presence of these disguised accusations from the details of the defense. In this instance, the analyst suspected that the caller was suffering from a self-accusation that lay just below the surface of awareness, something like the following: "The reason that you avoid counseling is that you're just afraid to face up to your problems." This is a lecture that sufferers have heard many times.

The ego analyst tried to open the conversation by taking the role of a tolerant authority. He explained why the accusation of cowardice did not fit the facts, saying, "It makes sense to me that you might not want to reveal yourself to a stranger, because people—particularly professionals—can make us feel bad by telling us what's 'wrong' with us." He added, "It seems reasonable to avoid any counselor who makes you feel worse." In this way, the assumed self-hating thought is neutralized or disarmed without ever pressuring the sufferer to face it.[7] His automatic self-accusatory opinion—that it is cowardly and irresponsible to distrust counseling—was partially relieved.

In other words, a simultaneous reduction in self-hate and increase in self-esteem occurred. Instead of hating himself for avoiding psychotherapy, the caller could see that it was a reasonable strategy to want to keep his own counsel. Caution with strangers was valid and even useful, rather than cowardly and self-defeating. And his behavior improved during that time of self-reflection because there was less guilt of the kind that drove him toward the bottle.

Finally, from his strengthened position against counseling, he could entertain the idea of actually entering therapy. Once the caller felt that it was reasonable to avoid counseling, he could discuss both sides of the question, "Should I try counseling or not?" The point here is that one can objectively explore both sides of issues only if one is reasonably free from pressure to reject one side of the debate. The reluctant caller could explore more specific fears of placing his trust in the counselor. For example, his fear that counseling would not work—because he might be beyond help—could be candidly discussed. In a nonjudgmental relationship wherein he would not be exhorted to overwhelm his negative feelings, he could tolerate this reflection, a prospect that had previously seemed impossible.

Subsequent clinical articles will demonstrate that, as treatment progresses, successively more extreme versions of self-blame are relieved by the analyst's nonjudgmental interpretations. Sufferers become more collaborative and less resistant than in conventional treatment precisely because the ego analyst consistently relieves guilt rather than subtly reintroducing it in instructions to behave according to the professional's principles. Eventually, therapist and client sufficiently relieve the self-blaming thoughts that motivate the client's excessive drinking.

No formal outcome studies of ego analytic treatment of alcoholics have been undertaken, but clinical experience speaks to an important negative evaluation that is likely to be made. Readers are likely to conclude that, like classical psychoanalysis, ego analysis is unable to produce a quick return to sobriety, whereas the indoctrinations of disease-oriented and behaviorist approaches are promoted as producing quick benefits and being cost effective. As Apfelbaum (1983) has clinically demonstrated in the field of sex therapy, ego analysis is adaptable to short-term contractual therapy. The author's case load currently includes three clients who had been diagnosed alcoholic by local clinics and who had each been through two twenty-one-day treatment programs in a five-year period. At present, each of these clients has abstained or controlled his drinking at safe levels for more than three months after receiving only an average of three one-hour treatments during a three-week period; and all are currently being maintained in one-hour-per-week therapy.

Summary

The clinical experience of ego analysts suggests that the self-abusive behavior that Vaillant (1983) and other disease theorists believe is biologically determined and maladaptive actually makes sense as a way of warding off intrapersonal and interpersonal problems that sufferers are currently incapable of solving. The relatively agonizing, alcohol-related problems experienced by sufferers can, when all of the relevant inner experiences are assembled, be less troubling to them than the difficulties they experience when sober, particularly the root difficulty of self-castigation.

An implication of this argument is that the theorist assume the considerable task of challenging the moralistic norms that have crept into psychiatric diagnostics and psychological thinking in general. Ego analysis offers a way to launch this challenge by explaining that sociopathy indicates self-hating thoughts that are even more severe than those experienced by obsessive people. Therefore, relief of guilt is a more reasonable solution to the problem of antisocial behavior, including alcoholism and other addictions, than the indoctrinations of the disease theorist and the cognitive behaviorist.

Notes

1. Fenichel asserted the authenticity of this shift and of its designation, saying, "All analysis is really ego analysis" (1941:166).

2. Apfelbaum (1966) has explained Freud's fundamental departure from id analysis, which remains in disguised form in contemporary ego psychology. Apfelbaum detailed Freud's abandonment of the concepts of inner entities, physical drive states, and the seething-cauldron view of impulses in favor of functions, psychological aims, and distorted derivatives of self-hate. Nevertheless, in contradistinction to Vaillant, both conventional and ego analytic psychodynamic theorists argue that emotion—especially psychological pain—is a major determinant of behavior.

3. See Zucker and Gomberg's (1986) challenge to Vaillant's research analysis that is based on methodological considerations as well as developmental personality theory.

4. See Loewald's (1952) observations on the ego psychology version of psychoanalysis. He stated that "psychoanalytic theory has unwittingly taken over much of the obsessive neurotic's experience and conception of reality and has taken it for granted as 'the objective reality'" (p. 448). Apfelbaum (1966) argued this observation is true of id analysis as well.

5. Wile (1981:48), an ego analyst, maintained that the behavioral therapist takes an "overly restricted view of positive reinforcement." Similarly, Marlatt (1978) committed to a narrow view of punishment: he does not acknowledge the complexity and extensiveness of guilt. According to Eisnitz (personal communication, 1980), "this reductionism is a consequence of social learning theorists' rigid insistence on precise and experimentally verifiable investigation and their complementary unqualified rejection of more speculative kinds of inquiry."

6. Fenichel (1941:176) clarified that "all defense is 'relative defense'; relative to one layer it is defense, and at the same time, relative to another layer it is that which is warded off."

7. This ego analytic interpretation differs significantly from the strategic therapist's paradoxically intended technique of reframing the resistance, i.e., pointing out its validity. The strategic therapist does not actually believe that defenses are sensible, whereas ego analysts do.

References

American Psychiatric Association. 1980. *Quick Reference to the Diagnostic Criteria from Diagnostic and Statistical Manual of Mental Disorders.* 3rd ed. Washington, DC: American Psychiatric Association.

Apfelbaum, B. 1966. On Ego Psychology: A Critique of the Structural Approach to Psycho-analytic Theory. *The International Journal of Psycho-analysis* 47:451–475.

———. 1983. *Expanding the Boundaries of Sex Therapy.* Berkeley: Self-published.

Bandura, A. 1977. *Social Learning Theory.* Englewood Cliffs, NJ: Prentice-Hall.

Blum, E.M. 1966. Psychoanalytic Views of Alcoholism: A Review: *Quarterly Journal of Studies on Alcohol* 27:259–299.

Farquhar, J.L., N. Maccoby, P.D. Wood, J.K. Alexander, H. Breitrose, B.W. Brown Jr., W.L. Haskell, A.L. McAlister, A.J. Meyer, J.D. Nash, and M.P. Stern. 1977. Community Education for Cardiovascular Health. *Lancet* 1:1192–1195.

Fenichel, O. 1941. *Problems of Psychoanalytic Technique.* New York: Psychoanalytic Quarterly.

———. 1945. *The Psychoanalytic Theory of the Neurosis.* New York: Norton.

Festinger, L. 1957. *A Theory of Cognitive Dissonance.* Stanford: Stanford University Press.

———. 1964. *Conflict. Decision and Dissonance.* Stanford: Stanford University Press.

Freud, S. 1923. The Ego and the Id., In J. Rickman, ed., *A Selection from the Works of Sigmund Freud.* Garden City, NY: Doubleday Anchor Books.

Jones, M.C. 1968. Personality Correlates and Antecedents of Drinking Patterns in Adult Males. *Journal of Consulting and Clinical Psychology* 32:2–12.

Kammeier, M.L., H. Hoffmann, and R.G. Loper. 1973. Personality Characteristics of Alcoholics as College Freshmen and at Time of Treatment. *Quarterly Journal of Studies on Alcohol* 34:390–399.

Loewald, H.W. 1952. The Problem of Defence and the Neurotic Interpretation of Reality. *International Journal of Psycho-Analysis* 33:241–253.

Marlatt, G.A. 1978. Craving for Alcohol, Loss of Control, and Relapse: A Cognitive-Behavioral Analysis." In P.E. Nathan, G.A. Marlatt, and T. Loberg, eds., *Alcoholism: New Directions in Behavioral Research and Treatment.* New York: Plenum Press.

———. In press. Alcohol, the Magic Elixir: Stress, Expectancy, and the Transformation of Emotional States. In Gottheil, ed., *Stress: Alcohol and Drug Interactions.* New York: Brunner/Mazel.

McCord, W., and J. McCord. 1960. *Origins of Alcoholism.* Stanford: Stanford University Press.

McFadden, J., and J. Peterson. 1986. Driven to Drink: A Nontraditional Approach to Excessive Drinking. Unpublished Book Proposal.

Milam J. 1983. *Under the Influence: A Guide to the Myths and Realities of Alcoholism.* New York: Bantam.

Shaw, S. 1985. The Disease Concept of Dependence. In N. Heather, I. Robertson, and P. Davies, eds., *The Misuse of Alcohol: Crucial Issues in Dependence Treatment and Prevention.* New York: New York University Press.

Stein, H.F. 1985. Alcoholism as Metaphor in American Culture: Ritual Desecration as Social Integration. *Ethos* 13:195–235.

Tahka, V. 1966. *The Alcoholic Personality.* Helsinki: Finnish Foundation for Alcohol Studies.

Vaillant, G.E. 1980. Natural History of Male Psychological Health, VIII: Antecedent of Alcoholism and "Orality," *American Journal of Psychiatry* 137:181–186.

———. 1983. *The Natural History of Alcoholism: Causes, Patterns, and Paths to Recovery.* Cambridge, MA: Harvard University Press.

Wile, D.B. 1981. *Couples Therapy: A Nontraditional Approach.* New York: John Wiley & Sons.

Zucker, R.A., and E.S. Lisansky Gomberg. 1986. Etiology of Alcoholism Reconsidered: The Case for a Biopsychosocial Process. *American Psychologist* 41: 783–805.

10

A Moral Vision of Addiction: How People's Values Determine Whether They Become and Remain Addicts

Stanton Peele

[John] Phillips is not altogether realistic about himself. He recalls that when he was a postman, he threw mail away because his mailbags were too heavy; as a graveyard plot salesman, he received down payments, pocketed the money and never recorded the transactions. Still, on page 297 of a 444-page book, in reporting how he skipped out on a $2,000 hotel bill, he writes, "My values were beginning to corrode under the prolonged influence of hard drugs" (Finkle, 1986:33).

Thomas (Hollywood) Henderson, the former Dallas Cowboy linebacker who has been jailed in California since 1984 on sex charges involving two teenage girls, will be released this week and has already been scheduled for a paid speaking tour to talk against drug and alcohol abuse. Henderson was an admitted drug user (*New York Times,* October 14, 1986:30).

Introduction

The scientific study of addiction has strongly opposed value considerations in addiction, regarding these as remnants of an outdated, religious-moral model. Behavior therapists, experimental psychologists, and sociologists hold this view in common with disease theorists who have championed the idea that a moral perspective oppresses the addict and impedes progress toward a solution for alcoholism and addiction. Many social scientists and others, however, believe the disease approach actually is just another form of the moral model, and that "the acceptance of the 'disease' concept . . . [has] covertly intensified rigid moralizing" (Fingarette, 1985:60). It has accomplished this by embodying the evil of addiction in the use of the substance—in any use of such drugs as cocaine and in any kind of drinking by those with alcohol problems—and by urging abstinence as if it represented a modern scientific and therapeutic invention.

Nonetheless, the aim of "demoralizing" addiction retains a strong appeal for liberal observers and for social and behavioral scientists. In fact, social researchers frequently bemoan the strong tendencies for both general populations and treatment personnel to continue to see addiction in moral terms even as most people ostensibly endorse the fashionable view of addiction as a disease (Orcutt et al., 1980; Tournier, 1985). In other words, as scientists, they wish to stamp out entirely people's continuing tendency to regard addiction as a reflection of the addict's moral qualities and to hold people responsible for addictive behavior. The view of this chapter, on the other hand, is that appetitive behavior of all types is crucially influenced by people's preexisting values, and that the best way to combat addiction both for the individual and the society is to inculcate values that are incompatible with addiction and with drug- and alcohol-induced misbehavior.

I sat with an older woman watching a television program in which a woman who directed a prominent treatment program described how, as an alcoholic in denial, she drank alcoholically throughout her years as a parent, thus raising six children who all either became substance abusers or required therapy as children of an alcoholic. The woman's argument was that she had inadvertently inherited her alcoholism from her two alcoholic grandfathers (a model of genetic transmission of alcoholism, incidentally, which no one has actually proposed). The woman I was sitting with clucked about how insidious the disease was that it could make a mother treat her children this way. I turned to her and asked: "Do you really think you could ever have gotten drunk and ignored your children, no matter how delightful you found drinking or how it relieved your tension or however you reacted to alcohol genetically?" Neither she nor I could imagine it, given her values as a parent.

Scientists have ignored successful, value-based personal and social strategies against addiction because of their uneasiness about making distinctions among value systems. Their reluctance is counterproductive and, put simply, wrong on the evidence. The evidence that a person's or group's values are essential elements in combatting addiction include the following areas of research: (1) the large group differences in the successful socialization of moderate consumption of every kind of substance; (2) the strong intentional aspects of addictive behavior; (3) the tendency for some people to abuse a range of unrelated substances and to display other antisocial and self-destructive behaviors; (4) developmental studies that repeatedly discover value orientations to play a large role in styles of drug use in adolescence and beyond; (5) the relationship of therapeutic and natural remission to personal value resolutions by addicts and to life changes they make that evoke values which compete with addiction.

How Do Some Groups Encourage Almost Universal Moderation and Self-Control?

The power of the group to inspire moderation of consumption is perhaps the most consistent finding in the study of addictive behavior. Even the most ardent supporters of the disease theory of alcoholism, including Jellinek himself, clearly indicated that cultural patterns are the major determinants of drinking behavior. Vaillant (1983), while defending the disease theory, claimed alcoholism had both a cultural and a genetic source. He noted that Irish-Americans in his core-city sample were seven times as likely to be alcoholic as were those of Mediterranean descent (Italians and Greeks, with some Jews). Clinical outcomes in this study, such as return to moderate drinking, were more closely tied to ethnic group than they were to numbers of alcoholic relatives, which Vaillant used as a measure of genetic determination of drinking.

Vaillant, like Jellinek, explained these data in terms of cultural differences in visions of alcohol's power and in the socialization of drinking practices. Yet this kind of explanation of group differences does not fit well with Vaillant's professed belief in inbred sources of individual drinking problems. Vaillant's ambivalence is indicated by his explanation for the large social-class differences in alcoholism he found: his core-city group had an alcoholism rate more than three times as great as that for his Harvard-educated sample. Vaillant suggested this discrepancy was due to the tendency for alcoholics to slide down the social ladder, in which case inherited alcoholism would be more prevalent in lower social classes. Among other problems with his explanation is its failure to take into account the ethnic differences in the composition of his two samples (almost entirely recent ethnic immigrants in the core-city group, predominantly upper-middle-class WASPs in the pre–World War II Harvard sample).

Vaillant's uneasiness about group differences in alcoholism rates is common among clinicians and other representatives of the dominant alcoholism movement in the United States, although it is certainly not limited to these groups. For example, a number of years ago the NIAAA published a popular poster entitled "The typical alcoholic American" that depicted a range of people from different ethnic, racial, and social groups, of different ages, and of both sexes. The point of the poster, obviously, was that anyone from any background could be alcoholic, a point often made in contemporary media presentations about alcoholism. Strictly speaking, this is true; at the same time, the poster ignores fundamental and major differences in alcoholism rates that appear with regard to almost every demographic category it depicted. Without an awareness of these differences, it is hard to imagine how a researcher or clinician could understand or deal with alcoholism.

One mark of the disbelief in social differences in alcoholism has been the tendency to hunt for hidden alcoholics in groups that ostensibly display few drinking problems. We are told regularly, for instance, that so many more men than women are in alcoholism treatment because the stigma attached to women's drinking problems prevents women from seeking treatment. In fact, indications are that women with drinking problems are *more* likely than men to seek therapy for alcoholism, as they are for all kinds of psychological and medical problems (Woodruff et al., 1973). Epidemiological investigations find that women have far fewer drinking problems than men by every kind of measure (Ferrence, 1980). Even researchers with biological and disease orientations find powerful sex differences in alcoholism. Goodwin et al. (1977), for example, found 4 percent of women with alcoholic biologic parents were alcoholic or had a serious drinking problem; the authors suggested that since from .1 to 1 percent of women in Denmark (where the study was conducted) were alcoholic, the findings hinted at a genetic component to female alcoholism, although the small number of female alcoholics discovered in the study forbad definitive conclusions.

Another group popularly singled out for denying their alcohol problems is the Jews. All surveys find Jews underrepresented among problem drinkers and alcoholics (Cahalan and Room, 1974; Greeley et al., 1980). Glassner and Berg (1980) conducted a survey of a Jewish community in an upstate New York city with the hypothesis "that low alcohol abuse rates among Jews resulted more from the ability to hide excessive drinking [and research methodology flaws] . . . than from actual drinking patterns of Jews" (p. 651). Among eighty-eight respondents, including both observant and nonpracticing Jews, Glassner and Berg discovered no problem drinkers. Even by accepting at face value all reports of Jewish alcoholics by zealous community alcoholism representatives, the researchers calculated an alcoholism rate far below that for Americans at large (less than 1 percent, probably closer to 1 in 1,000). Such research in no way discourages frequent claims that Jewish alcoholism is on the increase and may be rampant, and that Jews have an urgent need to deal with the denial brought on by the stigma they attach to alcoholism.

One particularly interesting cultural difference in alcoholism rates concerns Asian and Native American populations. That is, the large-scale alcohol problems often described among Indian and Eskimo groups have been attributed to the way these racial groups metabolize alcohol. Native Americans often show a quick onset of intoxication and a visible reddening from ingesting small amounts of alcohol. Unfortunately, while reliable racial differences in processing alcohol have been measured, these do not correlate with alcohol abuse (Peele, 1986b). In particular, Chinese and Japanese Americans, who have the same reactions to alcohol as do Native Americans, display according to some measures (such as alcohol-related crime and violence) the very *least* alcohol abuse among American ethnic and racial groups, measures by which Indians show the highest such rates.

What Accounts for Cultural Differences in Alcoholism?

The effort to explain Native American alcoholism by way of racial differences is, of course, another version of the denial of the importance of social learning in addiction. A related suggestion is that natural selection has weeded out those susceptible to alcoholism in groups that have a long history of drinking, and that this elimination of alcoholics in some races accounts for their lower alcoholism rates. Besides displaying a Lysenko-like optimism about the speed of genetic adaptation, this hypothesis neglects important elements in the history of drinking. Aboriginal Indian groups *did* drink beverage alcohol and therefore were available for a similar racial elimination of alcoholism; moreover, different Indian groups in Latin and North America have had very different experiences with problem intoxication, depending usually upon their relation to Caucasians (MacAndrew and Edgerton, 1969).

Jews, on the other hand, have been known as moderate drinkers since Biblical times—that is, from their first identification as a group distinct from the racially related Semitic populations that surrounded them (Keller, 1970). This analysis strongly suggests that their belief system from the beginning distinguished the Jews from their neighbors. Some theorists have speculated that Jewish moderation stems from the group's perpetual minority status and the premium this has placed on self-control and intellectual awareness (Glazer, 1952). Similar kinds of cultural explanations have been used to account for the notable drinking patterns of other groups. For example, Bales (1962) analyzed frequent problem drinking among the Irish as a reflection of a world view that is at once flamboyant and tragic. Room (1985) points out that Indian groups lack a value for self-control that would inhibit excessive drinking or drunken misbehavior.

Maloff et al. (1979) summarized the results of decades of social scientific observations of cultural drinking styles and other consumption practices in detailing cultural recipes for moderation. One rather remarkable element in cultural recipes for moderate consumption is illustrated by the cases of Jewish and Chinese-American drinking. As described by Glassner and Berg (1984: 16), "Reform and nonpracticing Jews define alcoholism in terms of psychological dependency and view suspected alcoholics with condemnation and blame." In other words, Jews guarantee almost universal moderation by explicitly rejecting the major contentions of the disease theory of alcoholism, including a belief in biological causation and the need for a nonpunitive attitude toward habitual drunkenness. Jews instead strongly disapprove of drunken misbehavior and ostracize those who do not conform to this standard of conduct.

The Cantonese Chinese in New York City, as described by Barnett (1955), employed a similar approach in disapproving of and applying powerful group sanctions to those who do not control their drinking. These people simply refused to tolerate loss-of-control drinking. As a part of his study, Barnett examined police blotters in the Chinatown district of New York. He found that, among 17,515 arrests recorded between 1933 and 1949, *not one* reported drunkenness in the charge. Are these Chinese suppressing alcoholism or simply its overt manifestations? Actually, since drunken arrest is a criterion for alcohol dependence in DSM-III, its elimination automatically eliminates a central element of alcoholism. All this is academic, however. Even if all these Chinese accomplished was to eradicate drunken misbehavior and violence in a crowded urban area for seventeen years, their model is one that the United States as a whole could emulate with great benefit.[1]

This Chinese case study stands in stark contrast to that of an Ojibwa Indian community in northwest Ontario studied by Shkilnyk (1984). In this community, violent assault and suicide are so prevalent that only one in four die of natural causes or by accident. In one year one-third of the children between ages 5 and 14 were taken from their parents because the parents were unable to care for the children when almost continuously drunk. This village was marked by a "cycle of forced migration, economic dependence, loss of cultural identity, and breakdown in social networks" (Chance, 1985:65), that underlay its self-destruction through alcohol. At the same time, the people of this tribe had an absolute belief that alcoholism was a disease they could not control. The title of this work, "A poison stronger than love," comes from a village resident who declared "The only thing I know is that alcohol is a stronger power than the love of children."

Can somebody seriously recommend converting Chinese or Jewish populations to the conception of alcoholism as an uncontrollable disease—one that is not indigenous to their cultures? What might we expect from such a conversion? MacAndrew and Edgerton (1969) surveyed cultural differences in attitudes toward alcohol in relation to drinking patterns. Their primary finding was that drunken comportment took a specific form in each society, a form that often varied dramatically from one cultural setting to another. Societies accepted that drunkenness led to certain behaviors and, not surprisingly, had a high incidence of such behaviors—including violence and alcoholic crime. In other words, societies have varying notions of both the degree and the results of loss of control caused by drinking, differences with major consequences for behavior. Similar differences in the belief that alcohol causes misbehavior have also been found to hold for individuals within U.S. culture (Critchlow, 1983).

The Causes and Consequences of the Denial of Social Forces in Addiction

The measurement of social variation in the addictive and appetitive behaviors often achieves an order of magnitude comparable to that Vaillant found between Irish- and Italian-American drinking styles. For example, in the case of obesity, Stunkard et al. (1972) found low-socioeconomic-status (SES) girls were nine times as likely to be fat by age 6 as high-SES girls. Is there a cultural bias against such social-scientific findings compared with results that are seen to indicate genetic or biological causality? If some biological indicator were found to distinguish two populations as well as ethnicity does in the case of alcoholism or SES does in the case of childhood obesity for women, the discovery would surely merit a Nobel Prize. Instead, in our society, we ignore, minimize, and deny socially based findings.

In other words, rather than Jews' denying their alcoholism, the alcoholism movement is practicing massive denial of social factors in alcoholism. We commonly read reviews of the literature that declare that research findings with regard to social differences run exactly counter to standard wisdom in the field. Thus, "The stereotype of the typical 'hidden' female alcoholic as a middle-aged suburban housewife does not bear scrutiny. The highest rates of problem drinking are found among younger, lower-class women . . . who are single, divorced, or separated" (Lex, 1985:96–97). Unemployed and unmarried women are far more likely to be alcoholics or heavy drinkers (Ferrence, 1980). Why are such findings regularly denied? In part, middle-class women (like Betty Ford) are eagerly sought as alcoholism patients because of their ability to pay for therapy and because their prognosis is so much better than that of lower-SES or derelict women.

Perhaps also in the United States this denial comes from a pervasive ideology that minimizes class distinctions. It is seen as an additional and unwarranted burden to the oppressed to announce that low-SES women are far more likely to be obese (Goldblatt et al., 1965), that low-SES men are far more likely to have a drinking problem (Cahalan and Room, 1974), and that the greater likelihood for lower-SES people to smoke has become increasingly pronounced as more middle-class smokers quit (Marsh, 1984). In general, social class is correlated with people's ability and/or willingness to accept and act on healthful recommendations. The health belief model finds that health behaviors depend on the person's sense of self-efficacy, the value the person places on health, and the person's belief that particular behaviors really make a difference to health outcomes (Lau et al., 1986).

The alternative to discussing such issues in terms of values is usually to ascribe addiction, alcoholism, and obesity to biological heritage. But what are the consequences of believing, as Vaillant (1983) claimed (with so little evidence), that low-SES people are more often alcoholic because their parents' alcoholism has propelled them downward economically and socially, and that they harbor a biological inheritance likely to perpetuate this trend? What should we make of the high incidence of alcoholism, drug addiction, cigarette smoking, and obesity among black Americans? Should we believe they have inherited these tendencies, either separately or as one global addiction factor? This thinking offers little chance for improving the lot of those who suffer the worst consequences of addiction.

In addition to less secure values toward health, lower socioeconomic status seems to be associated with the failure to develop effective strategies for managing consumption. The best illustration of this is the presence of high abstinence and abuse levels in the very same groups. For example, in the United States, the higher a person's SES, the more likely a person is both to drink at all and to drink without problems (Cahalan and Room, 1974). Low SES and minority racial status make people both more likely to abstain and more likely to require treatment for alcoholism (Armor et al., 1978). It is as though, in the absence of a confident way of drinking, people strive to avoid alcohol problems by not drinking at all. This strategy is highly unstable, however, because it depends mainly on the person's ability to remain outside drinking or drug-using groups throughout his or her lifetime.

It seems often that the secrets of healthful behavior are limited to those who already possess them. Many middle- and upper-middle-class people appear to gain this knowledge as a birthright, even when they endorse disease theories of alcoholism. Despite Vaillant's (1983) emphasis on the uncontrollable nature of alcohol abuse, an illustration accompanying the *Time* magazine piece on Vaillant's book showed the Vaillant family taking wine with a meal. The caption read: "Wine is part of the meal on special occasions for the Vaillants and Anne, 16, and Henry, 17. 'We should teach children to make intelligent drinking decisions'" (New Insights into Alcoholism, 1983: 64). In his book, Vaillant (1983:106) advised that "individuals with many alcoholic relatives should be . . . doubly careful to learn safe drinking habits," although he nowhere discussed how this is to be done.

When I observe public health officials, academicians, and the largely professional and managerial class of people I know, I find almost none smokes, most dedicate themselves to physical fitness and exercise, and hardly any have time for drinking or taking drugs in a way that leads to unconsciousness. I haven't attended a party in years where I have seen anyone get drunk. I am perplexed when these same people make public health recommendations or analyze addictions in a way that removes the locus of control for addictive behavior from the individual and places it in the substance—as when they concentrate on preventing people ever from taking drugs, treat alcoholism and comparable behaviors as diseases, and explain overweight as an inherited trait—all exactly opposite to the approach that works in their own lives. This anomaly marks the triumph of the very values and beliefs that have regularly been shown to lead to addiction; it is a stunning case of bad values chasing out good.

The explanation for this perverse triumph starts with the success of a minority of people with the worst substance abuse problems in converting the majority population to their point of view. For example, Vaillant (1983) explained how several alcoholics educated him about alcoholism, thereby reversing the point of view he previously held (Vaillant, 1977) and placing him in conflict with most of his own data. This triumph of bad values is due also to the dominance of the medical model in treatment for psychological problems in the United States—and especially the economic benefits of this model of treatment, residual superstitions about drugs and the tendency to convert these superstitions into scientific models of addiction (Peele, 1985), and a pervasive sense of loss of control that has developed in this country about halting drug abuse.

Do Human Beings Regulate Their Eating Behavior and Weight?

The idea that people regulate their consumption in line with personal and social values is perhaps most disputed in both popular and scientific circles in the case of obesity. People we know all the time strive but fail to achieve a desired weight. Strong evidence has been presented and widely publicized that weight and obesity are genetically determined. If this is the case, then the attempt to restrain eating to achieve a healthy, but biologically inappropriate, weight is doomed and is likely to lead to eating disorders like bulimia and anorexia that are rampant among young women. This view of the futility of conscious restraint of eating has been most emphatically presented by Polivy and Herman (1983).

Yet there are also strong commonsensical indications that weight is closely associated with social-class, group, and individual values: after all, the beautiful people one watches in movies, television, and performing music seem very much thinner (and better looking) than average. In this section, I examine the idea that weight and eating behavior are under cultural and individual control by tracing the work of three prominent researchers and their followers: (1) psychiatrist Albert Stunkard, who established that weight is greatly influenced by social group and yet who has sought to prove that weight is a biological inheritance; (2) social psychologist Stanley Schachter (and several of his students), who have striven to show through experimental research that eating behavior is irrational and biologically determined; and (3) physical anthropologist Stanley Garn, who depicts human weight levels as largely malleable and adaptable to social standards.

Albert Stunkard and the Inheritance of Overweight

Stunkard conducted some of his most important research on obesity as an epidemiologist with the Midtown Manhattan study, where he found low-SES women were six times more likely to be obese than were high-SES women (Goldblatt et al. 1965; see Stunkard et al., 1972). Differences in obesity rates were also apparent among ethnic groups in the Manhattan study; for example, obesity was three times as prevalent among Italian as English women. What emerged from these data, however, was the *flexibility* of weight level, because members of the same ethnic groups showed considerable movement toward the U.S. mean the longer they lived in the United States and the higher their socioeconomic status became. In other words, people (especially women) zeroed in on the U.S. ideal of thinness to the extent they became integrated into the mainstream of the U.S. middle class.

Stunkard (1976), however, expressed little faith in conventional psychological accounts of obesity and looked more toward a biological basis for overweight, even as he stressed behavior modification techniques for losing weight. Recently, Stunkard et al. (1986) elicited a tremendous media reaction when they found, in a study of Danish adoptees, that biological inheritance swamped any environmental effects in determining weight levels. Despite this discovery, Stunkard remained committed to a program of weight loss for high-risk populations who can be targeted for weight-control programs at an early age based on their parents' obesity (Why Kids Get Fat, 1986).

Stanley Schachter and His Students and the Social Psychology of Obesity

Stanley Schachter (1968), a pioneering social psychologist, extended his work on the cognitive determination of emotions to the idea that fat people labeled their hunger based on external cues, rather than on the actual state of their stomachs. That is, instead of deciding whether they were hungry based on how full they were, they heeded such cues as the time of day or presence of inviting food to make decisions about eating. Although the "externality" model of overeating initially showed promising results in a series of ingenious experiments, it later came under fire and was rejected by prominent students of Schachter who had collaborated on much of the externality model research in the 1960s and 1970s (cf. Peele, 1983). For example, Rodin (1981) repudiated the externality model of obesity primarily because there are externally oriented eaters at all weight levels.

Nisbett (1972) proposed that weight levels (as opposed to external eating styles) are set at birth or in early childhood, so that when weight descends below this level the hypothalamus stimulates eating until the natural weight level is regained. This is one version of the so-called set-point model, which has enjoyed tremendous popularity. Rodin (1981) rejected the set-point model based on research that shows women who have lost weight do not show greater responsiveness to food cues, as set-point predicts. Rodin herself, however, emphasized physiological factors in overweight and held out the possibility that "arousal-related overeating" can be explained "without relying on psychodynamic factors" (p. 368). She also noted the self-maintaining nature of overweight, a kind of inertial adaptation by the body that might be called a model of "relative set-point"—people tend to stay at the weight level they are at.

Despite the strong emphasis on inbred and physiologic causes of overweight that characterizes the writing and research of Schachter and such Schachter students as Rodin, Nisbett, and Herman, subjects in their research often appear spontaneously to achieve self-directed weight loss and desired weight levels. For example, Rodin and Slochower (1976) found that girls who reacted strongly to external cues gained more weight than others at a food-rich camp, but that these girls frequently managed to lose much of this weight before returning home, as though they were learning how to respond to their new environment in order to maintain their preferred weight. Schachter (1982) himself discovered long-term weight loss was a relatively common event. Sixty-two percent of his ever-obese subjects in two communities who had tried to lose weight had succeeded and were no longer obese, having taken off an average of 34.7 pounds and kept the weight off for an average of 11.2 years. This result strongly contradicted previous statements by Schachter, Nisbett, and Rodin, to wit, "Almost any overweight person can lose weight; few can keep it off" (Rodin, 1981:361).

Although the dominant view of obesity—even including this group of prominent social psychologists—has insisted on the biological determination of weight level and has strongly resisted the idea of social and individual regulation of weight, a body of literature supports the role of cognition and of parental socialization on eating and obesity. For example, Wooley (1972) found that both obese and normal-weight subjects did not regulate their eating based on the actual caloric content of the food they ate, but that they did respond to the amount of calories they *thought* this food contained. Milich (1975) and Singh (1973) discussed findings that indicate subjects may respond very differently in natural settings—where other matters are important to them—than they do in the typical laboratory settings where set-point and externality research have been conducted. Woody and Costanzo (1981) explored how learned eating habits (such as the types of food young boys eat) in combination with social pressures lead to obesity or its avoidance.

Stanley Garn and the Social Relativity of Eating Behavior

When leading *social-psychological* researchers espouse biogenic theories of obesity, we are not likely to find much space given to models of overweight and of eating behavior based on parental and cultural socialization and value-oriented or other goal-directed behavior (cf. Stunkard, 1980). The most comprehensive body of data opposed to reductionist models of obesity like set-point has been presented by an anthropologist, Stanley Garn. The primary point of departure for Garn (1985) is evaluating whether "fatness" changes or remains constant throughout the individual's lifetime, based on Garn's own and several other large-scale longitudinal investigations. Indeed, it is remarkable that both proponents of set-point and later revisions of the idea that obesity is intractable (such as Schachter, 1982) make no reference to epidemiological studies that directly test this question of constancy of weight levels and fatness.

These data contradict the set-point hypothesis in the most direct way possible. "Taking all of our data into consideration, and the more relevant data from the literature, it is clear that fatness level is scarcely fixed, even in adults. Some 40 percent of obese women and 60 percent of obese men are no longer obese one decade and two decades later. The percent of obese who become less than obese increases in succession for adolescents, for children, and finally for preschool children. Three-quarters of our obese preschoolers were no longer obese when they were young adults. To the extent that fatness level is not fixed for long we may have to reconsider some of the more popular explanations for obesity" (Garn, 1985:41). The finding that the earlier the age of initial assessment the less continuity there is with adult fatness particularly contradicts assertions like those by Polivy and Herman (1983) that those who do lose weight, such as Schachter's (1982) subjects, do not have genuine set-point obesity as measured by childhood fatness.

Garn (1985) also evaluated the question of inheritance of obesity and came to conclusions diametrically opposed to those announced by Stunkard et al. (1986), although Garn's work seems somehow to invite less media attention than the Stunkard group's. In general, Garn et al. (1984) also found continuities in parental-child fatness. However, this correlation peaked at age 18 and declined thereafter, as children left home. The correlation Garn found between adopted children and biological relatives decreased the earlier the age of adoption. Data like these have prompted Garn to propose the "cohabitation effect," based on the idea that "family-line resemblances in fatness, however striking, may be less the product of genes held in common than of the living-together effect" (Garn, 1985:20–21).

Resolving the Irresolvable—What Does Weight Have to Do with Values?

How do we account for the nearly opposite conclusions reached by Garn (1985) and Stunkard et al. (1986)? Perhaps these are due to different measurements—in Stunkard et al. the measure is body mass, which varies with height (and leg length), whereas in much of Garn's work (and Stunkard's Midtown Manhattan research) the measures were of *actual* fatness (such as triceps skin-fold thicknesses). Interestingly, in Stunkard et al.'s (1986) but not in Garn's (1985) data, childhood weight correlated far more with mother's than father's weight—a difference that would seem more the result of feeding habits than genetic inheritance. Nonetheless, despite their opposite points of departure, Garn and Stunkard have issued almost identical statements about the relevance of their findings: for Garn et al. (1984:33). "The largely learned family-line nature of fatness and obesity becomes important in the early diagnosis of obesity, the prevention of obesity, and in . . . fatness reduction."

Stunkard "suggests that the children of overweight parents could be targeted for intensive weight-control measures, particularly vigorous exercise programs. . . . Such notions are the backbone of . . . [Stunkard et al.'s] new weight-loss program for black teenage girls" (Why Kids Get Fat, 1986:61)—or, in other words, exactly the same group Stunkard et al. (1972) found to suffer obesity from a socioeconomic source. This popular news magazine story was accompanied by a photograph of a slender Stunkard and another thin researcher with an obese black woman, her husky husband, and their overweight daughter. Apparently, whatever the source of obesity, it infects underprivileged groups more readily and it becomes less likely when people are aware of the dangers of obesity and have the resources with which to combat it.

The most emphatic rejection of the idea that people successfully achieve desired weight levels through planned eating strategies was presented by Polivy and Herman (1983:52), who argued "for the forseeable future, we must resign ourselves to the fact that we have no reliable way to change the natural weight that an individual is blessed or cursed with." Instead, the effort to go below this preordained body weight by restraining eating is doomed to failure, a failure often marked by compulsive dieting, episodic binge eating, and subsequent guilt and self-induced vomiting that characterize bulimia (Polivy and Herman, 1985). Polivy and Herman's model is a complex one that emphasizes the role of cognitive factors in binge eating and that it is not weight loss per se but *dieting* as a method of weight loss that leads to eating disorders.

There are certainly strong grounds to say that the marketing of unrealistically thin images of beauty leads to bulimia, because people (usually young women) strive for a weight goal unobtainable through their ordinary eating habits. There is nothing that requires, however, that biological inheritance creates "natural" body weight or prevents people from being as thin as they like. Polivy and Herman's work has regularly found that all people restrain their eating—after all, most people don't eat banana splits for breakfast, no matter how delicious an idea this is in the abstract. Bulimia could as easily be described as the failure of some people's habitual eating habits to bring about desired weight and hence their need to rely on unsuccessful dieting techniques. On the other hand, people generally conform to cultural norms of weight and thinness, change their weight as they change social groups, and frequently (though not inevitably) bring their weight (and eating) in line with a desired self-image.

Harris and Snow (1984) found that people who maintained considerable weight loss (an average of 40 pounds) displayed little binge eating, in contrast to unsuccessful dieters who had lost weight and regained it. Apparently, there are better and worse ways to go about losing weight. We all know such stable examples of weight loss because they frequently appear on our television and movie screens, in the forms of entertainers and actors like Cheryl Tiegs, Victoria Principal, Judith Light, Lynn Redgrave, Dolly Parton, Joan Rivers, and Stephen Jay Gould, professional weight watchers like Jean Nidetch and Richard Simmons, and athletes like Joe Torre, Billie Jean King, John McEnroe, and Chris Evert. Perhaps no group of people has greater motivation and opportunity to become biologically new people than those who go before the public, and they regularly take up this opportunity. Polivy and Herman's pessimism and recommendation that people accept whatever weight they find themselves at lest they do themselves more harm than good represents more a world view than a proven empirical position (Peele, 1983).

Addiction as Intentional, or Value-Driven, Activity

My argument is that in a real sense, people select their weight and obesity levels in line with who they are. In particular, the continuous excessive eating or periodic binge eating that most correspond to addiction cannot be understood biologically. Yet a crucial image of addictive behavior is that it is uncontrollable. Otherwise, people would simply cease doing whatever it was (overeating, overdrinking) that caused them problems or brought about undesired results. Levine (1978) argued that the idea of loss-of-control drinking inaugurated the modern conception of addiction and was first used at the turn of the eighteenth century to explain excessive drinking. In recent years, loss of control à la the addiction model has become increasingly popular as an explanation for all sorts of self-defeating and self-destructive behavior (Room, 1985). Still, the concept of loss of control is nowhere more insistently marketed today than in the definition of alcoholism, most notably by Alcoholics Anonymous.

To challenge the notion of loss of control, as Marlatt and Gordon (1985) and others have done, is to reorient our thinking about addiction in a manner whose impact has not yet been fully explored. To begin with, that addicts often do things they regret and wish they could change does not distinguish their behavior from much ordinary behavior; nor does their desire to reorient the larger pattern of their life and their inability to do so. In the words of philosopher Herbert Fingarette (1985:63): the "difficulty in changing the large pattern [of alcoholism] is not an 'impairment' of self-control; it is a normal feature of anyone's way of life. . . . This is no mystery or puzzle, no rarity, no pathology or disease needing a special explanation." From this perspective, addiction is a medicalized version of an essential element in all areas of human conduct, an element that has been noted throughout history but that has for the most part been explained by concepts of habit and will or the lack of it.

Neither laboratory nor epidemiological experimentation provides support for the idea that alcoholics lose control of their drinking whenever they consume alcohol. That is, drinking alcohol does not inevitably, or even typically, lead to excessive drinking by the alcoholic. Moreover, experiments with alcoholics demonstrate that they drink to achieve a specific state of intoxication or blood alcohol level; that they are often self-conscious about this state, what it does for them, and why they desire it; and that even when they become intoxicated, they respond to important dimensions of their environments that cause them to drink less or more. In other words, although alcoholics often regret the effects of their drinking, they *do* regulate their drinking in line with a variety of goals to which they attach more or less value (cf. Peele, 1986).

The failure of loss of control to provide an explanation for chronic overdrinking is now so well established that *genetic* theorists posit instead that alcoholics inherit special temperaments for which alcohol provides welcome amelioration (Tarter and Edwards, this volume). In this and related views, alcoholics are extremely anxious, overreactive, or depressed, and they drink to relieve these states. Here the difference between genetic and social-learning viewpoints is solely in whether a mood state is seen to be inbred or environmentally induced and to what extent the theorist believes drinking is reinforcing because learning plays a part in interpreting the pharmacological effects of alcohol. But either perspective leaves a great deal of room for the intervention of personal choices, values, and intentions. Just because someone finds drinking relieves tension—even if this person is very tense—does not mean he or she will become an alcoholic.

The life study of alcoholism provides good support for the idea of alcoholism as an accumulation of choices. That is, problem drinkers do not become alcoholics instantaneously but instead drink with increasing problems over periods of years and decades (Vaillant, 1983). The development of clinical alcoholism is especially noteworthy because most problem drinkers reverse their drinking problems before reaching this point (Cahalan and Room, 1974). Why do some drinkers fail to reorient their behavior as over the years it eventually culminates in alcoholism? As Mulford (1984:38) noted from his natural processes perspective, "early acquired definitions of self as one who meets his responsibilities, who does not land in jail, and other self definitions that are incompatible with heavy drinking will tend to retard progress in the alcoholic process and accelerate the rehabilitation process." Mulford indicated here by *self-definition* the values by which one defines oneself.

Why Do the Same People
Do So Many Things Wrong?

Modern models of addiction have consistently overestimated the amount of variance in addiction accounted for by the chemical properties of specific substances (Peele, 1985). Although popular prejudice continues to uphold this view, *no data of any sort* support the idea that addiction is a characteristic of some mood-altering substances and not of others. For example, among the many fundamental reevaluations caused by examining narcotics use among Vietnam veterans was the finding that heroin "did not lead rapidly to daily or compulsive use, no more so than did use of amphetamines or marijuana" (Robins et al., 1980:217–218). A related finding was

> Heroin does *not* seem to supplant the use of other drugs. Instead, the typical pattern of the heroin user seems to be to use a wide variety of drugs plus alcohol. The stereotype of the heroin addict as someone with a monomaniacal craving for a single drug seems hardly to exist in this sample. Heroin addicts use many other drugs, and not only casually or in desperation. Drug researchers have for a number of years divided drug users into heroin addicts versus polydrug users. Our data suggest that such a distinction is meaningless (Robins et al., 1980:219–220).

Cocaine use is now described as presenting the same kind of lurid monomania that pharmacologists once claimed only heroin could produce; again, the explanation presented is in the "powerful reinforcing properties of cocaine" that "demand constant replenishment of supplies" (Cohen, 1985: 151). Indeed, "if we were to design deliberately a chemical that would lock people into perpetual usage, it would probably resemble the neurophysiological properties of cocaine" (Cohen, 1985:153). These properties demand that those who become dependent on the drug "continue using [it] until they are exhausted or the cocaine is depleted. They will exhibit behaviors markedly different from their precocaine lifestyle. Cocaine-driven humans will relegate all other drives and pleasures to a minor role in their lives" (Cohen, 1985:152).

Seventeen percent of 1985 college students used cocaine in the previous year; 0.1 percent of 1985 students used it daily in the previous month (Johnston et al., 1986). Former college students who used the drug for a decade typically remained controlled users, and even those who abused the drug showed intermittent excesses rather than the kind of insanity Cohen described (Siegel, 1984). Perhaps the key to these subjects' ability to control cocaine use is provided by research by Johanson and Uhlenhuth (1981), who found that members of a college community who enjoyed and welcomed the effects of amphetamines decreased their usage as it began to interfere with other activities in their lives. Clayton (1985) pointed out the best predictors of degree of cocaine use among high school students were marijuana use, truancy, and smoking and that even the very few people in treatment reporting cocaine as their primary drug of choice (3.7 percent) regularly used other drugs and alcohol as well.

These data indicate that we need to explore the user—particularly the compulsive user—for the key to addiction. Robins et al. (1980) constructed a Youthful Liability Scale for abuse from demographic factors (race, living in the inner city, youth at induction) and problem behaviors (truancy, school dropout or expulsion, fighting, arrests, early drunkenness, and use of many types of illicit drugs) that preceded drug user's military service and that predicted post-Vietnam use of all types of street drugs. Genetic-susceptibility models based on individual reactions to given drugs are unable to account for simultaneous misuse by the same individuals of substances as pharmacologically diverse as narcotics, amphetamines, barbiturates, and marijuana in the Robins et al. (1980) study or cocaine, marijuana, cigarettes, and alcohol in the Clayton (1985) analysis. Istvan and Matarazzo (1984) summarized the generally positive correlations among use of the legal substances caffeine, tobacco, and alcohol. These relationships are particularly strong at the highest levels of usage: for example, five out of six studies Istvan and Matarazzo cited have found 90 percent or more of alcoholics to smoke.

The relationships among negative health behaviors and addiction are not limited to correlations among drug habits. Mechanic (1979) found smokers were less likely to wear seat belts, while Kalant and Kalant (1976) found users of both prescription and illicit amphetamines suffered more accidents, injuries, and untimely deaths. Smokers have 40 percent higher accident rates than nonsmokers (McGuire, 1972). From the standpoint of these data, addiction is part of a panoply of self-destructive behaviors some people regularly engage in. Drunk drivers turn out to have more accidents and worse driving records than others even when they drive sober (Walker, 1986), suggesting that drunk driving is not an alcohol problem but one of drunk drivers' generally reckless and antisocial behavior. The disease model and behavioral theories both have missed the extent to which excessive and harmful substance use fits larger patterns in people's lives.

Drug Abuse as the Failure of Children to Develop Prosocial Values

The use of a combination of early-life factors to predict both heroin use and addiction to other drugs reinforces the results of a large (and growing) number of studies of adolescent drug use. Jessor and Jessor's (1977) pioneering work emphasized a kind of nonconformity dimension in predicting both drug and sexual experimentation. This factor seems rather too global, in that it confuses personal adventurousness with antisocial alienation (not to dismiss the possibility that adolescents can confuse these things). Pandina and Scheule (1983) constructed a more refined psychosocial index on which drug and alcohol-abusing adolescents showed high scores but on which "a large proportion of student moderate users did not display problematic or dysfuntional profiles" (p. 970). Further explorations in this area of research have indicated at least three interesting and potentially related dimensions associated with drug and alcohol abuse:

1. *Alienation.* Adolescents who abuse a range of substances are more isolated from social networks of all kinds. At the same time (perhaps as a result), they associate with groups of heavy drug users that reject mainstream institutions and other involvements connected with career success and accomplishment (Kandel, 1984; Oetting and Beauvais, this volume). Individual orientations in part *precede* the selection of group association, although group involvement then exacerbates individual inclinations in this direction.

2. *Rejection of achievement values.* Jessor and Jessor found that absence of achievement values strongly predicted drug use. In the Monitoring the Future study of the class of 1980, Clayton (1985) pointed out, second to marijuana use in predicting extent of cocaine involvement was truancy. Clayton speculated it was unlikely that cocaine involvement preceded truancy in these data, and thus the absence of a commitment to school attendance was a condition for drug abuse. Lang (1983) provided a summary of data indicating an inverse relationship between achievement values and substance abuse.

3. *Antisocial aggressiveness and acting out.* A relationship between antisocial impulsiveness or aggressiveness and alcoholism has been repeatedly noted. MacAndrew (1981) reported sixteen studies showing a higher (in some cases much higher) than 80 percent detection rate for clinical alcoholics through the MAC scale of the MMPI. The highest factor loading for the scale was "boldness," interpreted as "an assertive, aggressive, pleasure-seeking character," an example of "factor loadings that make alcoholics resemble criminals and delinquents" (MacAndrew, 1981:617). MacAndrew (1981) in addition noted five studies of clinical drug abusers that showed similarly high detection rates according to the MAC scale. MacAndrew (1986) has found a similar kind of antisocial thrill-seeking to characterize women alcoholics.

The MAC scale and similar measures are not measuring the consequences of alcohol and drug abuse. Hoffman et al. (1974) found the MAC scores for treated alcoholics were not significantly different from those the same subjects showed on entering college. Loper et al. (1973) also detected higher Pd and Ma scores on MMPI responses (indicators of sociopathy, defiance of authority, et al.) in college students who later became alcoholic. This finding is reinforced by similar results Jones (1968) obtained with young respondents through use of Q sorts.

These findings are so well established that the battle is to claim them for different domains of explanation. Genetic models of alcoholism now regularly incorporate the idea of the inheritance of impulsive, delinquent, and criminal tendencies. Tarter and Edwards (this volume), for example, postulated that impulsivity is the central element in inheritance of alcoholism. I have elsewhere summarized grounds for caution about such genetic models (Peele, 1986b). The crucial issue is the relationship between addiction as antisocial misbehavior and socialization processes and social values. Cahalan and Room (1974) found alcohol abuse was strongly related to antisocial acting out, but their data clearly identify this as a social phenomenon found among particular groups. The question I pose in this article is whether we see it as within our cultural control to minimize through social learning the expression of uninhibited aggression, sensation-seeking, and disregard for social consequences that characterize addiction.

The Commonplaceness of Natural Remission in Addiction

A crucial element in the disease myth of addiction, one used to justify expensive, long-term—and increasingly coercive and involuntary—treatment is the progressive and irreversible nature of addiction. According to one television advertisement, overcoming alcoholism on one's own is like operating on yourself. All data dispute this. Epidemiological research finds that people typically outgrow drinking problems, so that alcohol abuse decreases with age (Cahalan and Room, 1974). The data on drug abuse are identical, and less than one-third of men who have ever used heroin continue to do so throughout their twenties (O'Donnell et al., 1976). We have reviewed data such as Schachter's (1982) and Garn's (1985), which indicate that long-term weight loss is a common event. Yet perhaps the single greatest area of self-cure of addiction is smoking—approximately 30 million people have quit smoking, with 95 percent quitting on their own (USPHS, 1979).

Conventional wisdom about addiction denies this commonplace reality to such an extent that addiction and alcoholism experts often seem embarked on campaigns to attack their own data. For example, Vaillant (1983:284–285) combined data showing that a majority of alcohol abusers in his sample were in remission, hardly any due to treatment, and that his own hospital patients' outcomes after two and eight years "were no better than the natural history of the disorder" with an insistence that alcoholism be treated medically (Vaillant, 1983:20). Although he found the large majority of his natural-history population recovered from alcoholism without the assistance of AA (including even those who abstained), all of Vaillant's lengthy case studies indicated that this is impossible. (In further data from his study Vaillant has sent me, those who quit drinking by attending AA had higher relapse rates than those who quit on their own.)

Gross (1977:121) described the difficulties confronting the alcohol dependence model:

> The foundation is set for the progression of the alcohol dependence syndrome by virtue of its biologically intensifying itself. One would think that, once caught up in the process, the individual could not be extricated. However, and for reasons poorly understood, the reality is otherwise. Many, perhaps most, do free themselves.

Here an originator of the alcohol dependence syndrome, which emphasizes the self-perpetuating nature of the biological effects of alcoholism, is bewildered when it fails to explain the majority of the outcomes of alcoholism. The reasons most people moderate their substance use as they age are obvious. In terms of Mulford's (1984:38) natural process model:

> Time is moving the developing alcoholic out of the status of the "young man sowing wild oats." He is now expected to be a responsible husband, father, employee, and useful community member. It is no longer excused as "boys will be boys."

The medicalization and biologization of ordinary human development is a dangerous misunderstanding of the nature of human behavior. For example, Merrell Dow Pharmaceuticals has been placing full-page ads in major magazines indicating the basis of smoking is a *"physical dependence on nicotine. . . .* Because these effects can defeat even a strong willpower, your chances of quitting successfully are greater with a program that provides an alternative source of nicotine to help alleviate tobacco withdrawal"—that is, chemical detoxification under medical supervision. Schachter (1982), for one, found smokers who tried to quit on their own were two to three times more successful than those who sought professional help. In a review of the methods Schachter's subjects used to quit, Gerin (1982) reported that

> The techniques of the 38 heavy smokers who quit smoking for nearly seven years were less varied. Roughly two-thirds reported their only technique was deciding to stop. "I took the cigarettes out of my pocket," one said, "threw them away, and that was it."

How well would we expect the same smokers to do under a medically supervised withdrawal maintenance program extending over months in which the doctor and nicotine-weaning drug were seen as the agents of control?

It is not enough to say merely that self-cure in addiction has been discredited by professionals. Self-curers are now being *penalized*. When many baseball players revealed during a federal trial that they had used cocaine but had quit (reasons given were "I was getting older and had too much to lose" and that one player felt "cocaine played some part" in his slipping performance), baseball commissioner Peter Ueberroth ordered severe fines and other penalties. Yet players who admit they are "chemically dependent" and who submit to treatment are not penalized according to the policies of professional baseball and other sports. In this scheme, those who claim to be addicted or whose drug use becomes uncontrolled are better off than those who control their substance use or who quit on their own.

How Do So Many Quit Addictions without Our Help?

When we consider the elaborate and expensive treatments that have been created to eliminate addiction, we may marvel at the naive techniques self-curers employ. In the Schachter (1982) study

> it seems that these people lost weight when they made up their minds to do so, and managed to drop substantial poundage by eating smaller portions and less fattening food. People made comments like: "I just cut down, just stopped eating so much." To keep the weight off, they stuck to their regimens of eating less (Gerin, 1982:32).

Recall that these subjects had lost an average of 34.7 pounds and maintained this weight loss for an average of 11.2 years. Again, Schachter found those who did not undergo formal weight-loss programs stood a better chance of achieving remission, although weight loss was just as common for the super-obese (30 percent or more overweight) as it was for less overweight subjects.

In considering the banality and at the same time the idiosyncratic or personalized nature of people's methods for losing weight, it might seem that the best techniques are the ones people devise for themselves in line with their own life circumstances. Thus, every time a well-known personality loses weight, magazines rush to report the star's reduction secrets to others, although the methods may have worked primarily because they were developed by the person who relied on them in the first place. Similarly, founders of weight-reducing movements like Richard Simmons and Jean Nidetch point to themselves as examples of why everyone should follow their methods, when in fact they might as well instruct people to find the methods that make the most sense for them.

Possibly, larger processes of change may be the same for people whether or not they enter therapy (Waldorf, 1983) or whatever the area of addictive behavior they seek to modify. On the other hand, in a study of comparisons between treated and untreated smokers who quit, those who were treated relied more on behavioral-type methods for avoiding a return to smoking, while self-curers used more cognitive coping techniques (Shiffman, 1985). Those who were treated appeared to be rehearsing learned strategies, while self-curers seemed to look to themselves for a method—usually involving thinking about themselves and their situations—that worked. It could well be that different types of people resort to treatment or do it on their own. Wille (1983) found those who relied on treatment to quit narcotic addiction feared that they could not manage withdrawal by themselves.

Several accounts of the self-descriptions of alcoholics (Ludwig, 1985; Tuchfeld, 1981) and heroin addicts (Waldorf, 1983; Wille, 1983) who quit on their own have emphasized powerful and at the same time subtle existential shifts in attitudes about themselves and their addictions. That is, while the episode that prompted a change in their lives could be undramatic (unlike the hitting-bottom phenomenon usually described at AA), some such unexceptional event often triggered a powerful psychological reaction in the addict. These reactions were connected with other areas of their lives that addicts valued—for example, alcoholics who quit or cut back frequently mentioned the effect their drinking had on their families (Tuchfeld, 1981). The former addicts usually made changes in their work lives and personal associations that supported their new drug-free or nonaddict identities, just as such life shifts often added to their urge to quit.

Vaillant's (1983) summary of the treatment literature indicated that the same kinds of environmental, social, and life changes accompany and encourage remission from alcoholism due to treatment. For example, Orford and Edwards (1977) discovered improved working and marital conditions were most responsible for positive outcomes in alcoholism treatment. The work of Moos and Finney (1983) has in recent years signaled a whole new focus on the life context of alcoholics in treatment. Vaillant noted several surveys have found "that the most important single prognostic variable associated with remission among alcoholics who attended alcohol clinics is having something to lose if they continue to abuse alcohol" (p. 191). This is another way of saying that treated alcoholics do best when they have other involvements that are important to them and that are inconsistent with continued addiction.

Relapse Avoidance as Moral Certitude

Relapse prevention is currently a major focus of cognitive and behavioral therapies (Marlatt and Gordon, 1985; Brownell et al., 1986). Rather than concentrating on quitting an addiction (drinking, smoking, overeating, drug-taking), this model focuses on the internal and environmental forces that lead the individual to resume the addiction after having quit. The process of managing the urge to return to the addiction, particularly after the person has had one smoke, drink, or fattening dessert, is a special target for analysis and intervention. In Part I of Marlatt and Gordon (1985), Marlatt recommended balancing feelings of responsibility for and being able to control the addiction with avoiding guilt when the addict fails to do so and has a slip. The client can be wrecked either by overreacting with too much guilt or by denying the possibility of being able to control an urge to continue after having had a drink, smoke, etc.

Marlatt's sinuous and complex analysis—involving literally hundreds of pages—makes one pessimistic that any human being can safely steer a passage between the alternate shoals of assuming too much responsibility and guilt and not enough responsibility for his or her behavior. When some clients need to be brought into therapy, in Marlatt's view, to have another smoke but to be guided through feelings of powerlessness and guilt and reminded of how much they wanted to quit in the first place, we also may wonder what are the survival chances of their remission in the dangerous world out there. Are people ever able to get this straightened out on their own or are they forever obligated to belong to an AA, Weight Watchers, Smokenders group or else to return to their cognitive-behavioral therapist for lessons on relapse prevention? One wonders about the 25 million or so Americans who have managed this difficult passage on their own in the case of smoking alone.

Shiffman (1985) and others have studied coping strategies of those who have quit smoking successfully on their own, but these studies typically involve short-term follow-ups. In a larger time frame, reformed addicts may relinquish their original preoccupation first with withdrawal and then with relapse in order to become more concerned with broader issues like lifestyle and establishing and maintaining social networks. Wille (1983) found this postwithdrawal process was retarded for those in treatment, who were more preoccupied with and more dependent on therapy to keep them abstinent. Are these treated addicts manifesting differences they showed on entering treatment, or did treatment itself provoke such continued dependence? Interestingly, Waldorf (1983) found few differences between untreated and treated addicts in remission but for a tendency for untreated addicts not to believe abstinence was obligatory and to use heroin again without relapsing.

This difference suggests that therapy often serves the function of convincing addicts that a slip will cause them to relapse. Orford and Keddie (1986) and Elal-Lawrence et al. (1986) in England found that involvement with standard treatment programs and being convinced that controlled drinking was impossible were the main hindrances to resuming moderated drinking patterns. This may also explain why, in Vaillant's (personal communication,

June 4, 1985) data, membership in AA was associated with greater relapse than quitting by oneself because nearly all alcoholics drank again and those in AA were persuaded this meant they would resume alcoholic drinking. While clinicians in Marlatt and Gordon (1985) were at pains to encourage their patients' self-efficacy, these psychologists and others likewise indicate to patients that a great deal of therapeutic work needs to be performed to prevent the patients from relapsing.

The formerly obese subjects in Harris and Snow (1984) who averaged long-term weight loss of 40 pounds and who were not susceptible to eating binges show there is a further stage in addiction remission, one in which the person gets beyond devoting their major emotional energy to avoiding relapse. These reformed overeaters seem to have developed a new, stable image of themselves as nonobese people. Indeed, the mark of the cure of their addictive behavior is that they no longer need to rely on external supports to maintain their new behavior. Perhaps this is a goal to shoot for in therapy because it guarantees such stable recovery outcomes. The essential cure in this case is the development of a confident, natural approach to avoiding relapse—a kind of moral certitude about the opposing issues of guilt and responsibility. Is this state obtainable through current therapy practices, or is the individual obligated to develop such a secure moral sense of self on his or her own?

Both natural and treated remission express people's values about themselves, their worlds, and the choices available to them. Marsh (1984), based on a survey of 2,700 British smokers, found quitting smoking required that smokers "lose faith in what they used to think smoking did for them" while creating "a powerful new set of beliefs that non-smoking is, of itself, a desirable and rewarding state" (p. 20). While people may in some sense inadvertently become addicts, to continue life as an addict is an ultimate statement about oneself that many people are unwilling to make. The way they extricate themselves from addiction expresses additional values—about preferred styles of coping with problems ("For me to have to ask someone else to help with a self-made problem, I'd rather drink myself to death"; Tuchfeld, 1981: 631), how well they endure pain (such as withdrawal pain), or how they see themselves (after a difficult bout in defeating alcoholism, one of Tuchfeld's subjects declared, "I'M THE CHAMP; I'M THE GREATEST," p. 630).

Conclusion

We have disarmed ourselves in combatting the precipitous growth of addictions by discounting the role of values in creating and preventing addiction and by systematically overlooking the immorality of addictive misbehavior. In this way, scientists and treatment personnel contribute to the loss of standards that underlies our surge in addiction and criminal behavior by addicts. The steps we take—as in fighting the importation of drugs and introducing routine drug-testing—are exactly the opposite of the steps we need to take of creating more positive values among our drug-using young and holding people responsible for their drug use and other behavior. After the death of basketball star Len Bias, University of Maryland officials promised greater vigilance against drugs—even though they already had a model drug-testing program in place. Meanwhile, the University revealed Bias had failed all of his courses the previous semester.

Here a university made moralistic proclamations while indicating that it did not have the guts to insist that a student basketball player get an education. Universities also now regularly undermine their moral and intellectual integrity by sponsoring profitable programs on chemical dependence and other behavioral diseases, programs in which minimum standards of analytical thinking and academic freedom are disregarded (Peele, 1986a). At universities and elsewhere we have elevated the self-deception of the disease theory (Fingarette, 1985) to a place of scientific and academic honor. We mainly communicate with young people about drug use through irrational, anti-intellectual speeches, arguments, and programs (of the type typified by Dave Toma). This type of communication is most readily accepted by those with the most unsure values who are most likely to become addicted in the first place and to remain addicted despite such programs (Goodstadt, 1984).

Moral Outrages

On December 26, 1985, the ABC program *20/20* ran a segment on third-party responsibility for drunk-driving accidents. After drinking at a restaurant bar where he regularly got drunk, an alcoholic man ran head-on into another car and seriously injured its driver. Now "recovered," he claimed he was not accountable for his behavior after drinking and that the proprietor of the restaurant was to blame for the accident. The restaurant proprietor, the alcoholic, and the victim—who has been incapacitated since the accident—met to discuss the case before *20/20*'s cameras. Although she had previously indicated she held the drunk driver responsible for her pain and suffering, in an actual face-to-face confrontation with the two men, the victim blamed the restaurant owner. The frustrated proprietor could only repeat that he had no way of telling who was drunk at a crowded bar and who was not.

As a second part of this segment, the *20/20* producers arranged for a number of drinkers to be served by mock-bartenders at a Rutgers Center for Alcohol Studies' laboratory that simulates a bar setting. The point of the exercise was to show, à la research by Langenbucher and Nathan (1983), that for the most part people are not good judges of whether other people are intoxicated. Here the issue of whether a man should be held accountable for his actions in maiming another person was reduced to a technoscientific matter of the accuracy of judgments of the effects of alcohol on others. It seems that, like the victim herself, we cannot confront the essential moral issues involved and instead trivialize them by burying them beneath elaborate but irrelevant scientific methodology.

An article entitled "I still see him everywhere" (Morsilli and Coudert, 1985) has been reprinted regularly in *Reader's Digest* ads as "The magazine article most highly acclaimed by Americans in 1984." The article is by a father whose popular, outgoing 13-year-old son, a ranked tennis player in his age-group, was run down and killed by a hit-and-run driver. The driver, a 17-year-old girl, spent the day "drinking beer at a friend's house starting at ten in the morning, and later they switched to vodka." After killing the boy, she drove her car into a tree and was apprehended. "She didn't go to jail. Her three-year sentence was suspended. Her probation terms included regular psychological counseling, work at a halfway house and no drinking."

This case is an example of a trend in U.S. jurisprudence to replace jail sentences for crimes committed by alcoholics (and other addiction-related crime) with treatment. The crimes are not only drunk driving but felonies up to and including murder (Weisner and Room, 1984). The girl in this case may, as part of her work in a halfway house, serve as an educator, role model, and counselor for other young substance abusers. She may also (as have several young people who have killed people in drunk driving accidents) lecture ordinary school children and their parents about the dangers of drugs and alcohol. Drug and alcohol education programs regularly feature presentations by young reformed addicts and alcoholics. In this way, the emotionally crippled and morally infirm in our society are elected to positions of respect and moral leadership, based on the cultural self-delusion that addiction is a disease that may strike anyone (Fingarette, 1985), like the girl who spent her day drinking, got in her car, killed somebody, and then drove off.

Just Say No

In a nationally televised speech on September 14, 1986, Nancy and Ronald Reagan inaugurated a campaign against drug abuse in America. That campaign—like this article—emphasized positive values for young people but, unfortunately, it did so in a simplistic and a moralistic way that undermined from the start any chance it had to succeed. A keynote to the Reagan campaign (as promoted by the First Lady) has been the "Just Say No" program, whose aim is to have teenagers simply reject drugs whenever drugs are available. Of course, the idea that young people (and others) should not take drugs has been the staple of mainstream moral judgments for the last fifty years. Nonetheless, beginning in the late 1960s college and then high school students became regular consumers of drugs.

Indeed, the most notable aspect of the prohibitionist approach to drugs in this century has been its utter and abject failure first in preventing addiction and then (in the latter half of the century) in eliminating widespread drug experimentation (Peele, 1987). It seems an impossible dream to recall that for most of human history, even under conditions of ready access to the most potent of drugs, people and societies have regulated their drug use without requiring massive education, legal, and interdiction campaigns (cf. Mulford, 1984). The exceptions to successful self-regulation have come for the most part (as in the Chinese Opium Wars and in the drinking of Native American groups) as a result of cultural denigration brought on by outside military and social domination.

Now, in a country that is a major world power, we have completely lost faith in the ability of our society and its members to avoid addiction on their own. Just Say No and other government programs (along with much private advertising by treatment programs and research experts) incessantly convey the idea that people cannot be expected to control their drug use. It is remarkable under these circumstances that the vast majority of young drug users in fact do take drugs occasionally or intermittently without interfering with their ordinary functioning. Our official cultural attitude seems to be that this reality should be ignored and discouraged, with what results we can only guess. Meanwhile, the adoption of routine drug testing—coupled with increasingly compulsory treatment referrals—further infantilizes the drug-using population.

Nancy Reagan and her adherents have suggested that the Just Say No program could also be effective in discouraging teen pregnancy, which may actually be *the* social crisis of the 1980s. Teen-age child-bearing cost the nation $16.6 billion last year, a figure that grows with each cohort of pregnant teens. The problem is monumental among black teens and guarantees large-scale social failure for this group through the coming decades (which will provide a constant supply of drug addicts and alcoholics). Even considering only white Americans, the United States leads industrialized nations in teen births and abortions. This high rate of teen pregnancy occurs in this country despite the fact that U.S. teens are *not* more sexually active than those in other Western nations. "Overall . . . the lowest rates of teen-age pregnancy were in countries that had liberal attitudes toward sex [and] had easily accessible contraceptive services for young people, with contraceptives being offered free or at low cost and without parental notification" (Brozan, 1985:1).

These are not the policies endorsed by Nancy Reagan. Rather, the Just Say No program in the case of sex seems intent on reversing the worldwide trend toward earlier sexual intercourse. It seems safe to say that no official policy in this country will soon be built on accepting that the majority of teen-age girls will be sexually active. But moralizing against sexual activity has important negative consequences. A leading psychological investigator of contraceptive use by women noted that "unmarried women with negative attitudes toward sex tend to use less reliable methods of birth control—if they use them at all. . . . Women with such negative attitudes seem to have trouble processing information about sex and contraception and often rely on their partner to make decisions about contraception" (Turkington, 1986:11). In other words, just like problem drug users, they are unprepared to accept moral responsibility for their actions.

The Reagan logic is that all teen pregnancy is an unintended consequence of illicit sexual activity, just as addiction is thought to be an unintended consequence of drug use. However, many adolescents (particularly those in deprived settings) report seeking specific satisfactions from the pregnant role and motherhood, although these expectations are soon disappointed and replaced by the harsh reality of raising a child with inadequate resources. The solution to the problem of premature parenthood, like that of drug use, is to provide these adolescents with more substantial and enduring sources of satisfaction that will replace their search for a sense of personal value and accomplishment through self-defeating means. We need also have enough respect for people to acknowledge they have a right to certain life choices while insisting that they accept their responsibilities as potential parents, as members of our society, and as self-directed human beings who will live with the consequences of their actions.

By implacably (but unsuccessfully) opposing personal behaviors that offend us, like sexual activity and drug use, we avoid the essential task of teaching young people the values and skills they need to achieve adulthood. The issue is not only to get through to the large numbers of the young who seem not to be hearing us but to establish bedrock moral principles for our society. As it is, we seem to be falling further behind in creating a moral environment in which we want to live and in giving children a set of values that are adequate for such a world. Some of the values we need more of, as outlined in this chapter, are values toward health, moderation, and self-control; achievement, work, and constructive activity; larger purposes and goals in life; social consciousness, concern for the community, respect for other people, and mutuality in human relationships; intellectual and self-awareness; and acceptance of personal responsibility for our actions. These are the value choices that confront all of us, and not just drug users.

Note

1. The positive values the Jews and Chinese place on achievement and consciousness and their high levels of academic and economic success in the United States would also encourage sobriety. On the other hand, immigrant Jews in disadvantaged economic communities in the United States and ghettoized European Jews drank notably

less than their neighbors from other ethnic groups. In any case, the examples of American Jews and Chinese strongly oppose the argument that a judgmental and punitive approach *causes* alcoholism.

References

Armor, D.J., J.M. Polich, and H.B. Stambul. 1978. *Alcoholism and Treatment.* New York: Wiley.

Bales, R.F. 1962. Attitudes Toward Drinking in the Irish Culture. In D.J. Pittman and C.R. Snyder, eds., *Society, Culture and Drinking Patterns.* New York: Wiley.

Barnett, M.L. 1955. Alcoholism in the Cantonese of New York City: An Anthropological Study. In O. Diethelm, ed., *Etiology of Chronic Alcoholism.* Springfield, IL.: Charles C. Thomas.

Brownell, K.D., G.A. Marlatt, E. Lichtenstein, and G.T. Wilson. 1986. Understanding and Preventing Relapse. *American Psychologist* 41:765–782.

Brozan, N. 1985. U.S. Leads Industrialized Nations in Teen-Age Births and Abortions. *New York Times* March 13:1, C7.

Cahalan, D., and R. Room. 1974. *Problem Drinking among American Men.* New Brunswick, NJ: Rutgers Center of Alcohol Studies.

Chance, N.A. 1985. Questioning Survival, *Natural History* July:64–66.

Clayton, R.R. 1985. Cocaine Use in the United States: In a Blizzard or Just Being Snowed? In N.J. Kozel and E.H. Adams, eds., *Cocaine Use in America: Epidemiological and Clinical Perspectives.* DHHS Publication no. ADM 85-1414. Washington, DC: U.S. Government Printing Office.

Cohen, S. 1985. Reinforcement and Rapid Delivery Systems: Understanding Adverse Consequences of Cocaine. In N.J. Kozel and E.H. Adams, eds., *Cocaine Use in America: Epidemiological and Clinical Perspectives.* DHHS Publication no. ADM 85-1414. Washington, DC: U.S. Government Printing Office.

Critchlow, B. 1983. Blaming the Booze. The Attribution of Responsibility for Drunken Behavior. *Personality and Social Psychology Bulletin* 9:451–473.

Elal-Lawrence, G., P.D. Slade, and M.E. Dewey. 1986. Predictors of Outcome Type in Treated Problem Drinkers. *Journal of Studies on Alcohol* 47:41–47.

Ferrence, R.G. 1980. Sex Differences in the Prevalence of Problem Drinking. In O.J. Kalant, ed., *Research Advances in Alcohol and Drug Problems.* Vol. 5. *Alcohol and Drug Problems in Women.* New York: Plenum.

Fingarette, H. 1985. Alcoholism and Self-Deception. In M.W. Martin, ed., *Self-Deception and Self-Understanding.* Lawrence, KS: University of Kansas.

Finkle, D. 1986. Review of "Papa John," *New York Times Book Review* August 17:3.33.

Garn, S.M. 1985. Continuities and Changes in Fatness from Infancy through Adulthood. *Current Problems in Pediatrics* 15(2): entire issue.

Garn, S.M., M. LaVelle, and J.J. Pilkington. 1984. Obesity and Living Together. *Marriage and Family Review* 7:33–47.

Gerin, W. 1982. [No] Accounting for Results. *Psychology Today* August:32.

Glassner, B., and B. Berg. 1980. How Jews Avoid Alcohol Problems. *American Sociological Review* 45:647–664.

————. 1984. Social Locations and Interpretations: How Jews Define Alcoholism. *Journal of Studies on Alcohol* 45:16–25.

Glazer, N. 1952. Why Jews Stay Sober. *Commentary* 13:181–186.

Goldblatt, P.B., M.E. Moore, and A.J. Stunkard. 1965. Social Factors in Obesity. *Journal of the American Medical Association* 192:1039–1044.

Goodstadt, M.S. 1984. Drug Education: A Turn On or a Turn Off? In S. Eiseman, J.A. Wingard, and G.J. Huba, eds., *Drug Abuse: Foundations for a Psychological Approach*. Farmingdale, NY: Baywood.

Goodwin, D.W., F. Schulsinger, J. Knop, S. Mednick, and S.G. Guze. 1977. Alcoholism in Adopted-Out Daughters of Alcoholics. *Archives of General Psychiatry* 34:751–755.

Greeley, A.N., W.C. McCready, and G. Theisen. 1980. *Ethnic Drinking Subcultures.* New York: Praeger.

Gross, M.M. 1977. Psychobiological Contributions to the Alcohol Dependence Syndrome. In G. Edwards et al., eds., *Alcohol-Related Disabilities.* WHO Offset Pub. No. 32. Geneva: World Health Organization.

Harris, M.B., and J.T. Snow. 1984. Factors Associated with Maintenance of Weight Loss. Paper presented at the Meeting of the American Psychological Association. Toronto.

Hoffman, H., R.G. Loper, and M.L. Kammeier. 1974. Identifying Future Alcoholics with MMPI Alcoholism Scores. *Quarterly Journal of Studies on Alcohol* 35: 490–498.

Istvan, J., and J.D. Matarazzo. 1984. Tobacco, Alcohol, Caffeine Use: A Review of Their Interrelationships. *Psychological Bulletin* 95:301–326.

Jessor, R., and S.L. Jessor. 1977. *Problem Behavior and Psychosocial Development.* New York: Academic.

Johanson, C.E., and E.H. Uhlenhuth. 1981. Drug Preference and Mood in Humans: Repeated Assessment of d-Amphetamine. *Pharmacology Biochemistry and Behavior* 14:159–163.

Johnston, L.D., P.M. O'Malley, and J.G. Bachman. 1986. *Drug Use among American High School Students, College Students, and Other Young Adults.* DHHS Publication No. ADM 86-1450. Washington, DC: U.S. Government Printing Office.

Jones, M.C. 1968. Personality Correlates and Antecedents of Drinking Patterns in Adult Males. *Journal of Consulting and Clinical Psychology* 32:2–12.

Kalant, O.J., and H. Kalant. 1976. Death in Amphetamine Users: Causes and Estimates of Mortality. In R.J. Gibbins et al., eds., *Research Advances in Alcohol and Drug Problems.* Vol. 3. New York: Wiley.

Kandel, D.B. 1984. Marijuana Users in Young Adulthood. *Archives of General Psychiatry* 41:200–209.

Keller, M. 1970. The Great Jewish Drink Mystery. *British Journal of Addiction* 64: 287–295.

Lang, A.R. 1983. Addictive Personality: A Viable Construct? In P.K Levison, D.R. Gerstein and D.R. Maloff, eds., *Commonalities in Substance Abuse and Habitual Behavior.* Lexington, MA: Lexington Books.

Langenbucher, J.W., and P.E. Nathan. 1983. Psychology, Public Policy, and the Evidence for Alcohol Intoxication. *American Psychologist* 38:1070–1077.

Lau, R.R., K.A. Hartman, and J.E. Ware, Jr. 1986. Health as a Value: Methodological and Theoretical Considerations. *Health Psychology* 5:25–43.

Levine, H.G. 1978. The Discovery of Addiction: Changing Conceptions of Habitual Drunkenness in America. *Journal of Studies on Alcohol* 39:143–174.

Lex, B.W. 1985. Alcohol Problems in Special Populations. In J.H. Mendelson and N.K. Mello, eds., *The Diagnosis and Treatment of Alcoholism.* 2nd ed. New York: McGraw-Hill.

Loper, R.G., M.L. Kammeier, and H. Hoffman. 1973. MMPI Characteristics of College Freshman Males Who Later Become Alcoholics. *Journal of Abnormal Psychology* 82:159–162.

Ludwig, A.M. 1985. Cognitive Processes Associated with "Spontaneous" Recovery from Alcoholism. *Journal of Studies on Alcohol* 46:53–58.

MacAndrew, C. 1981. What the MAC Scale Tells Us about Men Alcoholics. *Journal of Studies on Alcohol* 42:604–625.

———. 1986. Similarities in the Self-Depictions of Female Alcoholics and Psychiatric Outpatients: Examination of Eysenck's Dimension of Emotionality in Women. *Journal of Studies on Alcohol* 47:478–484.

MacAndrew, C., and R.B. Edgerton. 1969. *Drunken Comportment: A Social Explanation.* Chicago: Aldine.

Maloff, D., H.S. Becker, A. Fonaroff, and J. Rodin. 1979. Informal Social Controls and Their Influence on Substance Use. *Journal of Drug Issues* 9:161–184.

Marlatt, G.A., and J.R. Gordon, eds. 1985. *Relapse Prevention.* New York: Guilford.

Marsh, A. 1984. Smoking: Habit or Choice? *Population Trends* 37:14–20.

McGuire, F.L. 1972. Smoking, Driver Education and Other Correlates of Accidents among Young Males. *Journal of Safety Research* 4:5 11.

Mechanic, D. 1979. The Stability of Health and Illness Behavior: Results from a 16-Year Follow-Up. *American Journal of Public Health* 69:1142–1145.

Milich, R.S. 1975. A Critical Analysis of Schachter's Externality Theory of Obesity. *Journal of Abnormal Psychology* 84:586–588.

Moos, R.H., and J.W. Finney. 1983. The Expanding Scope of Alcoholism Treatment Evaluation. *American Psychologist* 38:1036–1044.

Morsilli, R., and J. Coudert. 1985. I Still See Him Everywhere. *New York Times* April 23:28.

Mulford, H.A. 1984. Rethinking the Alcohol Problem: A Natural Process Model. *Journal of Drug Issues* 14:31–43.

New Insights into Alcoholism. 1983. *Time* April 25:64.69.

Nisbett, R.E. 1972. Hunger, Obesity, and the Ventromedial Hypothalamus. *Psychological Review* 79:433–453.

O'Donnell, J.A., H. Voss, R. Clayton, G. Slatin, and R. Room. 1976. *Young Men and Drugs: A Nationwide Survey.* DHEW Publication no. ADM 76-311. Washington, DC: U.S. Government Printing Office.

Orcutt, J.D., R.E. Cairl, and E.T. Miller. 1980. Professional and Public Conceptions of Alcoholism. *Journal of Studies on Alcoholism* 41:652–661.

Orford, J., and G. Edwards. 1977. *Alcoholism.* New York: Oxford University.

Orford, J., and A. Keddie. 1986. Abstinence or Controlled Drinking in Clinical Practice: A Test of the Dependence and Persuasion Hypotheses. *British Journal of Addiction* 81:495–504.

Pandina, R.J., and J.A. Schuele. 1983. Psychosocial Correlates of Alcohol and Drug Use of Adolescent Students and Adolescents in Treatment. *Journal of Studies on Alcohol* 44:950–973.

Peele, S. 1983. *The Science of Experience.* Lexington, MA: Lexington Books.

———. 1985. *The Meaning of Addiction: Compulsive Experience and Its Interpretation.* Lexington, MA: Lexington Books.

———. 1986a. Denial—of Reality and Freedom—in Addiction Research and Treatment. *Bulletin of the Society of Psychologists in the Addictive Behaviors* 5:149–166.

———. 1986b. The Implications and Limitations of Genetic Models of Alcoholism and Other Addictions. *Journal of Studies on Alcohol* 47:63–73.

———. 1987. The Limitations of Control-of-Supply Models for Explaining and Preventing Alcoholism and Drug Addiction. *Journal of Studies on Alcohol,* 48: 61–77.

Polivy, J., and C.P. Herman. 1983. *Breaking the Diet Habit: The Natural Weight Alternative.* New York: Basic.

———. 1985. Dieting and Binging: A Causal Analysis. *American Psychologist* 40: 193–201.

Robins, L.N., J.E. Helzer, M. Hesselbrock, and E. Wish. 1980. Vietnam Veterans Three Years after Vietnam: How Our Study Changed Our View of Heroin. In L. Brill and C. Winick, eds., *The Yearbook of Substance Use and Abuse.* Vol. 2. New York: Human Sciences Press.

Rodin, J. 1981. Current Status of the Internal-External Hypothesis for Obesity: What Went Wrong? *American Psychologist* 36:361–372.

Rodin, J., and J. Slochower. 1976. Externality in the Obese: The Effects of Environmental Responsiveness on Weight. *Journal of Personality and Social Psychology* 29:557–565.

Room, R. 1985. Dependence and Society. *British Journal of Addiction* 80:133–139.

Schachter, S. 1968. Obesity and Eating. *Science* 161:751–756.

———. 1982. Recidivism and Self-Cure of Smoking and Obesity. *American Psychologist* 37:436–444.

Shiffman, S. 1985. Coping with Temptations to Smoke. In S. Shiffman and T.A. Wills, eds., *Coping and Substance Use.* Orlando, FL: Academic.

Shkilnyk, A.M. 1984. *A Poison Stronger Than Love: The Destruction of an Ojibwa Community.* New Haven, CT: Yale University.

Siegel, R.K. 1984. Changing Patterns of Cocaine Use: Longitudinal Observations, Consequences, and Treatment. In J. Grabowski, ed., *Cocaine: Pharmacology, Effects, and Treatment of Abuse.* DHHS Publication no. ADM 84-1326. Washington, DC: U.S. Government Printing Office.

Singh, D. 1973. Role of Response Habits and Cognitive Factors in Determination of Behavior of Obese Humans. *Journal of Personality and Social Psychology* 27: 220–238.

Stunkard, A. 1976. *The Pain of Obesity.* Palo Alto, CA: Bull.

———. 1980. *Obesity.* Philadelphia: Saunders.

Stunkard, A., E. D'Aquili, S. Fox, and R.D.L. Filion. 1972. Influence of Social Class on Obesity and Thinness in Children. *Journal of the American Medical Association* 221:579–584.

Stunkard, A.J., T.I.A. Sorensen, C. Hanis, T.W. Teasdale, R. Chakraborty, W.J. Schull, and F. Schulsinger. 1986. An Adoption Study of Human Obesity. *New England Journal of Medicine* 314:193–198.

Tournier, R.E. 1985. The Medicalization of Alcoholism: Discontinuities in Ideologies of Deviance. *Journal of Drug Issues* 15:39–49.

Tuchfeld, B.S. 1981. Spontaneous Remission in Alcoholics: Empirical Observations and Theoretical Implications. *Journal of Studies on Alcohol* 42:626–641.

Turkington, C. 1986. Contraceptives: Why All Women Don't Use Them. *APA Monitor* August: 11.

U.S. Public Health Service. 1979. *Smoking and Health: A Report of the Surgeon General.* DHEW Publication no. PHS 79-50066. Washington, DC: U.S. Government Printing Office.

Vaillant, G.E. 1977. *Adaptation to Life.* Boston: Little, Brown.

———. 1983. *The Natural History of Alcoholism.* Cambridge, MA: Harvard University Press.

Waldorf, D. 1983. Natural Recovery from Opiate Addiction: Some Social-Psychological Processes of Untreated Recovery. *Journal of Drug Issues* 13:237–280.

Walker, H. 1986. Drunk Drivers Hazardous Sober Too. *Journal* (Addiction Research Foundation of Ontario) March: 2.

Weisner, C., and R. Room. 1984. Financing and Ideology in Alcohol Treatment. *Social Problems* 32:167–184.

Why Kids Get Fat. 1986. *Newsweek* February 3:61.

Wille, R. 1983. Processes of Recovery from Heroin Dependence: Relationship to Treatment, Social Changes and Drug Use. *Journal of Drug Issues* 13:333–342.

Woodruff, R.A., S.B. Guze, and P.J. Clayton. 1973. Alcoholics Who See a Psychiatrist Compared with Those Who Do Not. *Quarterly Journal of Studies on Alcohol* 34:1162–1171.

Woody, E.Z., and P.R. Costanzo. 1981. The Socialization of Obesity-Prone Behavior. In S.S. Brehm, S.M. Kassin, and F.X. Gibbons, eds., *Developmental Social Psychology.* New York: Oxford University.

Wooley, S.C. 1972. Physiologic versus Cognitive Factors in Short Term Food Regulation in the Obese and Nonobese. *Psychosomatic Medicine* 34:62–68.

Index

About the Contributors

Bruce K. Alexander, Ph.D., is professor of psychology and director of the Drug Addiction Research Laboratory at Simon Fraser University, Burnaby, British Columbia.

Fred Beauvais, Ph.D., is a senior scientist at Colorado State University, Fort Collins.

Kathleen L. Edwards is a graduate research assistant at the Western Psychiatric Institute and Clinic, Pittsburgh.

P. Joseph Frawley, M.D., is vice president of clinical affairs at Schick Shadel Hospital, Santa Barbara, California.

Kim Fromme is a graduate research assistant in the Addictive Behaviors Research Center at the University of Washington, Seattle.

Riley E. Hinson, Ph.D., is associate professor of psychology at the University of Western Ontario, London, Ontario.

Marvin D. Krank, Ph.D., is assistant professor of psychology at Mount Allison University, Sackville, New Brunswick.

Craig MacAndrew, Ph.D., is professor of psychology at the University of California, Irvine.

John McFadden is a clergyman and psychotherapist in Santa Rosa, California.

G. Alan Marlatt, Ph.D., is professor of psychology and director of the Addictive Behaviors Research Center at the University of Washington, Seattle.

E.R. Oetting, Ph.D., is professor of psychology and director of Western Behavioral Studies at Colorado State University, Fort Collins.

Cynthia S. Pomerleau, Ph.D., is a senior research associate in the Behavioral Medicine Program in the Department of Psychiatry at the University of Michigan, Ann Arbor.

Ovide F. Pomerleau, Ph.D., is professor of psychology and director of the Behavioral Medicine Program in the Department of Psychiatry at the University of Michigan, Ann Arbor.

Shepard Siegel, Ph.D., is professor of psychology at McMaster University.

Ralph E. Tarter, Ph.D., is associate professor of psychiatry and neurology at the University of Pittsburgh and the Western Psychiatric Institute and Clinic, Pittsburgh.

About the Editor

Stanton Peele is a visiting scientist, the Institute of Epidemiology and Behavioral Medicine, Medical Research Institute (San Francisco) and Alcohol Research Group (Berkeley). His most recent book is *The Meaning of Addiction,* published by Lexington Books in 1985. Dr. Peele has been a leading scholar in the addiction field and particularly in the study of commonalities in a wide range of addictions since the publication of his book *Love and Addiction* in 1975.